Anecdotes o...

The United States

E. D. Townsend

Alpha Editions

This edition published in 2019

ISBN : 9789389169232

Design and Setting By
Alpha Editions
email - alphaedis@gmail.com

This book is a reproduction of an important historical work. Alpha Editions uses the best technology to reproduce historical work in the same manner it was first published to preserve its original nature. Any marks or number seen are left intentionally to preserve its true form.

ANECDOTES

OF

THE CIVIL WAR

IN THE

UNITED STATES.

BY

BREVET MAJOR-GENERAL E. D. TOWNSEND,
LATE ADJUTANT-GENERAL, U. S. ARMY
(RETIRED).

NEW YORK:
D. APPLETON AND COMPANY,
1, 3, AND 5 BOND STREET.
1884.

COPYRIGHT BY
D. APPLETON AND COMPANY,
1883.

PREFACE.

Without desiring to lay any claim to that fondness for story-telling commonly attributed to garrulous old people, the author has very naturally often enjoyed the pleasure which the narration of incidents, some of them now known, perhaps, to no other person living, has seemed to afford his friends. The opinion, repeatedly urged on such occasions, that he ought to preserve in authentic shape some of these historical anecdotes, has at length induced him to reduce to form such as he made notes of at the time, or can now recall with accuracy. If they fall short of the expectations formed of one who was known to have filled positions of high responsibility in military councils during the most critical period of our country's existence, or fail to reveal some of the hidden reasons for certain measures, and the secret history of certain events, which he may be supposed to know, it must be attributed partly to his conviction that in some matters the information confided to him was intended never to be made known; and partly to the fact that, while his advice and experience were always submitted to the higher powers when called for, he abstained from seeking knowledge which it was dangerous to the success of critical enterprises to have disseminated more than was absolutely necessary, content with understanding enough to insure an efficient execution of the authority intrusted to him.

Now that the lapse of time has softened the memories of the great conflict, and, beneath the kindly intercourse daily becoming cemented between North and South, the whole country is rapidly growing in prosperity, wealth, and power, the acts of men who were violently assailed in the hour of heated strife can and ought to be viewed with justice and kindness. Especially is this so in regard to those who are now far enough beyond the reach of criticism—in the unknown world. It is the author's hope that nothing may be found in these papers contrary to that spirit of national charity.

CITY OF WASHINGTON, D. C., *June*, 1883.

CONTENTS.

CHAPTER I.
PRESIDENT BUCHANAN.

Secession of Massachusetts—The Irish soldier—Token of affection . 1

CHAPTER II.
GENERAL SCOTT'S LOYALTY.

Tribute of Hon. W. M. Meredith and others—Rumored resignation—Virginia's bid for his services—Testimony of Senator Douglas—"Always a Union man"—Parting with Governor Morehead—Renewed oath—"Views"—Southern estimate of them . . . 3

CHAPTER III.
DEFENSE OF WASHINGTON.

Floyd's policy—Plan to capture Fort Moultrie—C. P. Stone—Regulars and volunteers—J. S. Wadsworth—An old fogy—Assignment of officers to guard public buildings—General Sanford—His grand review 9

CHAPTER IV.
SURRENDER OF AUGUSTA ARSENAL, GEORGIA.

The point of honor 17

CHAPTER V.
A YOUTHFUL SCOUT.

Sleeping *en route*—March of the Seventh New York . . . 19

CONTENTS.

CHAPTER VI.
OCCUPATION OF THE BALTIMORE AND OHIO RAILROAD DEPOT.

Limited means of transportation—Groundless fear of navigating the Potomac River 21

CHAPTER VII.
APPREHENDED PERSONAL VIOLENCE TO GENERAL SCOTT.

Anonymous letters—Precautions—Demonstrations of respect—Suspicious characters—Threats of "cold steel" 22

CHAPTER VIII.
A ROMANCE.

A flag-hoisting—A test 28

CHAPTER IX.
ROBERT E. LEE—ARLINGTON HEIGHTS.

A painful interview—Occupation of Arlington—Easy shelling distance—Mrs. Lee's note 29

CHAPTER X.
NEUTRALITY OF KENTUCKY.

Simon B. Buckner—Correspondence with General McClellan—Anderson, Nelson, and Carter—An unsuccessful diplomat . . . 35

CHAPTER XI.
MOUNT VERNON.

Neutral ground—General Scott's order 38

CHAPTER XII.
GENERAL SCOTT AND THE STARS AND STRIPES.

A flag presentation—"Are ye all there?" 40

CONTENTS.

CHAPTER XIII.
EVENINGS AT GENERAL SCOTT'S HEADQUARTERS.

A civil lawyer—An exacting host—A kind heart—Seventy-fifth birthday—A romantic adventure—The cadet Gray—The hot breakfast . 42

CHAPTER XIV.
VALUE OF A SPOOL OF COTTON.

Capture of United States troops in Texas—Escape of French's battery, 48

CHAPTER XV.
COLONEL MARTIN BURKE—THE FRENCH LADY.

The American Bastile—Arbitrary arrests justified—Obedience to orders—A very respectable "French lady" 50

CHAPTER XVI.
THE FIRST BATTLE OF BULL RUN.

Scott's plan opposed to invasion—His proposed campaign down the Mississippi—"On to Richmond!"—An anxious night—A panic—Order out of chaos 55

CHAPTER XVII.
THE COMMAND OF THE ARMY.

General McClellan—Discipline of volunteers—Scott's choice for general-in-chief—His complaint against McClellan—McClellan succeeds Scott—His tribute to Scott—Halleck succeeds McClellan—An order bewitched 60

CHAPTER XVIII.
BALL'S BLUFF—RED RIVER.

Object of demonstration on Leesburg—Rigorous treatment of General Stone—The secret history—Colonel Raymond Lee—General Stone at Red River—Colonel Bailey's engineering—Capture and recovery of his vote of thanks 70

CONTENTS.

CHAPTER XIX.
SERVICE IN THE ADJUTANT-GENERAL'S OFFICE.

General Scott's retirement—Disposal of his staff—Detached duty of the adjutant-general—Several candidates 76

CHAPTER XX.
JULIUS P. GARESCHÉ.

Killed in battle—Official announcement of his death—His charities—Decorated by the Pope—A priest's eulogium 82

CHAPTER XXI.
ARMY OF THE POTOMAC COMMANDERS.

Generous spirit of Burnside and Lincoln—Plain language to Hooker—Swapping horses while crossing a river 85

CHAPTER XXII.
PRESIDENT LINCOLN.

A cavalry rifle—The nervous traveler and the donkey—"There is a man in there!" 89

CHAPTER XXIII.
SUNDRY PERSONS.

Quakers—Isaac's mode of warfare—A woman in man's clothes—A kind Southern woman—A secret society—"Knights of the Golden Circle"—Grenfel—Release of Confederate prisoners—A Southern clergyman—Greetings from the North—Chaplains—Bounty-jumpers—I. C.—V. R. 92

CHAPTER XXIV.
GENERAL FRANK P. BLAIR.

How to legalize an illegal order 105

CHAPTER XXV.

EARLY'S INVASION.

A false alarm—President Lincoln's narrow escape 108

CHAPTER XXVI.

THE SHENANDOAH VALLEY TROPHIES.

Sheridan's black horse—"To Early, in care of Sheridan"—A big scare—Lo, they were gone! 110

CHAPTER XXVII.

TRIP TO SAVANNAH.

A Sunday service—A salute at sea—Conference with colored ministers—Fort Fisher—Promoted while asleep 114

CHAPTER XXVIII.

AMNESTY.

Proclamation sent through the lines—Good fruits—"Dixie" . . 119

CHAPTER XXIX.

ILLUMINATION FOR THE CAPTURE OF RICHMOND.

Magic effect—A perverse eagle 122

CHAPTER XXX.

AD INTERIM.

Mr. Stanton's suspension—Not sustained—General L. Thomas appointed *ad interim*—Mr. Stanton resists—Colloquy—A lawyer's *ruse*—"Stand firm!"—Neutral ground—Another *ad interim*—A new Secretary 124

CHAPTER XXXI.

EDWIN M. STANTON.

"Always tying your shoe"—"Some one had been drinking"—The Secretary obeying orders—Blood enough shed—Malicious reports—Baptism—Kindly notice 136

CHAPTER XXXII.
THE COLORED MESSENGERS.
Datcher—Madison's portrait 142

CHAPTER XXXIII.
THE RECORDS OF THE ADJUTANT-GENERAL'S OFFICE.
Obstacle to capital-moving—Method of keeping records—Tracing a cotton claim—Tracing a soldier—Confederate archives—The Alabama 144

CHAPTER XXXIV.
A CASE OF CIRCUMSTANTIAL EVIDENCE.
The unknown man—Convincing proofs 152

CHAPTER XXXV.
ORIGIN OF MILITARY COMMISSIONS.
General Scott in Mexico—Martial law—Lieber's instructions . . 160

CHAPTER XXXVI.
MEDALS AND CORPS BADGES.
Medals of honor—Recommendations—"Kearny patch"—Red, white, and blue—Legal recognition—Legends—Devices . . . 164

CHAPTER XXXVII.
CONFEDERATE FLAGS.
Inevitable Stars and Stripes—The Southern Cross—The Stars and Bars—The battle-flag—The white flag—Its surrender to the Monitor—The black flag 197

CHAPTER XXXVIII.
FORT SUMTER.
A pleasure-trip—The programme—Fac-simile of Anderson's dispatch—The flag-raising—Festivities—News of the President's death . 210

CONTENTS.

CHAPTER XXXIX.
THE FUNERAL OF PRESIDENT LINCOLN.

Unparalleled grief—Guard of honor—Funeral-train—Lying in state—Mottoes and floral tributes—Imposing demonstrations—The veteran Scott—"Come home"—At the tomb—A long farewell . . 220

CHAPTER XL.
THE GRAND REVIEWS.

A vast camp—War-worn veterans—The Bummer Brigade—Final discharge 244

APPENDIX A.
GENERAL SCOTT'S "VIEWS."

Paper of December 29, 1860—Several confederacies—Garrison the forts—Paper of October 30, 1860—Solicitude for the Union—Paper of October 28, 1860—Holding the forts—Paper of March 3, 1861—Four alternatives—"Wayward sisters" 249

APPENDIX B.
PRECAUTIONS AGAINST ATTACK.

General Orders, No. 4, April 26, 1861 257

APPENDIX C.

Extract from Secretary of War's report to the President, December 1, 1862 258

APPENDIX D.
PLAN OF CAMPAIGN.

Original draft of letter to General McClellan, May 3, 1861 . . 260

APPENDIX E.
RETIREMENT OF GENERAL SCOTT.

Act to retire Lieutenant-General Winfield Scott—Correspondence . 263

CONTENTS.

APPENDIX F.
COLLOQUY WITH COLORED MINISTERS.
Minutes of colloquy at Savannah, Georgia 267

APPENDIX G.
DEATH OF JUSTICE E. M. STANTON.
Affidavits and statements of cause of death 275

APPENDIX H.
MILITARY COMMISSIONS.
General Scott's projet—General Orders, No. 287, September 17, 1847 . 279

ANECDOTES OF THE CIVIL WAR.

CHAPTER I.

PRESIDENT BUCHANAN.

Secession of Massachusetts—The Irish soldier—Token of affection.

PRESIDENT BUCHANAN was very fond of visiting the Soldiers' Home, near Washington. He sometimes, in the summer, occupied the quarters of one of the officers stationed there, with whom he was on terms of friendly intimacy. I was asked by this officer to meet the President at dinner one day in the fall of 1860. The Bishop of Maryland was also there. It was a delightful day, and I walked out, in order to enjoy the fresh air and exercise.

There were some twelve or fourteen persons at the dinner. The hostess sat at the head of the table, with the President on her right, and myself on her left. The bishop was on the left of the host, at the other end of the table. In the general conversation that ensued it happened that the probable action of the Southern States in the pending troubles was discussed. The opinion was expressed that several of them would secede. Already several officers of the army and navy from those States had resigned. Mr. Buchanan seemed to be much annoyed, and said little. Presently some allusion was made to Massachusetts, when the President said, with considerable warmth: "I wish Massachusetts would secede; she is practically already out of the Union by her action in the fugitive-slave matter." Now I, being a Massachusetts man, felt rather awkwardly at this. Questions as to what I ought to do coursed rapidly through my brain. Suddenly an inspiration seized me. Looking up at the President, who was directly opposite me, I said with mock humility, "Mr. President, if Massachusetts should secede, would it be my duty to resign from the army, sir?" There was a dead silence. The President looked a little confused, and asked, "Are you from Massachusetts?" "Yes, sir," said I; "but I have been a good deal in California, and became very fond of that State, which makes me sometimes feel like saying of it, as the Irish soldier did, when asked where he came from—'I was born in Ireland, sir; but I call Illinois me native State.'" This excited a good laugh, and the conversation afterward took a more general turn.

I hardly knew whether or not to congratulate myself on my hit; but after dinner the President showed that he took it in good part, for he asked me how I came out of town. On my saying I had walked, he offered me a seat in his carriage if I would ride into town with him. Of course the offer was accepted with pleasure. On the way, I piloted him to the Oak Hill Cemetery, in Georgetown, where he desired to see a monument he had ordered in memory of a favorite niece, who was interred there, and of whose gentle nature he spoke with feeling and affection. He asked my opinion of the monument, and remarked that he had not yet prepared the inscription, which was the only part unfinished, and that he feared he would hardly be able to attend to it properly before the time came for him to leave Washington. I offered to assist him in any way, and subsequently drew a plan of the monument, with the words of the inscription arranged on it, for his approval. I then attended to the cutting of the words and the setting up of the monument.

This ride was thus the prelude to one of those episodes in life where the tender emotions of the heart shine forth with most sweetness amid the stern perplexities and harsh criticisms which attend high public office. It caused me me ever to remember with very kind feelings the official parting with Mr. Buchanan, when, a few weeks after, he retired from the presidential chair.

CHAPTER II.

GENERAL SCOTT'S LOYALTY.

Tribute of Hon. W. M. Meredith and others—Rumored resignation—Virginia's bid for his services—Testimony of Senator Douglas—"Always a Union man"—Parting with Governor Morehead—Renewed oath—"Views"—Southern estimate of them.

For some unaccountable reason, efforts have been made, since General Scott's death, to throw doubts upon his real loyalty to the Union. In 1860 and 1861 much anxiety was felt to ascertain what course he would take. The papers of the day, however, furnished abundant evidence that the tribute paid in a letter of April 30, 1861, addressed to him by Alexander Henry, Horace Binney, W. M. Meredith, and others, was only just. This is an extract from that letter:

"At a time like this, when Americans, distinguished by the favor of their country, intrenched in power, and otherwise high in influence and station, civil and military, are renouncing their allegiance to the flag they have sworn to support, it is an inexpressible source of consolation and pride to us to know that the General-in-Chief of the Army remains like an impregnable fortress at the post of duty and glory, and that he will continue to the last to uphold that flag, and defend it, if necessary, with his sword, even if his native State should assail it."

The Charleston (South Carolina) "Mercury," of April 22, 1861, stated that "a positive announcement was made at Montgomery, Alabama,* that General Scott had resigned his position in the Army of the United States, and tendered his sword to his native State—Virginia. At Mobile, one hundred guns were fired in honor of his resignation." This shows something of the estimated value of the general's influence.

Many efforts were made to induce him to resign, but he never once wavered in his devotion to the Union, whatever may be thought of the wisdom of his views, which, like those of every one, may be open to criticism. On one occasion Judge Robertson, a small, thin, but venerable-looking man, came to Washington with two other Virginia gentlemen, to offer General Scott the command-in-chief of the Army of Virginia, together with an estate belonging to the Commonwealth, and esteemed the most valuable in Virginia, if he would abandon the United

* Then the capital of the Southern Confederacy.

States service and go with the South. The general listened in silence as Robertson feelingly recalled the days when they were school-boys together; and then spoke of the warm attachment Virginians always cherished for their State, and of their boasted allegiance to it above all other political ties. But, when he began to unfold his offer of a commission and estate, the noble old soldier stopped him, exclaiming: "Friend Robertson, go no further. It is best that we part here, before you compel me to resent a mortal insult." Robertson and his friends at once took their departure, and I saw them as they descended the stairs, looking much discomfited.

Senator Douglas delivered a speech in Ohio in which he said he had been asked whether there was truth in the rumor that General Scott was about to resign. "Why," said the Senator, "it is almost profanity to ask that question. I saw him only last Saturday. He was at his desk, pen in hand, writing his orders for the defense and safety of the American capital." The Senator then detailed a conversation he had had with Judge Robertson, in which the latter corroborated the account of the interview just narrated.

General Scott answered an inquiry from his old and valued friend, Senator J. J. Crittenden, as to his reported intention to resign: "I have not changed; always a Union man."

Just before actual non-intercourse between the sections, Governor Morehead, of North Carolina, an old friend of General Scott, came one morning to his office. He had been to Philadelphia to withdraw his daughter from school, and take her home while travel was yet uninterrupted. The interview between the old friends was very affecting. Both deprecated the prospect, so imminent, of a separation of the States. Not a suggestion was hinted that they might soon be together in the new confederacy, but their parting was evidently viewed by both as final. The Governor shortly arose and bade a mournful farewell. He then said his daughter, a sweet young lady, who was in a carriage below, wished very much to see General Scott once more, and asked if she might come. Of course, a ready assent was given, and she presently appeared. A few parting words of regret were spoken, and she, bending over the general as he sat in his chair, kissed him reverently on the forehead. Tears streamed down the cheeks of father and daughter as they silently withdrew.

On Monday, May 6, 1861, in obedience to orders from the War Department requiring all officers to specially renew their oath of allegiance to the United States, the oath was administered to General Scott in his office, and at the same time to his staff.

The famous sentence, "Say to the seceded States, 'Wayward sisters, depart in peace,'" has been quoted as if it stood alone, to indicate that General Scott favored secession. This is evidently unfair. The sentence referred to was the fourth *and last* alternative which it seemed to him was within reach of the President. It was contained in a letter of March 3, 1861, to the Secretary of State about to come into office, and which appeared in print without the general's sanction. As early as October, 1860, the "views" of General Scott upon "threatened" secession were published, and the four alternatives, afterward submitted to Mr. Seward, were a sort of supplement to those views. The three papers entire will be found in Appendix A. As interpreted by the light of frequent conversations during my service with the general, there is no doubt in my mind that he meant to show "*all solicitude for the safety of the Union,*" and by pointing out not what he would approve or desire, but what would probably occur, viz., the fatal division—not into North and South, but into four, and subsequently more, weak confederacies—to warn his countrymen against the dangers which seemed so imminently to threaten. Then, to prevent the possibility of secession, he declared: "In my opinion, all these works" (in Southern States) "should be immediately so garrisoned as to make any attempt to take any one of them by surprise, or *coup de main*, ridiculous"; and, with proper management, that "*there is good reason to hope that the danger of secession may be made to pass away without one conflict of arms, one execution, or one arrest for treason.*"

This was in October, 1860, before any events had occurred to show what the future would certainly bring forth. To be sure, the advice to send troops to reënforce the posts seems absurd in view of the very small number he reported as available. But, as in duty bound, when submitting his recommendations, he represented the full extent of his own resources, leaving it to the President to use his constitutional powers to provide the means. A few weeks later, when there was a will, a way was readily found to raise all the troops needed. There is an obvious reason why, in the agitated state of the public mind, General Scott ought not to have made a specific recommendation in writing on this head.

As to the Southern sentiment, it was seen in the furious denunciations of him in Southern papers when his real position came to be known. The secession estimate of his "views" was announced at the reception tendered to Mr. Floyd in Richmond, after he resigned his place in President Buchanan's Cabinet, in these words:

"The plan invented by General Scott to stop secession was, like all campaigns devised by him, very able in its details, and nearly certain of general success. The Southern States are full of arsenals and forts, commanding their rivers and strategic points. General Scott desired to transfer the army of the United States to these forts as speedily and as quietly as possible.* The Southern States could not cut off communication between the Government and the fortresses without a great fleet, which they can not build for years, or take them by land without one hundred thousand men, many hundred millions of dollars, several campaigns, and many a bloody siege. *Had Scott been able to have got these forts in the condition he desired them to be, the Southern Confederacy would not now exist.*"

This was the involuntary tribute paid to General Scott's "views" in the capital of that very State which he had repudiated for the Union. It was not intended to glorify him, but Mr. Floyd for thwarting him.

* The army had been unnecessarily scattered under Secretary Floyd's administration, and his assent was necessary to enable General Scott to draw in from remote posts companies now much more needed at the East.

CHAPTER III.

DEFENSE OF WASHINGTON.

Floyd's policy—Plan to capture Fort Moultrie—C. P. Stone—Regulars and volunteers—J. S. Wadsworth—An old fogy—Assignment of officers to guard public buildings—General Sanford—His grand review.

As early as January 2, 1861, the "New York Times" had the following statement: "It is now well known that military companies have been organized and drilled for months past in Maryland and Virginia, and that the distinct object of their organization is to aid in the seizure of Washington City in the interest of the disunionists, or the prevention by force of Lincoln's inauguration. Some of the less prudent of their leaders boast in private circles that they have five thousand well-armed and organized men ready to strike the blow instantly upon the concerted signal being given."

This statement perfectly agreed with information in possession of the War Department before Mr. Floyd left it. It is matter of surprise, under the circumstances, that Floyd should have permitted General Scott to assemble the military force he was able to bring to Washington for the defense of the capital. Other circumstances would seem to indicate either that Floyd had not at that time fully made up his mind what would be the drift of events; or that he had not decided what his own course should be; or else that he did certain things to conceal his ultimate designs.

Mr. Floyd resigned as Secretary of War in the last part of December, 1860. Within about a month before that time, Colonel Cooper being absent, I was in charge of the Adjutant-General's office. Going one day to the Secretary's room on some business, I met there Colonel R. E. DeRussy, Acting Chief of Engineers, who had been sent for by the Secretary. Mr. Floyd took from his table-drawer a letter, which he read aloud, from some one in Charleston, South Carolina, stating that an organized band of the young men of Charleston had formed a plan to capture Fort Moultrie by assault. There was but a small garrison of regulars there, wholly inadequate to defend the fort. The sand had been blown into the ditch until it had gradually filled it in some places to within a short space from the top of the wall, so as to make it an easy matter to scale the parapet. Suggestion was made by the writer that information, or instructions, should be conveyed in some form to the commanding officer, to the effect that, in case of an assault being made, only a nominal defense would be necessary, in view of the fact that the attack would be made by so consideraeble a number that the garrison could suffer itself to be overpowered, and surrender gracefully, without loss of honor, and thus avoid useless bloodshed. This was the way the Southern arsenals and small detached posts were all taken; though no intimation was given by the United States authorities that they might be surrendered at all. Having read the letter, Mr. Floyd asked Colonel DeRussy if there was any way at his disposal in which the sand could be cleared from the ditch. The colonel replied that there was a small but sufficient balance of appropriation which could be applied to that purpose, and he could have it done as if it were a part of the repairs he had been for some time putting on Fort Moultrie. The Secretary then gave orders that the work should be done without loss of time.

Although a grand organization of the entire militia force of the District of Columbia existed in general orders of the War Department, and plenty of regiments, brigades, and divisions were to be found *on paper*, yet the actual force consisted of two or three companies, pretty well drilled, and of a major-general and two brigadiers, whose physical capacity for active duty was at least doubtful. Moreover, most of the officers and men of the organized companies were either positive in their affiliation with the South, or openly declared they would not fire upon their relatives and friends from Maryland and Virginia, if arrayed against them, even to resist an attack upon Washington.

It happened that at this time Captain Charles P. Stone,* who was a distinguished graduate of the Military Academy, and had but a short time before resigned his commission in the Ordnance Department, was then in the city. Acting on the principle which all graduates from West Point recognize, Captain Stone offered his services to General Scott in any capacity where he could be useful. He was a Massachusetts man, and had served with credit under General Scott in the Mexican War. About the first of January, 1861, he was mustered into the United States service as colonel and inspector-general of the District of Columbia militia, under the legal organization, and was assigned to the military command of the District of Columbia, with authority to reorganize the volunteers of the District. He very soon disposed of the disloyal

* For several years past distinguished as the chief of military staff to the Khedive of Egypt.

and lukewarm elements, and had a small but compact body of men, who did excellent service.

Besides this force, Magruder's Light Battery, of the First United States Artillery, Barry's, of the Second Artillery, and a very fine battery, made up at West Point, of men, horses, and guns used in the instruction of cadets, and commanded by Griffin, also some foot-companies of artillery and some of infantry, which were within reach, were brought to Washington. Thus about three thousand men were collected there, barely enough to guard the public buildings and the approaches to the city.

Colonel Stone was indefatigable in posting his troops, and in collecting all the provisions he could get,* so as to

---

* At about this time, General Scott received a telegram from General James S. Wadsworth, in New York, asking him if a vessel-load of cheese would be acceptable. I well remember the expression of satisfaction with which the general directed a reply to be sent that it would be, for it was really a question of some concern whether the army commissary and the private grocery and provision stores would have subsistence enough for citizens and troops until the way could be opened from the North. The cheese arrived safely and was issued to the troops. General Wadsworth soon after entered the United States service, and after rendering much important aid in various capacities, and making himself exceedingly popular, was killed in battle. The name of Fort Richmond, on Long Island, near the entrance to New York Harbor, was changed to Fort Wadsworth in his honor. With this fort is connected, later, one of President Lincoln's humorous sallies. High officials of the navy proposed to the President that the military engineers should prepare Fort Wadsworth with sand-bags and others appliances, according to the latest ideas of defense against iron-clad ships with heavy armaments; and that an iron-clad ship should then try to batter it down. The experiment was to be tried of the relative powers of such a battery to destroy and of such a fortification to withstand. The President paid a visit to Secretary Stanton in his office, to ask his opinion of the scheme. Mr. Stanton sent for the then Chief of Engineers, General Delafield. He heard the whole plan in silence, and then said: "Mr. President, I do not perceive that any provision is made that my

stand a siege if necessary. He took large quantities of flour from the mills in Georgetown, the most of which he stored in the Capitol building. All the halls were soon barricaded with barrels, and the floors white with their contents.

Companies were quartered in the public buildings, with stores of ammunition and provisions. Picket-guards were posted at the bridges and highways leading into the District, and a concerted signal was announced, at sound of which the troops were to repair to certain rendezvous in case of attack.

It occurred to me that it would be a wise plan to assign a regular officer of rank to the charge and command of each public building and important section of the city. General Scott approving the suggestion, Colonel Stone and I arranged the details, which were given in an order of the general. Adjutant-General L. Thomas lived in Georgetown; to him was assigned the command of all the troops there, and the provision for guarding the bridges. He was always there at night. Major McDowell, assistant adjutant-general, who was the officer employed to muster volunteers into the United States service, was assigned to Capitol Hill, especially to take charge of the Capitol building. This became an important and exten-

---

fort shall be allowed to defend itself. This is one of our most costly permanent forts, and it is in complete order. I shall have no objection whatever to the test, if you permit me to man my batteries and fire back again; but I am not willing to stand by and see those expensive works knocked to pieces without their having a chance to give as good as they get." "That's right! that's right!" said the President; "why, they told me you were a good deal of an old fogy; but I like just such old fogy ideas as yours." It seemed that some persons had been advising the President to retire General Delafield, and put a younger officer at the head of his corps,

sive command, as soon as regiments of volunteers from the North arrived, for many of them were quartered there. McDowell so commended himself to Secretary Cameron, by his skillful management of these new troops, that a little later, with the influence of Mr. Chase, Secretary of the Treasury—like himself an Ohio man—he was selected to receive the commission of brigadier-general in the regular army.

Captain W. B. Franklin, Corps of Topographical Engineers,[*] who had charge of the extension to the Treasury building, then in process of erection, was assigned to that building. He collected there quite a magazine of supplies. For the defense of the President and the Executive Mansion I named several high officers, but Colonel Stone objected to each one. At last I asked him who was his choice. He replied, "I claim that post for myself, as the most responsible and dangerous." Colonel J. P. Taylor, commissary-general of subsistence, was assigned to the Patent-Office building; Captain A. A. Humphreys, Corps of Engineers, to the Smithsonian; Colonel Gareschè, assistant adjutant-general, to the War Department building. Some warm personal friends of President Lincoln formed a volunteer body-guard, to stay in the Executive Mansion.

The officers thus distributed attended to their regular duties in the day, but were at their posts every night to be in readiness for an emergency. Instructions for their guidance in such an event were issued in general orders. (See Appendix B.) The few troops we had were frequently marched in small bodies through the streets,

[*] Of this officer's balance of character, General Scott used to say that he was neither too fast nor too slow.

either in relieving guards, or for exercise, and thus an impression arose that their numbers were much greater than they really were. Several years after the war I was told by a citizen that such was the general belief, and that it was supposed we were constantly being reënforced by the troops seen marching to and fro.

There never was greater rejoicing than when the volunteers from the North began to arrive. The famous New York Seventh was the first to appear. It arrived April 27th, and its welcome will not soon be forgotten. It marched up Pennsylvania Avenue to the Executive Mansion, where it passed in review before the President, and thence to the War Department, where it was regularly mustered into service. After this, other regiments continued to arrive in quick succession. Major-General Sandford, long conspicuous in New York as an energetic and intelligent commander of a fine division of the State uniformed militia, received from General Scott a telegram, dated May 6, 1861, saying, "Send without delay every regiment of the New York quota in and about your city, as soon as equipped for service, to this place, *via* the ocean and the Potomac River." By untiring exertions, he forwarded his whole division, splendidly organized and equipped. In reference to his coming in person, General Scott telegraphed to him, on the 8th of May: "Nobody more highly estimates your value as a soldier than myself, and you will receive a hearty welcome from me. More than one brigade of your troops are here, and more expected. Your right to follow them and command them is unquestionable, but your presence will be attended with one disadvantage: we are in critical circumstances, and it would take weeks to make you as well acquainted with localities, officers, and men, as brevet Brigadier-General Mansfield, whom you would supersede as the commander of the department."

With an unselfishness worthy of commemoration, General Sandford waived this consideration, and soon followed his division, reporting in person in the latter part of May. He was received into the United States service, and placed in command of the New York troops and of Arlington Heights. General Scott was very much pleased at his soldierly tone, and at the orders he had given his troops in starting them from New York. Hearing that the Potomac River was closed by rebel batteries, he instructed them to proceed up the river in their transports, and, if molested by hostile batteries, to land in sufficient force, storm them, and disperse the enemy.

The first grand review that took place in the city of Washington was that of Major-General Sandford's division of ten thousand men. The troops marched before President Lincoln and Cabinet, and General Scott, who were seated on a platform erected on the sidewalk in front of the Executive Mansion. A large proportion of the regiments was composed of foreign citizens, who had evidently seen military service in their native countries, and being, as they were, all well dressed in uniforms of their own fancy, well drilled, and preceded by excellent bands, or drum-corps, the effect was much like a display of fine troops somewhere in Europe. It had a great influence in inspiring military enthusiasm and confidence, in strong contrast with the depression of our beleaguered state but a few weeks before.

The uniforms of several regiments, like the Zouaves, were new to Americans, and none the less striking. The

Garibaldi Guards presented a most picturesque appearance, in a rich foreign uniform, with *vivandières* attached to each company, marching on its right flank. As this regiment passed in review, nearly every man took from the muzzle of his musket, or from his breast, a small bunch of flowers, or of evergreens, and tossed it toward the stand. The *vivandières* did the same, and raised their hands to their caps in a graceful salute. The ground in front of the stand was thus completely strewed with flowers. One man, more enthusiastic than the rest, stepped from the ranks toward the stand and lodged a handsome bouquet directly in General Scott's lap. The next day there was a loud lament and complaint of this regiment from persons living near the encampment, that their gardens had been stripped of every flower and green sprig!

CHAPTER IV.

SURRENDER OF AUGUSTA ARSENAL, GEORGIA.

The point of honor.

IN the evening of the 23d of January, 1861, a telegram was received from Captain Arnold Elzey, Second Artillery, commanding Augusta Arsenal, Georgia, saying: "I am just officially informed by the Governor of Georgia, now in Augusta, supported by a superior military force, that Georgia, having resumed exclusive sovereignty over her soil, it has become his duty to require me to withdraw the troops under my command at the earliest practicable moment from the limits of the State. He declares his intention to take possession of the arsenal, and proposes to receipt for the public property and account for the same on adjustment between the State of Georgia and the United States of America. He further declares that the retention of the troops upon the soil of Georgia after remonstrance is, under the laws of nations, an act of hostility, claiming that the State now is not only at peace, but anxious to cultivate the most amicable relations with the United States Government, and that an answer from me to his demand is required at nine o'clock A. M. to-morrow. An immediate answer to this communication is respectfully requested."

I submitted this to General Scott as soon as it arrived. The general took me in his *coupé* to the residence of the Hon. Joseph Holt, Secretary of War, on Capitol Hill, to prepare a reply. The veteran, annoyed as he was at the idea of United States troops surrendering a post under any circumstances, was aware how hopeless an attempt at resistance would be, and yet, he insisted, the point of honor demanded that *at least a shot should be fired* before deliberately yielding even to an overwhelming force. How to convey this idea by telegraph to the commander of the arsenal, without exacting unnecessary bloodshed, was the question. After trying several forms, the following was agreed upon and sent that evening, in the hope that the officer to whom it was addressed would weigh it carefully, and that his soldierly instinct would enable him to see its drift:

"The Governor of Georgia has assumed against your post and the United States an attitude of war. His summons is harsh and peremptory. It is not expected that your defense shall be desperate. If forced to surrender by violence or starvation, you will stipulate for honorable terms and a free passage by water with your company to New York.   J. HOLT, *Secretary of War.*"

If Captain Elzey did not apprehend what was expected of him, it may perhaps be accounted for by his subsequently resigning and entering the Confederate service. His official report shows that early the next morning he sent to beg an interview with the Governor of Georgia, when he arranged terms for the immediate surrender of all public property except that of his company and its arms.

CHAPTER V.

A YOUTHFUL SCOUT.

Sleeping *en route*—March of the Seventh New York.

WHILE Northern troops were arriving daily at Annapolis, and their presence was greatly needed in Washington, they had to remain for some time inactive from want of ability to communicate orders to them. The roads were beset by rebel scouts, and the railroad was entirely controlled by unfriendly hands. Two or three officers attempted to make their way to Annapolis, but were obliged to turn back. At last a young son of Colonel Abert, Chief of the Corps of Topographical Engineers, undertook to convey a message. He bore orders to General B. F. Butler, who held a commission from the Governor of Massachusetts, and was the senior officer of the troops at Annapolis. Mr. Abert was familiar with the whole of that part of the country, and, though a mere stripling, he developed a rare coolness, bravery, and endurance, worthy a much older person. He started on foot, in his ordinary civilian dress, and, going across the country, struck the Annapolis Railroad not far from the Junction. He was frequently stopped, but, by his ready answers and evident knowledge of persons and localities, sustained his *rôle* of a Maryland citizen trying to get home to Annapolis. So completely did he deceive his interrogators that they helped him on the way, instead of impeding his journey. He was allowed to get on a platform-car bound for Annapolis, and very coolly lay down and went to sleep until he safely reached a point near the depot, when, to *evade arrest by the Yankees*, he got off and stole into town. From that time General Butler was regularly invested with the command, and the regiments began their march for the capital. Young Abert afterward received a commission in the regular army, and was a gallant officer.

The experience dreaded by the gentleman who came to ask General Scott what was the destination of the Seventh New York Regiment was not realized. The regiment was among the very first to reach Annapolis. In reply to the question what the general wished it to do, he said, "March to Washington." "March! why, general, its tracks will be marked with blood; it will have to fight its way through hordes of rebels!" "Fight, sir, fight! That is what the regiment came for! This is not a time to play soldier on parade!" The reality of the situation was at once perceived, and no further question was raised. The regiment marched, and would have fought, too, but it met no opposition.

CHAPTER VI.

OCCUPATION OF THE BALTIMORE AND OHIO RAILROAD DEPOT.

Limited means of transportation—Groundless fear of navigating the Potomac River.

On the morning of April 25th, as I happened to come out of the office opposite the War Department, Secretary Cameron drove to the door in a buggy. Seeing me, he turned his driver out, and invited me to take his place. Assuming the reins, I inquired, "Where shall I drive, sir?" "I wish," said he, "to go to the railroad depot as fast as possible." On reaching the depot, the first thing was to close the telegraph-office and lock it up, before the operator could send off a dispatch. Then we found Colonel Stone, who was at the depot, and, with the guard already stationed there, had been collecting all the extra rails and material he could find. The Secretary directed him to take possession of the depot, and all the small amount of rolling-stock and material there, and to hold it under military control.

While we were at the depot a small train arrived from Baltimore, which was taken. The engines and cars thus seized, with some few at Annapolis,* constituted for some

* Among these was the engine which had been taken to pieces by rebels and was put together again by the Massachusetts volunteer, who, being a machinist, recognized it as one he had helped to manufacture.

weeks the only means of land transportation for conveying troops from Annapolis. Several regiments destined for Washington had landed there, in consequence of the reports which had reached the North that the rebels had batteries on the Potomac which would sink any transports going up the river. The fact really was, that our gunboat flotilla made daily examination of Matthias Point, where the channel runs very near the shore, and of other dangerous places, and for a long time found no evidence of batteries, or preparations to erect them. But this information could not be conveyed in time to the troops on their way.

It was not long before volunteer troops enough were received into service to guard the line of communication from Philadelphia through Baltimore; and then engines and rolling-stock sufficient for all demands were rapidly put upon the route, and trains ran without fear of interruption. But, during the weeks of limited means, it was necessary to send an officer's guard with every train that moved to and from Washington.

CHAPTER VII.

APPREHENDED PERSONAL VIOLENCE TO GENERAL SCOTT.

Anonymous letters—Precautions—Demonstrations of respect—Suspicious characters—Threats of "cold steel."

EARLY in the commencement of the secession troubles, General Scott had lodgings at the house of Cruchet, a French caterer, on Sixth Street, opposite what was then the Unitarian Church, and is now the Police Court. One of his aides lodged on the opposite side of the street. A company of artillery, serving as infantry, was quartered a few blocks away, and a sergeant's guard detailed from this company was always on duty at the general's lodgings.

About this time, a large number of communications were received from several Northern States, Canada, Kentucky, and other parts of the South, and from Europe, especially from Germany, some of them anonymous, others signed with a name. All concurred in the declaration that a plot existed to assassinate President Lincoln and General Scott. They agreed singularly in the details, and sometimes in fixing the same dates for the attempt. The staff opened the general's mails, and we decided not to annoy him by telling him everything of this threatening character which we received, but only to inform him of so much of the contents of the communications as seemed necessary for him to know.

One of these letters was from a clergyman living in a most prominent secession city, and read as follows, the names being purposely left blank:

―――――, *February 14, 1861.*

General WINFIELD SCOTT.

RESPECTED SIR: A man by the name of ――― was taken suddenly ill at the ――― Hotel, and, desiring the services of a minister, I was called in. He had hardly time to confess to me that he was an accomplice to a most diabolical scheme of undermining and blowing up the Capitol on the Ides of March. I am constrained by his request to write you immediately, hoping that you may succeed in frustrating so diabolical a plan.

I am, truly yours,

————————,
Rector Church of ————.

So many of these statements agreed in affirming that the general would be attacked on a certain Thursday, that I could not help feeling unusual apprehension, and I determined to leave nothing undone to defeat the diabolical plot. The evening before that Thursday, one of the aides, who had been to the general's quarters, called at my house and told me the general wished to see me. In order to be prepared with any official information that might be required, I asked if he had mentioned why he wished to see me. The aide replied no, but he thought the general felt a little uneasy at being alone, so far away from where all the officers lived, the aide who was quartered near him being temporarily absent in New York. I went down at about eight o'clock, and found, as had been suggested, that I was merely wanted for company. I now thought it best to tell the general frankly that we apprehended an attempt on his life the next night, and wished he could be persuaded to move on the morrow to some lodgings near the War Department, where immediate access could be had to him. He at first made light of it, said that he felt quite secure with his guard, and that he did not place much reliance on the anonymous letters. I urged upon him that we had no right in such times to disregard even such sources of information, but when so many, coming from places so far apart, agreed in such a singular and circumstantial manner in their assertions, I thought it an imperative duty to use extraordinary precautions. At length he consented that I should procure him suitable lodgings, and agreed to move the next day. I remained with him till eleven o'clock, after offering to stay all night and keep watch by him, to which he would not listen. Then I gave the guard minute cautions and instructions. The sergeant was, on the occurrence of anything unusual, to send immediately to the company quartered near, and dispatch a messenger for me. The next morning I engaged the kind offices of Captain Palmer, of the Corps of Engineers, who had more leisure than I, to hunt up new quarters for the general. He found very comfortable ones at Mrs. Duvall's, a house —No. 159 (*old series*)—still standing back in a yard, on the south side of Pennsylvania Avenue, between Seventeenth and Eighteenth Streets. I dined with the General at Cruchet's Thursday evening, and after dark we drove in his *coupé* to Mrs. Duvall's. The headquarters company was moved to a house on Seventeenth street, opposite the War Department. The sergeant's guard was stationed in an out-building in the yard of the general's quarters, where it could hear orders conveyed in a whisper, and sentinels were posted in the yards in front and rear of the house. The back yard extended through to G Street, near its junction with Seventeenth, and the whole company could hear an alarm-shot, and in two minutes be at the general's side.

For several nights, until arrangements were made for an aide to lodge in the house, I rested on a sofa in the outer room, next the general's chamber, with sword and revolver at hand, fully expecting that some attempt would be made upon us. Nor shall I ever be convinced that anything prevented it except the evident state of preparation and watchfulness which was maintained. Every half-hour in the night I visited the sentinels and took observations of the neighborhood. There was a wood-yard on each side of the house, and frequently in the night the peculiar secession whistle was heard, coming from some one in these yards. I would then send out a patrol to search these yards. There were discharges of guns frequently in the night, and the inmates of the house heard bullets strike against its brick walls. The gentlemen boarders, among them a young clergyman, were at their request furnished with fire-arms, and they would have used them to good effect in the general's defense, so enthusiastic was their veneration for him.

Whenever General Scott alighted from his *coupé* to pass to his office, lines were formed by persons, generally in humble life, who removed their hats, and frequently uttered a fervent " God bless you, general!" as he passed them. Sometimes dark-visaged men would be seen on the corners of the street, intently scrutinizing him; and we were told by a stable-keeper near by that on two or three occasions very suspicious-looking men had asked him all sorts of questions as to where the general lived, how many officers he had on his staff, and what sort of looking men they were; and that he had once seen them take notes after such a conversation.

There was a young officer of cavalry attached to the general's staff as an extra aide. He was quite proud of his uniform and of his fine horsemanship, and certainly was a good-looking fellow. I had heard that there was a company formed near Tenally Town, back of Georgetown, which was drilling at night under suspicious circumstances. As this young officer was intimately acquainted in Georgetown and vicinity, I directed him to go out cautiously and try to ascertain the facts, without letting his mission be known. He could not forego the gratification of displaying his uniform and military trappings to his old friends, so out he galloped in complete martial equipment. He went to a store-keeper whom he knew, and believed to be a Union man, and bluntly inquired of him about what he wanted to ascertain. The man told him he had heard there was such a company under drill, but he did not know much about it. He promised to ascertain and let him know in a day or two if he would go out again. "But," said he, "when you come again I advise you to come in citizen's dress, or else to bring a guard with you. All General Scott's staff are known and marked, and, some of these times, if they don't look out, they will get an inch of cold steel in them."

These were some of the incidents that occurred every day, especially about the middle of April, 1861, which kept us vigilant night and day. No wonder that for weeks we lived in the constant expectation that, as we proceeded on our way from the general's quarters to our own, often late at night, we might at any time be assailed from behind a tree, or from some dark alley.

CHAPTER VIII.

A ROMANCE.

A flag-hoisting—A test.

AMONG the early arrivals of troops at the capital were the First Regiment of Rhode Island Infantry, commanded by Colonel Ambrose E. Burnside (afterward general and Senator), and Captain Charles H. Tompkins's battery of Rhode Island Artillery. Governor William Sprague accompanied these troops, to be soon followed by others from his State, as commander-in-chief of the whole. The Governor wore a military dress, was attended by a staff, and by his presence and example, no less than by the excellent organization and equipment of his command, did much toward creating the enthusiasm and pride which inspired the whole body of troops and the loyal among civilians. The infantry regiment was quartered in the Department of the Interior, over which building the United States flag was hoisted on the 3d of May, amid the acclamations of a large assemblage, the regiment parading in front, and its band playing patriotic airs.

Governor Sprague was remarkably youthful in appearance, and generally thought to be handsome. This, with his modest, dignified manners, made him quite popular. Some of the most piquant of romances notoriously originate during the stirring times of war, and so the handsome and chivalric young Governor soon became the object of harmless gossip in connection with the beautiful daughter of the Secretary of the Treasury. This young lady was the belle of the time, and her father's estimate of her was readily accepted in addition to her more patent charms: "She is a *good* daughter," he said, in reply to some complimentary allusion to her. The report of this engagement, not then acknowledged, did not fail to be discussed in General Scott's military family. The general himself, having a high regard for both parties, made some kind remarks referring to it. It happened one day, on the occasion of some display of troops, that the young lady, with her father, appeared on the street in an open landau. As they stopped near General Scott's office, the gallant veteran went to the carriage to pay his respects. As they were chatting, Governor Sprague came up and joined the group. Soon after, in his quarters, the general again referred to the report of the engagement, and said: "Did you observe the young lady during that interview? I watched her narrowly, and she bore the test admirably; no sign of emotion was betrayed by her." He evidently took as much interest in the affair as the younger men.

CHAPTER IX.

ROBERT E. LEE—ARLINGTON HEIGHTS.

A painful interview—Occupation of Arlington—Easy shelling distance—Mrs. Lee's note.

ROBERT E. LEE was colonel of the Second (now Fifth) Regiment United States Cavalry, stationed in Texas. He had commanded that military department, and in April, 1861, was on leave of absence. General Scott knew that he was at Arlington Heights, at the house of his father-in-law, Mr. Custis, and one day asked me if I had seen or heard of him lately. I replied in the negative, except that he was on leave and at Arlington Heights. Said the general, "It is time he should show his hand, and, if he remains loyal, should take an important command." I then suggested that I should write a note to Lee, and ask him to call at the general's headquarters. "I wish you would," replied the general. The note was written, and the next day, April 19, 1861, Colonel Lee came to the office. The general's was the front room of the second story. His round-table stood in the center of the room, and I had a desk in one corner. The aides were in an adjoining room, with a door opening into the general's. When Lee came in I was alone in the room with the general, and the door to the aides' room was closed.* I quietly arose, keeping my eye on the general, for it seemed probable he might wish to be alone with Lee. He, however, secretly motioned me to keep my seat, and I sat down without Lee having a chance to notice that I had risen. The general having invited Lee to be seated, the following conversation, as nearly as I can remember, took place:

General Scott. You are at present on leave of absence, Colonel Lee?

Colonel Lee. Yes, general, I am staying with my family at Arlington.

General Scott. These are times when every officer in the United States service should fully determine what course he will pursue, and frankly declare it. No one

---

* General Cullum thinks he was also in the room with the general, and present at this interview, but I am quite confident no one but myself witnessed the conversation between General Scott and Colonel Lee.

should continue in government employ without being actively engaged. (*No response from Lee.*)

General Scott (after a pause). Some of the Southern officers are resigning, possibly with the intention of taking part with their States. They make a fatal mistake. The contest may be long and severe, but eventually the issue must be in favor of the Union. (*Another pause, and no reply from Lee.*)

General Scott (seeing evidently that Lee showed no disposition to declare himself loyal, or even in doubt). I suppose you will go with the rest. If you purpose to resign, it is proper you should do so at once; your present attitude is an equivocal one.

Colonel Lee. General, the property belonging to my children, all they possess, lies in Virginia. They will be ruined if they do not go with their State. I can not raise my hand against my children.

The general then signified that he had nothing further to say, and Colonel Lee withdrew. The next day, April 20, 1861, he tendered his resignation, and it was accepted the 25th. General Scott made no remark upon the subject, but he was evidently much grieved at thus parting with a man of whom he had been justly proud, and for whom he had cherished the highest personal regard. He had no more devoted or efficient staff officer than Lee was in the Mexican War.

It was probably near the same day as the interview with General Scott that the following incident, related to me by the late General Shiras, occurred. Shiras was in the office of Adjutant-General L. Thomas when Colonel Lee came in there. Standing on the side of the table opposite where Thomas was sitting, Lee said, "General

Thomas, I am told you have said I was a traitor!" Thomas arose, and, looking him in the eye, replied: "I have said so; do you wish to know on what authority?" "Yes," said Lee. "Well, on the authority of General Scott!" Lee muttered, "There must be some mistake," turned and left the room.

Colonel Lee's family remained at their home, the Custis mansion, Arlington Heights, for some time after. They would doubtless have been treated with respect by our people had they chosen to continue their residence there. The cause of their hasty departure was the intelligence that the heights were to be occupied and fortified by the Union forces.

On the evening of May 2d there was a conference at General Scott's headquarters, in which the commander of the troops in Washington, General Mansfield, participated. The subject considered was the general defense of the city of Washington. Among the points discussed was the Heights of Arlington, and whether it commanded the city. The next day General Mansfield reported as follows:

"We now come to the city, and Georgetown, and arsenal, exposed to the Virginia shore. Here I must remark that the President's house and department buildings in its vicinity are but two and a half miles across the river from Arlington high ground, where a battery of bombs and heavy guns, if established, could destroy the city with comparatively a small force, after destroying the bridges. The Capitol is only three and a half miles from the same height at Arlington, and at the aqueduct the summits of the heights on the opposite shore are not over one mile from Georgetown.

"With this view of the condition of our position, it is clear to my mind that the city is liable to be bombarded at the will of an enemy, unless we occupy the ground which he certainly would occupy if he had any such intention. I therefore recommend that the heights above mentioned be seized, and secured by at least two strong redoubts, one commanding the Long Bridge and the other the aqueduct, and that a body of men be there encamped to sustain the redoubts, and give battle to the enemy if necessary. I have engineers maturing plans, and reconnoitring further. It is quite probable that our troops assembled at Arlington would create much excitement in Virginia; yet, at the same time, if the enemy were to occupy the ground there, a greater excitement would take place on our side, and it might be necessary to fight a battle to disadvantage."

It may be supposed there was no little commotion among the chief men when it was ascertained that any public building in Washington could be so easily shelled from Arlington. General Scott was in the habit of writing short "*bulletins*," as he called them, daily to the President. These were copied by a young officer, a relative of the Lee family, in whom the general took an extraordinary interest, and whom he supposed he had warmly attached to himself by many signal favors. The general made the result of General Mansfield's investigation of Arlington the subject of his bulletin, immediately after its receipt, and informed the President of the determination taken to prepare a column to go over at an early day to occupy the heights. For prudential reasons this bulletin was copied by another person, and it was not intended that the young aide should know anything about it. He had been warned not to cross the river to visit his relatives. By accident the general left this bulletin on his table, and the young man read it. He doubtless made it known to Mrs. Lee.*

In a day or two the general received from her the following note:

"ARLINGTON, *May 5th* [*1861*].

"MY DEAR GENERAL: Hearing you desired to see the account of my husband's reception in Richmond, I have sent it to you. No honor can reconcile either of us to this fratricidal war, which we would have laid down our lives freely to avert. Nor can it ever terminate *now* till *every* heart in the whole South ceases to beat, or they obtain the justice they demand. Whatever may happen, I feel that I may expect from your kindness all the protection you can in honor afford. More I would not ask, or expect. Nothing can ever make me forget your kind appreciation of Mr. Lee. If you knew all you would not think so hardly of him. Were it not that I would not add one feather to his load of care, nothing would induce me to abandon my home. Oh, that you could command peace to our distracted country!

Yours in sadness and sorrow,
"M. C. LEE.

"Lieutenant-General SCOTT."

When the heights were taken possession of, on the 24th of May, the Custis mansion was found abandoned. It has never been reoccupied by the family. As the war progressed, its absolute necessity as a fortified point induced the Government to erect several earthworks around the

* He left the service a very short time after, and before he could be possessed of any important secrets.

Custis estate. The estate itself was converted in part into a national cemetery, and in part into a depot for the Signal Service, and it still remains in that use.

CHAPTER X.

NEUTRALITY OF KENTUCKY.

Simon B. Buckner—Correspondence with General McClellan—Anderson, Nelson, and Carter—An unsuccessful diplomat.

It is well known with what anxiety the position which the State of Kentucky would occupy in the great contest was regarded by both sides. The effort from the beginning was, if possible, to keep it neutral. But this could not be. Its geographical location made it too important a strategical region to prevent a desperate struggle for its possession. Simon B. Buckner, a graduate of West Point of the class of 1844, and a native of Kentucky, played rather a conspicuous part in its earlier councils of the war. He resigned from the army in 1855, and settled in Kentucky. In 1861 he was Inspector-General of the State, and commanded its Home Guards under Governor Magoffin.

In June, 1861, some letters of General Buckner were published in the Louisville (Kentucky) papers, stating that he had entered into an arrangement with General McClellan, at Cincinnati, to the following effect:

"The authorities of the State of Kentucky are to protect the United States property within the limits of the State, to enforce the laws of the United States, in accordance with the interpretations of the United States courts, as far as those laws may be applicable to Kentucky, and to enforce, with all the power of the State, our obligations of neutrality as against the Southern States, as long as the position we have assumed shall be respected by the United States.

"General McClellan stipulates that the territory of Kentucky shall be respected on the part of the United States, even though the Southern States should occupy it; but, in the latter case, he will call upon the authorities of Kentucky to remove the Southern forces from our territory. Should Kentucky fail to accomplish this object in a reasonable time, General McClellan claims the same right of occupying given to the Southern forces. I have stipulated in that case to advise him of the inability of Kentucky to comply with her obligations, and to invite him to dislodge the Southern forces. He stipulates that, if he is successful in doing so, he will withdraw his forces from the territory of the State as soon as the Southern forces shall have been removed."

In the middle of June following, General Buckner called into the service of the State some companies, in view of an excitement at Columbus, Kentucky. He stated to their commander, in assigning him to command the force:

"Its general object will be to carry out the obligation of neutrality which the State has assumed in the contest now impending on our borders."

Supposing that at this time Buckner was acting in good faith to preserve neutrality, yet in the above extracts may be found some provisions which would make it easy to array Kentucky on the side of the South before the contingency in which the United States troops might enter the State could be acted on. If he desired to use it for that purpose, much valuable time could be gained by that Governor who, in April, replied to the call of the War Department for volunteers, "I say, emphatically, Kentucky will furnish no troops for the wicked purpose of subduing her sister Southern States." General McClellan's version of the agreement was to the effect that Buckner repeatedly solicited an interview with him, and when it took place it was strictly private and personal; that he gave no pledge on the part of the United States authorities that United States troops should not enter Kentucky, but the only understanding, so far as he knew, was that Confederate troops should be confined to Confederate soil, so far as Kentucky was concerned.

In May, 1861, General Robert Anderson was assigned to the command of the Military Department of Kentucky, he being a native of the State; and Lieutenants Nelson and Carter, of the navy, also natives, were commissioned brigadier-generals of United States volunteers, and sent there. The object in sending these officers was that they might exert their influence in organizing the State militia in the interest of the Union, so that the Governor would have a reliable military force under his authority, sufficient to cause the neutral attitude of the State to be respected. Anderson was also intended to be a safe counselor to the Governor, in reference to any military movements that might be made, and to take command if the United States should have to take part in them.

In August Buckner was in Washington. He talked very cautiously about the affairs of Kentucky, and seemed anxious to create the impression with the Government that he was laboring zealously for the Union. The President was at one time on the point of conferring upon him (subject, however, to General Anderson's approval) the commission of brigadier-general of volunteers; but, for certain reasons, this was not done, and he returned to Kentucky without such credentials. Soon after his return he began to act under the commission of a general officer from the Confederate Government. With the two commissions, to use as circumstances might dictate, he could, if so disposed, have raised a very respectable body of recruits for the Confederates.

CHAPTER XI.

MOUNT VERNON.

Neutral ground—General Scott's order.

IN May, 1861, there were rumors that the bones of Washington had been moved from Mount Vernon. The report caused quite a sensation North and South. The estate was in charge of a lady who resided there. Through her means an understanding was brought about between Union and secession people of all classes that the domain should be regarded as strictly neutral ground, to which both parties should have equal right. Upon a representation made by this lady, General Scott, glad to find there was still one bond of union left—the name of Washington—issued the following order:

GENERAL ORDERS, No. 13.
HEADQUARTERS OF THE ARMY,
WASHINGTON, *July 31, 1861.*

It has been the prayer of every patriot that the tramp and din of civil war might, at least, spare the precincts within which repose the sacred remains of the Father of his Country. But this pious hope is disappointed. Mount Vernon, so recently consecrated anew to the immortal Washington by the ladies of America, has already been overrun by bands of rebels who, having trampled under foot the Constitution of the United States—the ark of our freedom and prosperity—are prepared to trample on the ashes of him to whom we are all mainly indebted for these mighty blessings.

Should the operations of war take the United States troops in that direction, the general-in-chief does not doubt that each and every man will approach with due reverence, and leave uninjured, not only the tomb, but also the house, the groves, and walks which were so loved by the best and greatest of men.

WINFIELD SCOTT.

By command:
E. D. TOWNSEND, *Assistant Adjutant-General.*

No case of trespass was ever known to occur after the neutrality of the domain was once established.

CHAPTER XII.

GENERAL SCOTT AND THE STARS AND STRIPES.

A flag presentation—" Are ye all there ? "

As the general was one day sitting at his table in the office, the messenger announced that a person desired to see him one moment with a gift he had for him. A German was introduced, who without flourish made known that he had been commissioned by a house in New York to present to General Scott a small silk banner. It was very handsome, of the size of a regimental flag, and was made of a single piece of silk, stamped with the stars and stripes in their proper colors, instead of being composed of different pieces stitched together, as is usually the case. The German said the manufacturers were desirous of offering some token of the great respect in which General Scott was held, and of their sense of his importance to the country in that perilous time. The general was highly pleased, and, in accepting the gift, assured the donors that the flag should hang in his room wherever he went, and finally enshroud him when he died. As soon as the man departed, the general desired that the stars might be counted, to see if *all* the States were represented. They were "*all* there." The flag was forthwith draped between the windows, over the lounge where the general frequently reclined for rest during the day. It went with him in his berth when he sailed for Europe, after his retirement, and enveloped his coffin when he was interred at West Point.

This incident was a remarkable illustration of Mrs. Sigourney's lines which appeared in the "National Intelligencer" about that time:

STARS IN MY COUNTRY'S SKY.

Are ye all there? Are ye all there,
　　Stars of my country's sky?
Are ye *all* there? *Are ye all there,*
　　In your shining homes on high?
"Count us! count us," was their answer,
　　As they dazzled on my view,
In glorious perihelion,
　　Amid their field of blue.

I can not count ye rightly;
　　There's a cloud with sable rim;
I can not make your number out,
　　For my eyes with tears are dim.
Oh! bright and blessed angel,
　　On white wing floating by,
Help me to count, and not to miss
　　One star in my country's sky!

Then the angel touched mine eyelids,
　　And touched the frowning cloud;
And its sable rim departed,
　　And it fled with murky shroud.
There was no missing Pleiad,
　　'Mid all that sister race;
The Southern Cross gleamed radiant forth,
　　And the pole-star kept its place.

> Then I knew it was the angel
> Who woke the hymning strain
> That at our dear Redeemer's birth
> Pealed out o'er Bethlehem's plain;
> And still its heavenly key-tone
> My listening country held,
> For all her constellated stars
> The diapason swelled.   L. H. S.

HARTFORD, CONNECTICUT.

CHAPTER XIII.

EVENINGS AT GENERAL SCOTT'S QUARTERS.

A civil lawyer—An exacting host—A kind heart—Seventy-fifth birthday—
A romantic adventure—The cadet Gray.

THE President, Secretaries of War, State, and Treasury used often to drop in at General Scott's office, or at his quarters in the evening. When the President came, the general would always rise and insist on his taking the big arm-chair, which himself had been occupying. He would then recount to him the military movements of the day, and they would discuss some matter of interest, either of a military or political character. Sometimes nice questions would arise on international law as applicable to the peculiar relations between the contending sections. On such occasions the general showed that he had not forgotten his early education as a civil lawyer, but through life had continued to read until he had become really profoundly learned in that profession.

The general always expected one or more of the staff to dine with him, and to be at his quarters all the evening. Then, too, the officer commanding the troops in the District, and other high officers, would call to communicate with him, so he was always informed of everything that was going on. If there was no business, he was fond of relating anecdotes. They were always interesting, though the staff did not uniformly enjoy them, because they had so often heard some of them, after a fatiguing day, in a room heated by a six-burner gas-chandelier in midsummer. And, to say truth, the general had fallen into a way of speaking very slowly, with sometimes long pauses between his words. In short, these occasions were sometimes quite trying, for the general was exacting; he not only required auditors, but strict attention from them, and he sometimes showed impatience when he thought they were wanting. One evening I had a dull headache, and sat with my hand shading my eyes from the bright gas-light. Suddenly the general stopped in the midst of a sentence, and said sharply, "Colonel Townsend is now asleep!" I looked up in some surprise, and said, "Oh, no, general, I hear every word you say, but I have a headache, and the gas hurts my eyes." With a changed tone he said, "Oh, pardon me," and went on with his story. At another time he was in a terrible mood. We all thought the dinner of rich jowl, of which he was especially fond, was at fault. He snapped up every one who said a word. The District commander soon excused himself, saying he must go home and get a cup of tea. When he withdrew, the general said, "I don't like tea-sops." So each one came in turn for some hit. All this time I had escaped by keeping silent. At last I brought it on myself from the very fear that he would remark on my silence. He was speaking of peculiarities of pronunciation in different States, and illustrating them by examples. Coming to Virginia, he repeated the words, "Go up-*stars*." "Now," thought I, "is a good time to show that I am an appreciative listener," so I added, in a pleasant voice, "And shut the *do*." He turned fiercely upon me and said: "What has that to do with it? I have not come to that yet." Said I quietly, but in a decided tone: "I beg your pardon, sir; I'll not interrupt you again." He saw I was justly displeased, and immediately changed his manner. After this the evening passed much more agreeably, and the general did not make another petulant remark. I received a vote of thanks from the rest of the staff for this involuntary *coup*, and the general never showed any displeasure at it.

At one time I was sorely afflicted with "Job's comforters," which seriously interfered with my necessary activity. One evening, when my right wrist was thus nearly disabled, the general desired me to write a dispatch at his dictation. I usually wrote as rapidly as he spoke, but on this occasion I was obliged to ask him to wait a moment until I could overtake him. He made some remark about my not being as prompt as usual, but when he knew the reason he offered to take the pen himself. These trifling incidents illustrate the kind heart always showing itself amid the general's peculiarities.

Thursday, June 13, 1861, General Scott's seventy-fifth birthday, was marked by the presentation to him of a handsome bouquet by his staff. The general was much gratified, and spoke in complimentary terms of us, as "the staff of his old age."

EVENINGS AT GEN. SCOTT'S QUARTERS.

One or two of the anecdotes related by the general at the evening *soirées* will be found interesting here.

A ROMANTIC ADVENTURE.—General Scott was captain of artillery in 1812. He was ordered with his horse-battery to march to the Northern frontier, where he laid the foundation of his fame. He had an excellent first sergeant, who took pains to keep men, horses, and material in the highest order, and he was very proud of his splendid battery. On the march, as the battery was passing through a valley, the road lay close to the base of a high hill. At a sudden turn in the road Captain Scott, mounted on his spirited charger, came directly in front of a very attractive young woman, who was quite alone. The unexpected appearance of this formidable military display, seemingly ready to trample her under foot, threw the young lady into a great state of alarm. She turned pale, and seemed about to faint. Instantly the gallant captain sprang from his horse, and said some reassuring words, at the same time encircling her waist with his arm, as was evidently necessary to support her in her state of agitation. And so, the path between the foot of the hill and the road being very narrow, and the danger great that she might receive injury from the horses or wheels, she turned about to go home. The captain walked by her side and conversed pleasantly with her, not deeming it prudent the while to remove his supporting arm. They parted at her home, with modest expressions of thanks from the young lady.

Many years after, Captain Scott, now become general, with world-wide fame, was journeying in a private conveyance over the same road. Late at night, in a pelting storm, he stopped at a wayside inn, and asked lodgings and a supper. The landlord made some difficulty about even admitting him, alleging that he had no good accommodations, and could not provide a supper at that hour. After a short parley the traveler announced himself as General Scott, commander of the army, traveling on urgent military duty. He had come a long way that day, was weary and hungry, and the night was inclement. In an instant the door was thrown open, and the guest was shown to a parlor where in a twinkling a bright fire crackled on the hearth, and very soon after a smoking supper was served in good style, the host himself acting as waiter. After supper the general was ushered to the best chamber, where all things were arranged for his comfort. The next morning, at breakfast, the host addressed him with—" General Scott, you are the only man in the world of whom I am jealous. I don't know but my wife thinks more of you than she does of me. She would like to còme in and see you." The general had no conception who the fair lady could be, but he begged that he might have the pleasure of greeting her. In the tidy, good-looking matron who was thus introduced he recognized the pretty young woman of the hill-side adventure.

THE CADET GRAY.—Another anecdote of the general's is interesting as accounting for the gray uniform which has so long been the pride of West-Pointers. While preparing at Buffalo, in the summer of 1814, for the campaign in Canada, General Scott wrote to the quartermaster-general for some new uniforms, especially overcoats, for his men. Having received in reply the information that they could supply him with nothing which he required, but that he could have some overcoats of a light-gray color, very comfortable, though not the regulation uniform, he at once ordered them. Thus it happened that his command was clad in this dress when it crossed to Canada to meet the British under General Riall. General Scott, having been ordered to advance upon the British camp at Chippewa, moved in that direction on the morning of July 4th. In his march he encountered a body of the enemy, which, after some skirmishing, withdrew toward its main camp, and was rapidly and persistently pursued by Scott with his grays, whom the British commander mistook for volunteers, because of their uniform. When nearly overtaken, the British crossed Street's Creek and broke down the bridge behind them. When the Americans came to the bridge, and found their object foiled by its destruction, they could not repress their impatience and disappointment, for this alone prevented the battle of Chippewa, which was so handsomely won the following day, from being fought on the 4th of July.

After the battle, the British commander, who had been so hotly pursued, told General Scott he could not account for the good discipline of the *volunteers* before whom he had been forced to retreat so rapidly, or for the pertinacity of the pursuit, until he ascertained that his adversary really commanded a fine body of regulars, and remembered that anxiety to celebrate the anniversary of their independence had incited them.

It was in honor of this brigade and its commander that the gray became the famous "cadet gray."

Major-General Jacob Brown, in his report of the battle of Chippewa, said: "Brigadier-General Scott is entitled to the highest praise our country can bestow; to him, more than any other man, I am indebted for the victory of the 5th of July. His brigade has covered itself with glory."

CHAPTER XIV.

VALUE OF A SPOOL OF COTTON.

Capture of United States troops in Texas—Escape of French's battery.

AT the time of the outbreak of the rebellion, Major-General David E. Twiggs, a Louisiana man, was in command of the Military Department of Texas. A large proportion of the regular army was serving within that department, distributed in small bodies over an immense tract of country. The Government was persuaded that Twiggs secretly acted in concert with the Texan authorities, and suffered them to beleaguer the Union troops in every direction, so that no measures could be taken to prevent their surrender in detail to overwhelming numbers. Thus very nearly all the officers and enlisted men were put under a strictly worded parole not to serve in any capacity during the whole war, unless exchanged. Some, but not all, of the immediate staff serving under Twiggs were stanch in their loyalty to the Union, and they did what they could under the adverse circumstances which enveloped them. Among these was one of the best of men, Major William A. Nichols, assistant adjutant-general. As chief of the staff he could do much by foreseeing and providing for emergencies before they occurred. It was through his contrivance that a valuable battery of artillery escaped from the State and was saved to the Government.

In a note to me, dated March 7, 1861, Major Nichols says: "I send you a spool of cotton to show what *shifts* we were put to. It contains an order to French (William H. French, who commanded the battery) to '*cuidar*' (take care) for his guns—find it." The spool of cotton presented exactly the appearance of any ordinary one; but on removing the label pasted over the end and concealing the hole which passes through the center of the spool, I discovered a small roll of thin paper, on which was written the following order:

"HEADQUARTERS DEPARTMENT OF TEXAS,
"SAN ANTONIO, *February 10, 1861.*

"*The Commanding Officer, Fort Duncan.*

"SIR: Move instantly with the artillery companies upon Brazos Santiago; take your arms, guns, and necessary equipments and camp equipages; leave your horses on embarkation. The formal orders have been intercepted. Texas will demand the guns of the batteries. A steamer will be ready to take you by sea."

Not only were the movements of the army closely watched by the Texans, but some of Twiggs's staff took service against the Government, and did all in their power to wrest everything of value from the loyal officers, and convey it to the Texan authorities. In order to evade such vigilance, the wife of Major Nichols managed to send the spool containing the order to the wife of the British consul, at Eagle Pass, inclosing it in a letter, in which she asked that it be conveyed to Major French. This lady dispatched it by a Mexican boy, who safely delivered it, and French's sagacity guided him to its real object. He skillfully eluded the beleaguerers, and saved all his guns.

CHAPTER XV.

COLONEL MARTIN BURKE—THE FRENCH LADY.

The American Bastile—Arbitrary arrests justified—Obedience to orders—A very respectable French lady.

EARLY in the summer of 1861, when things were rapidly developing toward the rebellion, a new power, not hitherto exercised in this country, was exerted for the public safety. Persons were arbitrarily arrested and confined under military guard, on evidence satisfactory to the General Government that they were guilty of acts of a disloyal and dangerous character. It devolved upon the Secretary of State, in the first instance, to indicate who should be thus put in confinement. He made the arrests through his marshals, and they were turned over to General Scott, who held them at Fort Lafayette, in New York Harbor. By a natural association of ideas, both with the name and this use of the fort, it soon acquired the title of "the American Bastile."

This new and arbitrary power struck the Secretary of State with much force, and he once remarked to General Scott that he found it hard to realize that he had only to touch a bell and order the arrest of Mr. A. B., and in a short time to hear that A. B. was accordingly imprisoned at Fort Lafayette. The military justification of this measure and the extreme caution with which the power was exercised are ably set forth in Mr. Stanton's report as Secretary of War, dated December 1, 1862. (See Appendix C.)

The officer assigned to the immediate command of Fort Lafayette, specially selected by General Scott for that duty, was Colonel Martin Burke, of the regular artillery. The Secretary of State had heard the general's frequent jocose allusions to the colonel in terms which evinced perfect confidence in his vigilance and fidelity. One day he asked, "Who is this Colonel Martin Burke, of whom you seem to think so highly?" The general replied: "He is one of my regulars, sir; a veteran well known in the army." "Will he surely obey these extraordinary orders we are giving?" "You may rely on that, sir. Colonel Martin Burke is famous for his unquestioning obedience to orders. He was with me in Mexico, and, if I had told him at any time to take out one of my aides-de-camp and shoot him before breakfast, the aide's execution would have been duly reported." This created a hearty laugh, and brought some comical expressions to the faces of the aides present. Martin Burke was thenceforth a synonym for unquestioning obedience.

As might be supposed, Colonel (afterward brevet Brigadier-General) Burke was involved in some trouble on account of civil processes sought to be served on him, to avoid which he confined himself within his chain of sentinels almost as closely as he kept his prisoners. He once received a summons to attend as a witness before a court-martial at Fort Columbus, in New York Harbor, about nine miles from his post. He wrote to headquarters to inquire what it was his duty to do, saying he feared arrest by the civil authorities under an attachment which had been issued against him for not producing a prisoner in court on a writ, but which could not be served at the military post. This, he said, might prevent his obeying the summons of the court-martial. He suggested that, if it was deemed important enough for him to go, he might possibly escape arrest by traveling by water at night. His concern was, not about the arrest, but about a possible obstacle to his obeying his orders to appear as a witness.

The following are the instructions which were given for Colonel Burke's guidance:

HEADQUARTERS OF THE ARMY,
WASHINGTON, *July 19, 1861.*

Lieutenant-Colonel MARTIN BURKE, *U. S. Army, Fort Hamilton, N. Y.*

SIR: The general-in-chief directs that you assume command of Forts Hamilton and Lafayette, New York Harbor, taking quarters at the former place.

Orders have been given for the confinement of certain political prisoners and prisoners of war in Fort Lafayette, and a guard has been detailed for their custody, the officers of which will be quartered with the guard in the same fort. The general directs that you give orders to the following purpose:

1. That the prisoners be securely held, and that they be allowed every privilege consistent with this end, and be treated with all kindness.

2. That a record be kept of the names, dates of confinement, and release of the prisoners.

3. That the prisoners be permitted to provide themselves with such comforts as they require.

4. That an exact account be kept of the subsistence, etc., furnished the prisoners of war.

I am, sir, very respectfully,
Your obedient servant,
E. D. TOWNSEND,
Assistant Adjutant-General.

Among the most noted and troublesome of Colonel Burke's guests at Fort Lafayette was a certain Captain or Colonel Thomas, who held a commission from the Confederate Government. He had the *aliases* of "Zarvona" and "The French Lady." The latter was given him from the following incident, which illustrates his daring character, the account of which is taken from the "Baltimore American" of July 2, 1861:

"The steamer Saint Nicholas was captured in the Potomac River by a party of secessionists. The steamer left Baltimore, having on board about fifty passengers. Among those who went aboard previous to her departure was a very respectable 'French lady,' who was heavily veiled, and, pleading indisposition, she was immediately shown to her state-room, where she was kindly cared for by the females on board. There were also a party of about twenty-five men dressed in the garb of mechanics, carrying with them carpenters', tinners', blacksmiths', and other tools. When near Point Lookout, the 'French lady' appeared on deck, not in crinoline, but in the person of a stalwart man, who was immediately surrounded by the party of mechanics above alluded to. Captain Kirwan of the steamer demanded an explanation, when the 'lady-man' informed him that he designed confiscating the steamer and going on a privateering expedition. Finding himself overpowered, Captain Kirwan was compelled to submit, and the boat was handed over to the man and his crew, who took possession, and proceeded to run the steamer to a point known as 'The Cone,' on the Virginia shore. Upon landing at that place, the steamer was boarded by a body of about one thousand Virginia troops, when the passengers were landed and allowed to go on their way."

A short time after, Thomas and eight of his men were recognized as passengers on board the Mary Washington, *en route* from Fair Haven, Anne Arundel County, to Baltimore. It happened that Captain Kirwan and two of his officers were passengers at the same time, as were also two police-officers who had gone to Fair Haven to arrest another man. The captain of the Mary Washington, on making the discovery, was directed by the police-officers to land at Fort McHenry. Perceiving this intention, Thomas boldly attempted to overawe the officers. He drew his pistol, and, calling his men to his aid, peremptorily demanded that the boat should proceed up to Baltimore. But the party of officers and passengers against him was too strong, and Thomas was compelled to keep quiet. When the steamer reached Fort McHenry, the commanding officer was informed of the capture of Thomas, and sent a guard to receive and confine him. But he had disappeared, and could not be found for over an hour, when he was at last dragged from a bureau-drawer in the ladies' cabin.

Being small in stature he had managed thus to conceal himself.

During his confinement in Fort Lafayette he was constantly making trouble in some way. He once actually attempted to escape by throwing himself overboard, although he could not swim, with nothing to depend on but some empty tin cans arranged for floats.

CHAPTER XVI.

THE FIRST BATTLE OF BULL RUN.

Scott's plan opposed to invasion—His proposed campaign down the Mississippi—"On to Richmond!"—An anxious night—A panic—Order out of chaos.

In the early part of secession, General Scott was much opposed to fighting a battle within the seceded States, or to any display of military force which would lead to one. He reasoned that there were many Union and many neutral people in all the States, who, if they had time, would assert their principles and eventually overrule the more active secessionists. He frequently expressed himself to the President, and other influential men, in these terms: "If you will maintain a strict blockade on the sea-coast, collect your revenues on board cutters at the mouths of the harbors, and send a force down the Mississippi sufficiently strong to open and keep it free along its course to its mouth, you will thus cut off the luxuries to which the people are accustomed; and when they feel this pressure, not having been exasperated by attacks made on them within their respective States, the Union spirit will assert itself; those who are on the fence will descend on the Union side, and I will guarantee that in one year from this time all difficulties will be settled. But, if you invade the South at any point, I will guarantee that at the end of a year you will be further from a settlement than you are now."

The general's plan for the Mississippi was, to have gunboats built for the purpose, and to organize an army of Western volunteers, the whole force to rendezvous at Cairo, Illinois. McClellan was his choice for the command; Rosecrans, and some other "rough-vigor fellows," as he styled them, to have subordinate commands. I had often heard him detail this plan, and, on his declaring his intention of corresponding with General McClellan about it, I offered to draft the letter. I think it no mean compliment that the general should have assented, for he was always in the habit of doing such things himself. How much was left of my draft of the letter may be seen by the copy (Appendix D), with the alterations which the general made with his own hand. His erasures and interlineations were made with red ink.

In answer to the cry, "On to Richmond!" General Scott used to say that he was familiar with the country to be passed over; that it was hardly possible for inexperienced troops to make the march. They would have to haul all their supplies with them, for "they would find every house deserted; not a cow, or a chicken, or an accidental pig on the entire route." The bridges would be all broken down, and the marshy banks would prevent their being forded without becoming perfect quagmires.

THE FIRST BATTLE OF BULL RUN. 57

These delays and discouragements would be too much for undisciplined volunteers.

But, at last, the pressure for an advance upon Richmond became so great that the general, in deference to the wishes of higher authority, did all in his power to make preparations which would lead to success. Brigadier-General McDowell had served for some years on General Scott's staff, and was therefore well known to him. McDowell, having been assigned to the command which was eventually to fight the battle of Bull Run, was directed to prepare a plan for a movement toward Manassas, with estimates of the force he would need, and for all his supplies. The plan was to include a possible battle. While McDowell, with headquarters at Arlington Heights, was organizing and disciplining his regiments, he matured his plans, and made maps to illustrate them. They were repeatedly gone over with General Scott, until they were brought into the best possible shape. Then he was invited to unfold them to the President, in presence of the Cabinet, General Scott and his staff, and others, of whom General Fremont was one. The President received the company in the library of the Executive Mansion. General McDowell spread his map on the table, and demonstrated his plan with a clearness and precision that would have done credit to any West-Pointer at his last annual examination. Criticisms were invited from any one present; and the President specially asked General Fremont if he found any objection, or could suggest any improvement. Not a word was offered, and the whole scheme was approved. From that time active preparations were made for the movements which culminated in the battle of Bull Run, July 21, 1861.

The entire night of that 21st of July was spent by the President and Cabinet, and some military officers, at General Scott's quarters. The telegraph-office in the War Department, a short distance off, was in momentary receipt of dispatches from the field. At first, the success of the Union arms seemed assured. Then came tidings of a reverse; then of a panic, and *rout*. Then followed in quick succession details of the disaster, and rumors, with earnest appeals to guard the capital. I sat near the door of the general's room, to receive and read aloud the messages as they were delivered. At last came one in which the death of Colonel Cameron, brother of the Secretary of War, was reported. As I read aloud, not knowing what was to follow, I pronounced the words: "Colonel Cameron—" and then perceived that the sentence immediately came, "*was killed*." I had just time to stop abruptly, look at the Secretary a moment, and then finish the sentence in a low voice. This was the only preparation for the shocking announcement of his brother's death that could be given.

The following day was for a time a scene of such confusion and panic as required no ordinary nerve to encounter. General Scott was firm and unwavering as a rock. When reports were brought him that the rebels were advancing unopposed on Washington, and would soon be on the Long Bridge, the old soldier would calmly look at the informant and reply: "It is impossible, sir! We are now tasting the first fruits of a war, and learning what a panic is. We must be prepared for all kinds of rumors. Why, sir, we shall soon hear that Jefferson Davis has crossed the Long Bridge at the head of a brigade of elephants, and is trampling our citizens under foot! He has no brigade of elephants; he can not by any possibility get a brigade of elephants!" Thus from our general-in-chief emanated a remedy for panic which soon began to tell. We knew that there were some brigades, the one composed of the regulars, the one commanded by Colonel Keyes, and others, which remained entire, and occupied positions guarding the approaches to Washington. Meantime the general's aides occupied themselves in bringing order out of chaos. Placards were posted in conspicuous places designating rendezvous for the several organizations, and commanding all officers and men immediately to repair to them. As men straggled individually, or in squads, into town, they were directed where to go, and rations were provided for them there. Some of the general's staff went round to the hotels, and peremptorily ordered all the officers they found there to join their regiments immediately, on pain of arrest, their names and regiments being taken down. In this way, by nightfall things assumed a more orderly shape, and patrols, kept up throughout the day and night, soon suppressed all fear of disorders. For a time, however, there is little doubt that, had a squad of men, mounted on *black horses*,* appeared on the Long Bridge, or in the streets of the city, there would have been a stampede worthy of a flock of sheep.

The discussion of this battle is left to those who assume to write a strictly military history. There were fruitful elements of failure, however, without attributing blame to any one concerned. Panics will sometimes unaccountably seize the bravest veteran troops. What won-

* The Virginia troop of "Black-horse" had been a bugbear for some weeks.

der, then, that this great panic should have overtaken brigades and divisions composed of regiments some of which had not been three weeks in service, and were not sufficiently drilled to be able to wheel from a flank-march into line without breaking their ranks; brigades and divisions which had never been manœuvred as such, and which never saw the officers sent to command them until on the night before, or on the very morning of, the battle! It is rather a matter of wonder that an army should have done even so well, under such circumstances, as this one did at the outset.

CHAPTER XVII.

THE COMMAND OF THE ARMY.

General McClellan—Discipline of volunteers—Scott's choice for general-in-chief—His complaint against McClellan—McClellan succeeds Scott—His tribute to Scott—Halleck succeeds McClellan—An order bewitched.

IMMEDIATELY after the battle of Bull Run, General McClellan was summoned to Washington by the Secretary of War. In compliance with orders from the same source, he assumed his first command near Washington, under the title of the "Division of the Potomac," July 27, 1861. On his arrival in Washington he had a long interview with General Scott at his quarters. I was not present in the room, but waited outside to get a chance for a word with him as he passed out. I had just time to say: "I want to give you a hint about the state of things here. You will find splendid material for soldiers sadly in need of discipline. You will be beset on all sides with applications for passes, and all sorts of things, and if you yield to the pressure your whole time will be taken up at a desk, writing. You can from the outset avoid this; another officer can do it as well in your name. The troops want to see their commanding general, and to be often inspected and reviewed by him. Another thing: there is here a fine body of regulars; I would keep that intact, as a sort of 'Old Guard.' It may some time save you a battle." He took what I said kindly. Perhaps he never thought of it again, but it is certain that he pursued exactly that course. His splendid military evolutions while organizing and equipping his army will not soon be forgotten.

Some of the volunteer regiments came to Washington admirably provided. There were, especially, two from New Hampshire. They had complete clothing, arms and accoutrements, and tents. Their wagons were arranged like store-rooms, with boxes for their various supplies. They had also very good bands of music. Their religious services were very impressive. The regiments were drawn up in a hollow square, with the chaplain in the middle, and, while the bands played hymns which he gave out, the men sang them. Their rendering of "Old Hundred" was truly grand. But, with all this excellent material, the want of military instruction was apparent in such incidents as this: It was no unusual thing to see a sentry, when an officer in uniform passed his post, seated on a stone, with his musket between his feet. On the approach of the officer, aware that some complimentary recognition was expected, he would awkwardly raise his hand to his cap, while he continued sitting. General McClellan was not long in changing all this, and in forming a thoroughly disciplined army.

McClellan was not General Scott's first choice for general-in-chief of the army, to succeed him on his retirement. As the time approached when he purposed giving up the command, he frequently expressed anxiety to hear that General Halleck had arrived from California, where he had long been residing. He remarked that he should feel quite easy to turn over his responsibilities to Halleck as major-general, commanding the army. While General Scott held McClellan in high estimation for some junior command, he preferred Halleck, as being ten years older, and therefore presumably having riper judgment, besides having known accomplishment in theoretical knowledge of military law and practice.

The very day (July 22, 1861) that the Secretary of War, through the adjutant-general, telegraphed to McClellan, at Beverly, Virginia—" Circumstances make your presence here necessary. Charge Rosecrans, or some other general, with your present department, and come hither without delay"—General Scott, in ignorance of that dispatch, telegraphed to McClellan, " Remain in your command, instead of going to the valley of the Shenandoah." General McClellan naturally felt when he took command of the Army of the Potomac, that he had been put in direct communication with the War Department, and he therefore did not always observe the "channels of correspondence" which were usual. General Scott soon observed this, and, not willing to have his authority ignored so long as he remained general-in-chief, he gave me an autograph *projet* of a general order to issue, the last but one that went to the army in his name. It was this:

THE COMMAND OF THE ARMY.

GENERAL ORDERS, No. 17.
HEADQUARTERS OF THE ARMY,
WASHINGTON, *September 16, 1861.*

There are irregularities in the correspondence of the army which need prompt correction. It is highly important that junior officers on duty be not permitted to correspond with the general-in-chief, or other commander, on current official business, except through intermediate commanders; and the same rule applies to correspondence with the President direct, or with him through the Secretary of War, unless it be by the special invitation or request of the President.

By command of Lieutenant-General Scott:

E. D. TOWNSEND,
Assistant Adjutant-General.

General Scott afterward addressed a more pointed communication to the Secretary of War, in which his feelings as to General McClellan's course, and as to his choice of a successor, are unmistakably set forth:

HEADQUARTERS OF THE ARMY,
WASHINGTON, *October 4, 1861.*

Hon. S. CAMERON, *Secretary of War.*

SIR: You are, I believe, aware that I hailed the arrival here of Major-General McClellan as an event of happy consequence to the country and to the army. Indeed, if I did not call for him, I heartily approved of the suggestion, and gave it the most cordial support. He, however, had hardly entered upon his new duties, when, encouraged to communicate directly with the President and certain members of the Cabinet, he in a few days forgot that he had any intermediate commander, and has now long prided himself in treating me with uniform neglect, running into disobedience of orders of the smaller matters—neglects, though, in themselves, grave military offenses. I read and speak in the face of the following facts :

To suppress irregularity, more conspicuous in Major-General McClellan than in any other officer, I publish the following facts :

[Here follows General Orders 17, above quoted.]

With this order fresh in his memory, Major-General McClellan addressed two important communications to the Secretary of War, on respectively the 19th and 20th of the same month, over my head, and how many since to the Secretary, and even to the President direct, I have not inquired, but many, I have no doubt, besides daily oral communications with the same high functionaries, all without my knowledge.

Second. To correct another class of grave neglects, I the same day caused to be addressed to Major-General McClellan the following order :

HEADQUARTERS OF THE ARMY,
WASHINGTON, *September 16, 1861.*

To Major-General MCCLELLAN, *U. S. Army, commanding the Department of the Potomac:*

The commanding general of the Army of the Potomac will cause the position, state, and number of troops under him to be reported at once to general headquarters, by divisions, brigades, and independent regiments or detachments, which general report will be followed by reports of new troops as they arrive, with the dispositions made of them, together with all the material changes which may take place in said army.

By command of Lieutenant-General Scott:
(Signed)   E. D. TOWNSEND,
Assistant Adjutant-General.

Eighteen days have now elapsed, and not the slightest response has been shown to either of these orders by Major-General McClellan. Perhaps he will say, in respect to the latter, it has been difficult for him to procure the exact returns of divisions and brigades. But why not have given me proximate returns, such as he so eagerly furnished the President and certain Secretaries? Has, then, a senior no corrective power over a junior officer in case of such persistent neglect and disobedience?

The remedy by arrest and trial before a court-martial would probably soon cure the evil. But it has been feared that a conflict of authority near the head of the army would be highly encouraging to the enemies and depressing to the friends of the Union. Hence my long forbearance; and continuing, though but nominally, on duty, I shall try to hold out till the arrival of Major-General Halleck, when, as his presence will give me increased confidence in the safety of the Union, and being, as I am, unable to ride in the saddle, or to walk, by reason of dropsy in my feet and legs and paralysis in the small of the back, I shall definitely retire from the command of the army.

I have the honor to remain, with high respect, your most obedient servant,
WINFIELD SCOTT.

Thus the old war-chief to the last asserted his authority, and illustrated the maxim of "the ruling passion strong in death."

Meantime, McCleilan went on acquiring more and more popularity as the "young Napoleon of our army." On General Scott's retirement, General Orders, No. 94, of November 1, 1861, announced that "the President is pleased to direct that Major-General George B. McClellan assume command of the Army of the United States." This constituted him general-in-chief *vice* Scott. In assuming the command, McClellan, in General Orders, No. 19, of November 1, 1861, thus gracefully alluded to the retiring lieutenant-general:

"The army will unite with me in the feeling of regret that the weight of many years, and the effect of increasing infirmities, contracted and intensified in his country's service, should just now remove from our head the great soldier of our nation—the hero who in his youth raised high the reputation of his country on the fields of Canada, which he hallowed with his blood; who in more mature years proved to the world that American skill and valor could repeat, if not eclipse, the exploits of Cortez in the land of the Montezumas; whose life has been devoted to the service of his country; whose whole efforts have been directed to uphold our honor at the smallest sacrifice of life—a warrior who scorned the selfish glories of the battle-field when his great abilities as a statesman could be employed more profitably for his country; a citizen who in his declining years has given to the world the most shining instance of loyalty in disregarding all ties of birth and clinging still to the cause of truth and honor. Such has been the career, such the character, of WINFIELD

Scott, whom it has long been the delight of the nation to honor, both as a man and a soldier. While we regret his loss, there is one thing we can not regret—the bright example he has left for our emulation. Let us all hope and pray that his declining years may be passed in peace and happiness, and that they may be cheered by the success of the country and the cause he has fought for and loved so well. Beyond all that, let us do nothing that can cause him to blush for us; let no defeat of the army he has so long commanded embitter his last years, but let our victories illuminate the close of a life so grand." *

General McClellan's command of the whole army was terminated by the "President's War Order, No. 3," dated "Executive Mansion, Washington, March 11, 1862," as follows:

"Major-General McClellan having personally taken the field at the head of the Army of the Potomac, until otherwise ordered, he is relieved from the command of the other military departments, he retaining command of the Department of the Potomac."

The Government now thought it would try its own hand at commanding-in-chief. This lasted until July 11, 1862, when the following order issued from the Executive Office:

"*Ordered*, That Major-General Henry W. Halleck be assigned to command the whole land-forces of the United States, as general-in-chief; and that he repair to this capital so soon as he can with safety to the positions and

* General Scott died the 29th of May, 1866. He thus lived to fulfill this devout and eloquent prayer.

operations within the department now under his special charge."

After the Peninsular campaign, when the Army of the Potomac was withdrawn, and principally merged in General Pope's army, General McClellan was for a time left without any defined command. On the 2d of September, 1862, a draft of an order was received from General Halleck's office in the following form, and was duly issued accordingly:

GENERAL ORDERS, No. 122.
    WAR DEPARTMENT, ADJUTANT-GENERAL'S OFFICE,
      WASHINGTON, *September 2, 1862.*

By direction of the President, Major-General McClellan will have command of the fortifications of Washington, and of all the troops for the defense of the capital.

By order of the Secretary of War:
      E. D. TOWNSEND,
      Assistant Adjutant-General.

In this form copies were made, and some of the morning papers published the order. Later in the day, a memorandum from General Halleck's office directed that the form of the order be corrected so that it would read as follows:

GENERAL ORDERS, No. 122.
    WAR DEPARTMENT, ADJUTANT-GENERAL'S OFFICE,
      WASHINGTON, *September 2, 1862.*

Major-General McClellan will have command of the fortifications of Washington, and of all the troops for the defense of the capital.

By command of Major-General Halleck:
      E. D. TOWNSEND,
      Assistant Adjutant-General.

The difference in form consisted in omitting allusion to the authority of the President and of the Secretary of War, and substituting that of General-in-Chief Halleck.

There was probably some supposed political significance attached to this. At any rate, Secretary Stanton, by whose directions the order had already been given to the newspapers for publication, desired me to see that the order in the new form should appear in all the papers which had already published it, and that the Washington "Evening Star" should be sure to have it in the corrected form. I accordingly saw the editor of the "Evening Star," handed him a copy, communicated to him the Secretary's wish, and cautioned him against the possible contingency of the order having been already set up in its erroneous form from a morning paper. He promised to see to it, and I returned to the department satisfied that no mistake could possibly occur. To my amazement, in the afternoon the Secretary handed me a copy of the "Star," in which was the order in the objectionable form. Going to the "Star" office, I taxed the editor with not heeding what I had tried to impress upon him. He sent for a copy of the paper, then lying on the counter for sale, and I confess to being somewhat dazed when I there saw the order unmistakably in its *right* form. I began to think, for the first time, that there must be some truth in the existence of witches. The explanation was, that the order had been copied from the morning papers, and a very few *proof* copies of the "Star" had been struck off before the correction was made, which was immediately done when my manuscript was received, and all the main edition of the paper was quite correct. As luck would have it, the few copies of first proof fell into the hands of the newsboy who had sold one to the Secretary's messenger!

This circumstance illustrates the untiring vigilance which Mr. Stanton exercised over even comparatively trivial matters under his control.

CHAPTER XVIII.

BALL'S BLUFF—RED RIVER.

Object of demonstration on Leesburg — Rigorous treatment of General Stone—The secret history—Colonel Raymond Lee—General Stone at Red River—Colonel Bailey's engineering—Capture and recovery of his vote of thanks.

In the fall of 1861, Brigadier-General Charles P. Stone proposed to General Scott to permit him to take a brigade and make a demonstration along the line of the canal toward Harper's Ferry. Extensive flour-mills in Georgetown, upon which we mainly depended for breadstuffs, were owned by friends of Stone, and from them he learned that the fine wheat-harvest in the Leesburg district could probably be brought into Georgetown, if a show of force were made by the Government, under color of which the farmers might sell their harvest to their usual customers. Stone thought that such a demonstration, besides guarding the canal, might be continued toward Harper's Ferry, so as to co-operate with the column opposite that point, in compelling the Confederates to evacuate Harper's Ferry, then held by them. And so it resulted.

The disastrous action of Leesburg, or Ball's Bluff, October 21, 1861, in which Colonel E. D. Baker was killed, has given rise to much controversy. Stone was arrested soon after, and for a long time was kept in close confinement. Indeed, from that hour bad fortune seemed to persecute him until it broke him up, and forced him out of the service.

Whatever may be the true military aspect of his case, there must have been some reason, not openly declared, for the rigorous and unusual treatment to which he was so long subjected. Perhaps a clew may be found to it in the following facts: A part of Stone's command was composed of Massachusetts regiments.* Being strongly

---

* After the "Ball's Bluff" affair, a reference was made in the papers to the colonel of the Twentieth Massachusetts Regiment, which, being quite characteristic of the man, deserves to be perpetuated. It was as follows:

"Colonel Raymond Lee and staff were furnished with a skiff to make their escape. The colonel gallantly refused, and gave orders to use it for conveying the wounded across the river. It was filled with wounded, who reached the Maryland shore in safety, and the humane and gallant officer was taken prisoner."

Colonel Lee was taken to Richmond and confined as a prisoner of war in Libby Prison. A sequel to this incident was given in a Boston paper of July, 1882, and is authentic:

"On the 10th of November, 1861, General Winder, with his staff, visited the officers' prison, and read to the prisoners an order from Benjamin, the Confederate States Secretary of War, directing the selection of seven officers of highest rank, to be held as hostages for the officers and crew of the letter of marque Lady Jeff Davis, who had been convicted of piracy in a United States court. Those selected were to be confined in a cell of the common jail, and to be executed, if the officers of the privateer were executed by the United States Government. Slips of paper containing the names of all the officers were placed in a tin tobacco-box, and the fated names were drawn from the box upon command of General Winder by ex-Congressman Ely, who was captured at the first battle of Bull Run, and was confined with the Union officers. General Lee, then Colonel Lee, was

opposed to slavery, some of the men expected Stone, also a Massachusetts man, to take active part against it. In those early days of the war, the question of the negro status was a very troublesome one. No authority whatever had yet been assumed by the General Government which militated against the Constitution as it then stood. It was deemed of the first importance to treat the border slave States, not in secession, with much caution on this delicate point. They were to be held in the Union by careful policy, as well as by military occupancy. Accordingly, the orders given the several commanders of our forces were to surrender to their owners any slaves found by their masters in our camps, and claimed by them, provided they belonged to States not in rebellion. All who escaped from the rebel States were held to be free, as "contraband" of war.

It happened, when Stone's forces retreated across the river from Leesburg, that some few colored men came

one of the 'elected,' and the slip of paper drawn from the box designating him had on it only the words 'Colonel Lee.' The fate of the officers selected was not then determined, being contingent upon the action of the United States authorities with regard to the convicted people of the Lady Jeff Davis. This slip of paper with his name upon it was given to Colonel Lee, who indorsed upon the back of it that it was the ballot he drew in the lottery of life and death, and put it in a letter written to his family, which was allowed to be forwarded.

"On the 14th of November the officers designated as hostages were removed to the county jail, where they were detained about three months under rather disagreeable conditions. About the middle of February, 1862, the Confederate States Government, having received information that the Lady Jeff Davis people had been remanded as prisoners of war, the hostages were transferred from the jail to the prison assigned to prisoners of war, and on the 22d of that month they were put on board a flag-of-truce boat to be transferred to a United States steamer in neutral waters."

over with them. I personally had from two of them the following statement: These men were brothers to an admirable *free* woman who lived in my family as nurse. The rest of her family belonged to a Mr. Smart, who owned a large mill at Leesburg. The woman, being at the North with my family, sent to ask me to give her two brothers some of her wages, they being then at the house of a relative in Georgetown. I went for the purpose, saw the men, and asked them to tell me the facts about their coming over the river at the time of Stone's retreat. They said they became mixed up with the troops in their retreat across the river, and hardly knew how they happened to go over; that General Stone sent for them and told them they were perfectly free to go where they pleased, and that, if they desired, they could be employed in the camp. They replied that they did not come over intentionally; that Mr. Smart was a good master, and allowed them often to work for themselves; that he had a considerable sum of their money in his keeping; that their parents, wives, and children were all in Leesburg, and they wanted to go back to them. General Stone then promised to send them over with a flag of truce he was about to dispatch, and they returned of their own free-will.

Some of the Massachusetts volunteers, hearing that these men had been sent back, wrote to Governor Andrew, complaining that this United States officer was surrendering fugitive slaves to their masters. Governor Andrew sent orders to his colonels not to permit any slaves who took refuge within their camps to be surrendered. He also wrote a strong remonstrance against such policy by the Government, to the Massachusetts Senator,

Sumner. General Stone, having been shown Governor Andrew's instructions to the Massachusetts colonels, wrote to the Adjutant-General of the Army protesting that those regiments, having been mustered into the service of the General Government, and placed under his command by lawful authority, could not be permitted to receive instructions from the Governor of the State, from whose control they had entirely passed. This letter was rather injudiciously forwarded to Governor Andrew by the adjutant-general, though never intended by the writer for the Governor's eye. Senator Sumner, on receipt of the Governor's remonstrance, denounced General Stone on the floor of the Senate. Thereupon, Stone wrote him a strong letter, justifying himself, and remonstrating against being thus arraigned in a place where he could not defend himself. This brought a storm about Stone's ears, and there were even many persons who at last became convinced that he was disloyal. The many political friends of Colonel Baker, seriously feeling his loss, were perhaps ready to believe anything to the prejudice of the leader of the ill-fated expedition which cost his life. Stone's rigorous incarceration may have been due to these causes. At all events, he was held without trial, although he repeatedly and earnestly asked for the charges against him, and for an inquiry or trial.

At length he was released from arrest, though suffered to remain without a command, until in April, 1863, General Banks, who was commanding an army in the Southwest, wrote to the general-in-chief, Halleck, urging the pressing need of general officers of experience, and earnestly requesting that Brigadier-General Charles P. Stone be ordered to report to him immediately. He added that he had entire confidence in General Stone's zeal and ability, and would himself be responsible for his conduct. Upon this, Stone was ordered to General Banks. He became his chief of staff, and it is said to be greatly due to his skill and indefatigable exertions that the Red River disaster was not even more serious than it was.

A fleet of gunboats co-operated with General Banks in his Red River expedition, in May, 1864. Owing to a fall in the water, the boats came near being lost above the falls, at Alexandria, but they were extricated by "the indefatigable exertions of Lieutenant-Colonel Bailey (Fourth Wisconsin Volunteers), acting engineer of the Nineteenth Army Corps, who proposed and built a tree-dam of six hundred feet across the river at the lower falls, which enabled all the vessels to pass in safety the back-water of the Mississippi, reaching Alexandria, and allowed them to pass over the shoals and the obstructions planted by the enemy to a point of safety."

For this valuable service Colonel Bailey received a vote of thanks by Congress. I had the resolutions elegantly engrossed on parchment by one of the clerks in the adjutant-general's office, who was an accomplished penman—an artist in his way—and sent them to Colonel Bailey, in a tin case made for the purpose, with his name conspicuously painted on the outside. It is probable a vessel, by which the case was sent over part of the route, was captured by a rebel cruiser. The receipt of it was not acknowledged by Colonel Bailey. A year afterward a rebel vessel was captured by a United States war-steamer off Cuba. Among the articles found in her was the tin case containing Colonel Bailey's resolutions.

It was forwarded to Washington, and again sent on its journey to its rightful owner, with a letter giving an account of its adventures.

CHAPTER XIX.

SERVICE IN THE ADJUTANT-GENERAL'S OFFICE.

General Scott's retirement—Disposal of his staff—Detached duty of the adjutant-general—Several candidates.

THE interview between President Lincoln and his Cabinet and General Scott, which took place at the general's quarters, in the afternoon of November 1, 1861, when he retired from active service, under the provisions of a special act of Congress, was one of the most impressive ever witnessed. (The act and interesting correspondence relating to the retirement will be found in Appendix E.)

The general's military family accompanied him to New York, and bade him farewell on board the steamer in which he embarked for France.

Some of the staff supposed, from the terms of President Lincoln's pledge, that they were in some way to be personally attached as a military family to the commander-in-chief of the army and navy. The President, however, fully redeemed his promise to provide for them, by asking what they desired, and granting their requests. Colonel Van Rensselaer was made inspector-general in the regular army, and besides brevetted brigadier-general. The other aides received appointments as general officers of United

States volunteers, except Colonel Wright, who was a major of the regular cavalry, and was retained as additional aide-de-camp, with rank of colonel, to General McClellan. I returned somewhat later than the rest of the general's staff, and after they had been provided for, having to collect and forward to Washington the records of army headquarters, which had been left in New York. On reporting to the President, he asked what I desired. I replied that I did not think it right to indicate for what duty I was most required, but was ready for any orders that might be given me. The President remarked that doubtless the chief of my department would suitably assign me; so I then went to report to the new general-in-chief, General McClellan, fully expecting to follow Generals Cullum and Hamilton, who had gone to join General Halleck in the Army of the West. When General McClellan directed me to report to Adjutant-General L. Thomas for duty in the office, I could not forbear saying, "General, I have been a long time on duty there, and hoped now to have a turn in the field." The general replied that my peculiar experience was needed to systematize matters in the office, which had fallen into confusion.

The army had suddenly grown from ten thousand to over one hundred thousand, and the business had proportionally augmented. Several newly appointed officers of the department had gone on duty there for a few weeks, and, before they had time to learn the routine, had been detached to the field. Colonel Garesché—than whom no better officer or purer man ever lived—had been the senior assistant, and, though he labored incessantly, it was impossible for him to keep up with the general business, aided only by inexperienced officers, while he at the same time was in charge of the immense and complicated branch of the military commissions. Accordingly, the mails of several days were unopened; piles of letters, some of which had been acted on and others not, were all mixed together in confusion. The few clerks were struggling on, without system or much concert, to dispose of what pressed most at the moment. The rooms and hall were filled during office hours with volunteers from the front, who came to get sick-leaves, or discharges, each one, in his impatience to go home, clamoring for the earliest attention. It required a week of *extra hours'* work to clear away the wreck and assort the papers. Then the duties of the clerks were arranged so that two would not be doing the same thing while other things were left undone. The military hospitals in and around the city supplied abundance of superior clerks, who had left banks and counting-houses to volunteer, but whose physique was not equal to their ambition for the exposed life of a soldier. So, in a few weeks, matters were in such shape that no business need be neglected.

Adjutant-General Thomas had a very difficult place to fill. Secretary Cameron relied on him greatly in the management of military affairs, so suddenly and so vastly brought into the most prominent of all functions of the Government. It was at that time thought important that as much *éclat* as possible should be given to the arrival of volunteer regiments which came to re-enforce the army, and the adjutant-general was called upon to make addresses, present flags, etc., at the various camps around the capital. This state of things threw much of the immediate conduct of the office upon me as the senior assistant.

When the Hon. Edwin M. Stanton became Secretary of War, affairs had settled down to stern work, and glorifying ceased to be such a prominent element in military life. It happened that one day, at about one o'clock, Mr. Stanton sent word that he desired to see the adjutant-general. I answered the call, saying: "The adjutant-general has stepped out for a moment; can I do what you require?" He replied, "It appears to me he steps out quite often"; and then he handed me a paper he wished attended to. After this he often sent for me individually, and at last, in March, 1863, he ordered General Thomas away to muster out a large body of volunteers at Harrisburg. As soon as he returned from this duty, the Secretary found some other detached service for him. Finally, he sent him to Kentucky, and other States, with a roving commission to organize colored regiments, and look after abandoned lands and property. He did not come back to the office, and I was thus informally left in charge. This was a most uncertain and consequently embarrassing position to be placed in, and the only course was to do whatever seemed right, without waiting to ascertain what were the views of the adjutant-general, when he should return.

The first intimation that this was to be a permanent arrangement was, when one day the Secretary sent for me to be introduced to a certain prominent gentleman, to whom I was requested to administer the oath of office as a brigadier-general of volunteers. The Secretary then remarked, "I wish you to know Colonel Townsend, for you will receive orders from him as adjutant-general." It has since transpired that Mr. Stanton was early dissatisfied with General Thomas for some reason, and looked around to find some one suitable to put in his place. He gave situations in the War Office to several persons, probably with a view to having them on trial, meanwhile leaving me in charge of the adjutant-general's office as the senior assistant. It would seem that he was once very near appointing a colonel of the line, who had applied for the place, and had been highly recommended to him. He introduced this officer to me, and instructed me to put one of my juniors in the office, with all his clerks, under his orders, and to give him any other assistance he might call for. Something made me suspect that this was a first step toward giving this colonel of the line full charge over the whole adjutant-general's office. So I waited until he had withdrawn, when I said: "Mr. Secretary, it is necessary that I should clearly understand what relations Colonel —— is to bear to my office. He can not lawfully exercise any of the functions of the adjutant-general, which are defined by statute. In the personal absence of the head of the department, his duties devolve properly upon his next junior, and, as such junior, I can not receive orders from a colonel of the line. The assistant adjutant-general, whom you have directed to report to Colonel ——, has some of the duties which by law are under the adjutant-general; do you intend that Colonel —— shall now have supervision over them?" The Secretary replied curtly that he should require all officers to obey his orders. In answer, I made no question on that point, but said it was necessary, in such an unusual and rather complicated arrangement, that I should fully understand the intent and scope of his orders, and that he should be informed what their bearing would be. Meanwhile, the Secretary had time to ponder what I had said. He then told me he had brought Colonel —— into the War Office to take charge of a class of business that required more attention than I could give it; that there were claims enough set up against the Government for military supplies, etc., to swamp the Treasury, if the just were not separated from the unjust; and he expected me and the officers under me to help Colonel —— in examining them, in every way we could. To this, of course, I assented, the more readily as that class of cases was quite foreign to my duties. Colonel —— was supplied with two or three clerks; his business at once took such a shape that neither he nor I interfered with each other, and we continued for several years in the most harmonious relations. Whatever were the Secretary's original intentions, the result was perfectly satisfactory to me, for I was never superseded, but enjoyed to a gratifying extent the "great War Secretary's" confidence.

Riding with Secretary Stanton in his carriage, at the funeral of General Totten, Chief of Engineers, in April, 1864, I alluded to an interview with him on a certain Sunday in July, 1862, before I had really been placed in charge of the adjutant-general's office, when I pleaded with him to let me go from the department to field-service according with my rank. He remembered the circumstance, and that he had then complimented me by saying that my long familiarity with the working not only of his department, but of other branches of the Government, was too necessary to him to allow him to comply. He remarked that no reproach could justly attach to me for the line of duty in which I had been employed; that no officer had been more laborious from first to last, and that I had successfully met a weight of responsibility which could be appreciated only by a few persons.

Such commendation ought, perhaps, in reason, to be considered as sufficient justification for having foregone the more ambitious pursuit of fame in a more brilliant but not more useful sphere of professional service; especially as it came from one of the most exacting of public officers.

CHAPTER XX.

JULIUS P. GARESCHÉ.

Killed in battle—Official announcement of his death—His charities—Decorated by the Pope—A priest's eulogium.

WHILE commanding the Department of the Cumberland, in 1862, General Rosecrans sent an urgent request that Colonel Gareschér might be ordered to report to him. Gareschér added his own wish to this solicitation, and he was ordered. He arrived in time to be of material assistance in organizing the army which, after varied fortunes, defeated Bragg at Stone River. In a brief dispatch from that battle-field, General Rosecrans said, "We have to deplore the loss of Lieutenant-Colonel Gareschér, whose capacity and gentlemanly deportment had already endeared him to all the officers of this command, and whose gallantry on the field of battle excited their admiration."

At the outbreak of the rebellion he was the senior

assistant in the adjutant-general's office. In announcing his death to the officers of his department the adjutant-general said:

"His ability and untiring industry have left their impress on the elaborate records over which he presided; and the universal and unfeigned regret at his loss, so freely expressed by all who came in contact with him, is a touching evidence of his value as an officer and his worth as a man. Just and uncompromising in his official conduct, he was yet courteous, obliging, and affable. Possessing a chivalric spirit, with a high order of professional attainment, he hastened to embrace the first opportunity given him to enter on a more brilliant sphere of action, and reported to Major-General Rosecrans as his chosen chief of staff, in time to render essential aid in organizing the army with which the field of Murfreesboro was won. At a critical moment, on the 31st of December, when the general, with his staff, dashed forward to restore the tide of battle, which was turning against our arms, 'the noble Colonel Garesché' was instantly killed by a cannon-ball.

"What lot can be more enviable to a soldier than his! Of singularly spotless private character, faithful in the observance of his obligations as a Christian, and devoted in his leisure hours to the exercise of benevolent acts, honored and beloved in his profession, he died as a true hero, and is mourned with a depth and sincerity of grief not often betrayed."

Garesché was a very devout Roman Catholic, and fully lived up to his professions. There was no end to his unostentatious charities, which he usually performed after his tedious office-hours were over. He started the society of St. Vincent de Paul in Washington, and was one of its most active members, visiting and ministering to the poor and the sick. It is related of him that, at the risk of his own life, he once held in his arms an infant belonging to a poor family, while a priest baptized it, though the child was ill of small-pox. The Pope was informed of his extraordinary zeal, and sent him a medal of some charitable order. This he always wore on his breast.

His remains were brought to Washington for interment. There they were honored with an imposing funeral, attended by an immense concourse. The ceremonies took place at St. Aloysius Church. The presiding priest pronounced an eloquent eulogium upon him, in which he thus described his death:

"The battle, which had raged furiously, was going against our arms, and all seemed lost. Colonel Garesché had used almost superhuman efforts to cheer on the troops, and, seeing that they were yielding ground, he retired for a brief space to some bushes, where he was perceived kneeling as in earnest prayer. It is believed that he then offered up his own life as a sacrifice, if God would give him a victory. Immediately after, General Rosecrans and himself received the blessed sacrament, from a priest who attended the army as chaplain to the general. Colonel Garesché then rushed into the thickest of the fight, and was killed by a cannon-ball, which took off his head. Thus he fell, while at that moment the body and blood of his Lord was coursing through his veins."

CHAPTER XXI.

ARMY OF THE POTOMAC COMMANDERS.

Generous spirit of Burnside and Lincoln—Plain language to Hooker—Swapping horses while crossing a river.

THE battle of Antietam, Maryland, was fought by the Army of the Potomac, under General McClellan, September 16 and 17, 1862. General Burnside was ordered to relieve General McClellan November 5, 1862. He commanded at the battle of Fredericksburg, December 13, 1862. In his preliminary report to General Halleck, he explained the reasons why he had moved sooner and on a different plan from what had been indicated by the President, and attributed his want of success to fog and other unexpected causes of delay, which gave the enemy time to concentrate his forces. With singular frankness he says:

"To the brave officers and soldiers who accomplished the feat of thus recrossing in the face of the enemy, I owe everything; for the failure in the attack I am responsible, as the extreme gallantry, courage, and endurance shown by them were never exceeded, and would have carried the point had it been possible.

"The fact that I decided to move from Warrenton on to this line, rather against the opinion of the President, Secretary, and yourself, and that you have left the whole movement in my hands without giving me orders, makes me the more responsible."

President Lincoln, not to be outdone in generosity,

published, from the Executive Mansion, this address to the Army of the Potomac:

"I have just read your commanding general's preliminary report of the battle of Fredericksburg. Although you were not successful, the attempt was not an error, nor the failure other than an accident. The courage with which you, in an open field, maintained the contest against an intrenched foe, and the consummate skill and success with which you crossed and recrossed the river, in face of the enemy, show that you possess all the qualities of a great army, which will yet give victory to the cause of the country and of popular government. Condoling with the mourners for the dead, and sympathizing with the severely wounded, I congratulate you that the number of both is comparatively so small.

"I tender to you, officers and soldiers, the thanks of the nation. ABRAHAM LINCOLN."

January 25, 1863, the President relieved General Burnside from the command, at his own request, and assigned General Hooker in his stead. Hooker was wounded at Antietam, and was for a time at St. Elizabeth Hospital, near Washington. There were rumors about town, immediately after Antietam, that McClellan was to be removed; and it was persistently averred that Hooker would succeed him. But Burnside came first, and Hooker relieved Burnside the 26th of January, 1863.

On that same day the President addressed to General Hooker that singular communication, in which he told him:

"You are ambitious, which, within reasonable bounds,

does good rather than harm; but I think that, during General Burnside's command of the army, you have taken counsel of your ambition, and thwarted him as much as you could, in which you did a great wrong to the country and to a most meritorious and honorable brother officer. I have heard, in such way as to believe it, of your recently saying that both the army and the government needed a dictator. Of course it was not for this, but in spite of this, that I have given you the command. Only those generals who gain successes can set up dictators. What I now ask of you is military success, and I will risk the dictatorship."

When Hooker had made his grand movement across the river to Chancellorsville, by which he put his army between Lee and Richmond, compelling Lee to offer him the chance for a flank attack in his retreat, he issued a short order, saying:

"It is with heart-felt satisfaction the commanding general announces to the army that the operations of the last three days have determined that our enemy must either ingloriously fly, or come out from behind his defenses and give us battle on our own ground, where certain destruction awaits him."

Did not this give promise of the "military success" asked by the President? Happening to meet General Totten, Chief of Engineers, the morning after, he told me that he had been depressed by the failure of so many enterprises of late, but Hooker's order had quite put him in heart again. I was a classmate of Hooker's, and knew him too well to participate in General Totten's hopefulness. I remarked that it was certainly a masterly movement that had placed the Army of the Potomac in its present position, but I was afraid Hooker, though brave, and a good corps commander, had not the ready genius to be able to manage an army on the battle-field, against either Jackson, Longstreet, or Lee, singly, and still less against all three together. Alas! so it happened.

This first prognostication having been justified by the event, there was good reason for apprehension when it was known that Lee's army was in full march toward Maryland and Pennsylvania, and that Hooker was hastening to intercept it.

On the 27th of June the Secretary desired me to detail an officer to carry dispatches to the Army of the Potomac. He was to report at the department at seven o'clock in the evening. I thought it well for me to be there also at that time, and was accordingly ready to sign an order, which General Halleck brought to my room for that purpose. It is a good rule never to sign a paper without looking at its purport, so I read:

"By direction of the President, Major-General Joseph Hooker is relieved from the command of the Army of the Potomac, and Major-General George G. Meade is appointed to the command of that army, and of the troops temporarily assigned to duty with it."

As he left the room, General Halleck said, "That is a good order, isn't it?" To which I replied, "This is the first time I have drawn a long breath for several weeks."

The general who won the great battle of Gettysburg was thus invested with his command while his army was in full march toward the field of battle, and while he was in ignorance of the strength or whereabouts of the different corps composing it. "An exception proves the rule," they say; so Mr. Lincoln happily this time made an exception to his rule, " It is a bad plan to swap horses while crossing a river."

CHAPTER XXII.

PRESIDENT LINCOLN.

A cavalry rifle—The nervous traveler and the donkey—" There is a man in there!"

ONE day, I went to the Executive Office to see the President on some business. There were two other persons in the room. One was apparently a Western farmer, who had a sort of breech-loading rifle he had invented for cavalry service. Though he was not a mechanic, his gun showed much ingenuity and some originality. He was eager to exhibit it to the President, while the latter was anxious to converse with his other visitor. The President greeted me in his cheery manner, and said I had come just in time to examine the new invention, and advise the man, better than he could, what to do with it. I drew the inventor to the farther side of the room, and heard the explanation of his weapon, and all his story about it.

It consisted of a common musket-barrel, bent in a curve so as to pass over the shoulder, and thus serve at once as a stock to the rifle and a sling to suspend it by. This part of the rifle was also a magazine which would carry some twelve or fifteen cartridges. A spiral spring was arranged inside, so that every time a cartridge slid into the chamber from the magazine, another was pressed into its place ready for the next loading. At the junction of the barrel with the magazine-stock were the lock and the chamber, which received one cartridge all ready for discharge. By pressing a small button, a spring was pushed back so that the stock part could be made to turn just far enough to admit of a cartridge sliding from the magazine into the chamber. The communication between the magazine and chamber was shut off when the stock returned to its place, and the spring connected with the button flew back and fastened it securely. Thus, the rifle hanging over the shoulder, muzzle down—the man's arm passing through the curved stock—would be instantly loaded, with one hand, by pressing the button, turning the stock long enough for a cartridge to slide from the magazine to the chamber, and then letting it fly back to its place. By raising the piece with the arm on which it was suspended, and pressing it against a brace across the curved stock, which fitted the shoulder, aim could be taken and the trigger pulled. I hardly thought the invention would stand the test of a certain number of discharges, as our service arms have to do, and really did not feel willing to be the first to fire it off; but I listened with much interest to the owner, and then advised him to show it to the chief of ordnance, who was accustomed to examine such things, and who would tell him whether it would answer the purpose. The man bade the President good-day, and went out, so far well pleased. I never heard of his gun again, so it was not adopted.

After the inventor had gone, and the President had finished his conversation, in a recess by a window, with his other visitor, he related to us one of his characteristic stories. There was a gentleman traveling for his health, who was suffering greatly from nervousness and want of sleep. While journeying in Egypt, he was terribly annoyed by the braying of a donkey, used in transporting his baggage, which was tied every night near his tent. At last the dragoman told the master of transportation that his donkey must be kept at a distance, where his noise would not disturb their employer. Whereupon the man proceeded to stop the braying by tying a string with a heavy stone attached to the donkey's tail. The donkey immediately dropped his ears, hung his head, and remained quiet through the night. The next morning, when the stone was taken off, the donkey raised his head, shook his ears, and gave one good, long bray, like Baron Munchausen's trumpet when the frozen tunes thawed out.* I do not remember the application which Mr. Lincoln made of this story.

An old friend of Mr. Lincoln once related to me another of his stories which shows not a little of his character. This gentleman was conversing with the President at a time during the war when things looked very dark. On taking leave, he asked the President what he should say to their friends in Kentucky—what cheering news he could give them of him. Mr. Lincoln replied: "That reminds me of a man who prided himself greatly on his game of chess, having seldom been beaten. He heard of a machine, called the 'Automaton Chess-Player,' which was beating every one who played against it. So he went to try his skill with the machine. He lost the first game, so with the second, and the third. Then, rising in astonishment from his seat, he walked around the ma-

---

* The baron's marvelous story of the trumpet proves, after all, to have been only a prophetic vision of the modern phonograph.

chine and looked at it a few minutes. Then, stopping and pointing at it, he exclaimed, 'There is a man in there!' Tell my friends," said Mr. Lincoln, drawing himself up to his full height, " there is a man in here! "

This was no spirit of bravado. It was to reassure his friends, by showing them that he was not wavering or discouraged, but was determined to rise above every adverse event, and act his part manfully. It was on such occasions, when a great resolve was uppermost in his mind, that the true majesty of Mr. Lincoln appeared in his face and form. I think Vinnie Ream failed in her statue, representing him as presenting his Emancipation Proclamation to the world, by overlooking this trait. The statue, with head somewhat bowed, and a look as of doubt, does not seem to bring out the stern and lofty sentiment which, at such a moment, his whole presence, head erect, and mouth compressed, would have exhibited; showing that he realized the full responsibility, and courageously assumed it.

CHAPTER XXIII.

SUNDRY PERSONS.

Quakers—Isaac's mode of warfare—A woman in man's clothes—A kind Southern woman—A secret society—" Knights of the Golden Circle "—Grenfel—Release of Confederate prisoners—A Southern clergyman—Greetings from the North—Chaplains—Bounty-jumpers—I. C.—V. R.

THE FRIENDS.—The draft sometimes brought me in contact with a class of citizens who do not often resort to the War Department of the Government. The law did not, at first, absolutely exempt any one on account of religious scruples, for it would have been easy to manufacture such things to order. But, after every draft, Isaac Newton, Commissioner of the Department of Agriculture, who was a Quaker, was sure to usher in a pleasant-looking party of his Friends, to ask the discharge of some relatives, because of their creed, which was averse to war. They were always reasonable, and quiet in their earnestness, and seldom failed to effect their object. It sometimes happened that the young men drafted would be sent to the field before their release could be obtained. There were instances in which they passively underwent stern punishment, obeying everything they were told to do, except to go through any of the forms of using weapons. Some of these cases were so genuine that they were quite touching, and awakened strong sympathy. The difficulty lay in discriminating between those who were Quakers indeed and Quakers by pretense. But whenever the worthy Isaac appeared, with a band of his brothers and sisters, clad in their plain garb, the men never removing their hats, and all addressing one as "thou" and "thee," the cases were always genuine. One of the elder men, who came with a party on this errand, was afterward a member of a Quaker committee in charge of some Western Indians, under General Grant's plan of parceling the tribes among different religious denominations. This man never failed to drop in for a friendly chat, whenever he was called to Washington on his Indian business.

Isaac Newton dressed in ordinary citizen's clothes. He was a burly old gentleman, and seemed always in a good humor. Speaking once of scruples about fighting, I asked him if he believed it proper strictly to carry out the letter of Scripture, and under no circumstances to resist. "Oh, no," said he, "there are other ways of resisting besides fighting." Then he related an incident, where he met a man in a wagon, at a narrow part of the road, and the man, seeing he was a Quaker, refused to turn out for him, but stopped directly in the road. Isaac asked him kindly to turn out, and the man gruffly refused. Then he said, "Friend, if thou wilt not turn thy horse, I will turn him for thee." So he took the horse's head to turn him, when the man jumped out and ran as if to attack him. On this, Isaac seized him by the arms above the elbow, held him as if in a vice, and quietly said, "Friend, if thou dost resist, I will shake thee." So he gave him a shake as a sample, and the man, perceiving how powerful and resolute the Quaker was, apologized, and turned his horse as far out as he could. "I did not strike him!" said Isaac.

A FEMALE SPY.—In war-time as in peace, very ludicrous things sometimes happen, as well as things most serious. Among the distinguished individuals confined in the Old Capitol Prison, at Washington, was a young female who was arrested in man's clothes, which it was supposed she had donned as a cloak for her assumed office of spy. She was a good secessionist, at any rate, and had no friends in the city to supply her with appropriate clothing, so she had to remain as she was. It was at last reported to me that she was very much mortified about her raiment, and kept in bed all the time rather than appear in it, after she had been detected. Out of respect to her sex, I mentioned her dilemma to that most worthy, true-hearted Presbyterian divine, Dr. John C.

Smith, and suggested that his wife might be disposed, as a charity, to visit the little spy, and provide her with female apparel. Some time after, the doctor told me that Mrs. Smith had been to see the woman, had found her in bed, and much mortified at her condition; but in the course of the interview she had betrayed such a bitter, rebellious spirit, and hatred of the Government, that Mrs. Smith was disgusted with her, and came away declaring she might remain in bed, or wear her male garb until it dropped off, before she would minister to such a temper. I do not know what afterward became of her.

A REFUGEE.—Soon after the close of the war, a middle-aged woman, from North Carolina, came to Washington, on her way to Cincinnati. She had two stout, healthy-looking children, a boy and girl. She was loyal throughout the war, and was noted for her kindness to the Union prisoners who were kept at Salisbury. On one occasion, when a party was going by her door, on the way to be exchanged, a poor, weak, emaciated fellow was thrown down by the throng, and trampled upon so that he was taken up nearly dead. This good woman took him into her house, and tenderly nursed him, until in a few days death came to his relief. She then buried him in her own garden, had his grave nicely sodded, and a paling put around it.

As she could find no means of support in her native State, she was going North, in hopes of getting employment. Ascertaining that her resources were exhausted, the Secretary of War gave her some pecuniary aid, and transportation to Ohio.

It is not improbable that this woman belonged to a

secret society, which operated in Western North Carolina and East Tennessee, where there were many Union people. The society had forms of initiations, and signs, by which its members recognized each other. Its object in general was to aid and endeavor to restore the Union. Many soldiers of the Confederate armies worked with it, and quite a number of Union prisoners of war escaped and were concealed and safely guided within the Union lines by its means. It was said that President Lincoln knew of it, and was even initiated as a member.

GRENFEL.—A secret organization, composed of disaffected persons both in the North and South, existed throughout the war. It went under various names, such as "Knights of the Golden Circle," "Order of American Knights," "Sons of Liberty," etc. Its objects were to aid in every possible way the cause of disunion. It had both a civil and a military organization, under a regular system of government. The fruits of the civil branch were often seen, but, although the military branch was ready at any time to take part, the opportunity did not present itself within the Union lines. Some of its members were officers of the Confederate service. Its plan, constitution, and secret signs became known in 1864, and were discovered through the confessions of members under arrest, through documents, and through other means. In the summer of 1864 a plot was concocted to release over eight thousand Confederate prisoners of war, who were held at Camp Douglas, Chicago, Illinois. After their release, they were to engage in pillaging and burning the city. A considerable number of persons, known to be in active sympathy with the South, were observed to be in Chicago, about the time of the convention which met there in August. As a precaution, a re-enforcement was sent to the guard at the prison-camp, which thwarted the designs upon it. Afterward, at the time of the election in November, the presence again in the city of noted rebels, and certain positive information which had been gained of the plot, induced the Government to arrest some seven or eight of the leaders and bring them to trial before a military commission. Quite a large amount of arms and ammunition was seized at the time of the arrest.

Among the persons arrested in November was a Colonel G. St. Leger Grenfel, an Englishman, one of those many foreign adventurers who came to this country to take part with one side or the other. The charges on which he was tried were, conspiring, in violation of the laws of war, to release the rebel prisoners of war confined, by authority of the United States, at Camp Douglas, near Chicago, Illinois; and conspiring, in violation of the laws of war, to lay waste and destroy the city of Chicago. He pleaded not guilty, but was convicted, and sentenced to be hanged. The British minister and others interested themselves for him, and strong efforts were made to get him off entirely. The President commuted his sentence to imprisonment for life, at hard labor, at the Dry Tortugas, Florida, and he was accordingly sent there.

Grenfel was a fine-looking man, with the manners of a rather pompous gentleman. He was very bad-tempered, and disposed to give all the trouble he could. At the Tortugas, his *hard labor* consisted in the care of a small vegetable-garden, planted for the benefit of the prisoners. This he destroyed by watering with salt water. He abused every indulgence which was vouchsafed to him through the solicitation of friends abroad. At length, he used money sent him, and which he was permitted to receive to ameliorate his condition, in bribing a sentry. One very stormy night in March, 1878, he, with the sentry and three other prisoners, escaped from the island in a small boat. Their departure was soon discovered, and a revenue-cutter, which was lying at the Tortugas, cruised for several days in every direction, to capture them, but without success. The United States consuls at Havana and other places on the coast were instructed by telegraph to look out for the fugitives, but they were never after heard of. It is supposed that their craft was swamped in the violent storm, and in that dark night they all perished. About a year after, inquiry was made by Grenfel's relatives in Europe for him, which indicates that he did not return to his own country, and increases the probability that he was drowned.

About the time of Grenfel's escape, an absurd report was started that the United States Government had been keeping over one thousand Confederate prisoners of war confined at the Dry Tortugas. Inquiries were made of the Government concerning missing relatives supposed to be among those prisoners. The fact is, *all* Confederate prisoners of war were set free by exchange, or on parole, as soon as fighting had fairly ceased in 1865.

A SOUTHERN CLERGYMAN.—In 1861, before non-intercourse between the two sections was rigidly enforced, a certain clergyman of the Protestant Episcopal Church came from Philadelphia, where he had a parish, and called upon General Scott, asking a pass to go to Richmond. He said he was a native Virginian, and that he thought, if he returned to Richmond to stay, he might do some good in alleviating the troubles of war, especially among the colored population. The pass was given, and he went South.

In 1865, after fighting was over, this gentleman came again to Washington, and was introduced to me by a former acquaintance. He spoke of the deep concern which the Southern Episcopalians felt about their future relations with the Church at the North. The war had forced them into an apparent separation, but, now that the causes were removed, what would be exacted of them to secure a reunion? He had received very many letters from all parts of the Southern States, asking information and advice.

The General Convention was to sit at Philadelphia, in October of that year. I unhesitatingly replied to the reverend gentleman that there was no manner of doubt that the only thing his Southern brethren had to do was to repair at the proper time to Philadelphia, and quietly take their seats as usual, the bishops in the House of Bishops, and the clerical and lay delegates in their House. I was certain that, if they would go, the only question would be—not are you sorry for what you have done, but—have you come sure enough to fill your vacant places? I told him they would be received with open arms; and, in proof of my position, instanced the many strong expressions I had heard from public men, like Messrs. Stanton and Henry Wilson, of a desire that all the people of the South would with alacrity return to a cordial support of the Union, without coercion, or penalties of any sort. He took leave with many protestations of gratitude, and declared he should go back to his people with my words of encouragement, and urge them to do as I suggested. A few weeks after, I saw him again in Washington, when he presented me with a copy of the address of the Bishop of Virginia to his diocesan convention, in which the bishop recommended the election of delegates to the approaching General Convention. He told me that many churchmen at the South had received the assurances I had given him with great satisfaction, and that it had gone far to relieve their anxieties.

When the General Convention assembled, some few of the Southern churchmen attended, simply as spectators. Wherever they were recognized they were most cordially received. In the Upper House a bishop discovered one of his Southern brethren in a pew of the church. After a short, whispered conference with the few nearest him, he rose, went to the pew, seized his old friend by the hand, and insisted that he should accompany him back to his seat. There he was met by the entire body with unfeigned joy, and urged to take his seat as one of them.

This session of the General Convention, in 1865, was made memorable by the reunion of all the dioceses of the Protestant Episcopal Church in the United States. The Rt. Rev. R. H. Wilmer, who had been consecrated under the constitution of the Southern Church during the war, was recognized as of the Episcopate, on his merely signing an equivalent to the usual promise of conformity. The Bishop-elect of Tennessee was consecrated, without the delay of submitting his name to each separate diocese; and this was the easy adjustment of all external appearance of division.

SOME CHAPLAINS.—In the plan of organization adopted by authority of the President,* one chaplain was allowed to each regiment of volunteers, to be "appointed by the regimental commander on the vote of the field officers and company commanders on duty with the regiment at the time." There was a provision added that "the chaplain so appointed must be a regularly ordained minister of some Christian denomination." This last clause was not always properly heeded; and so it came to pass that, although as a rule army chaplains were fit and earnest men, some were occasionally invested with the office who had little appreciation of its spirit, and no training in the execution of its duties.

The uniform prescribed for chaplains was a plain black frock-coat, with standing collar, and one row of nine black buttons; plain black pantaloons, black felt hat, or army forage-cap, without ornament. On occasions of ceremony, a plain "*chapeau-de-bras*" was authorized to be worn.

The exceeding simplicity of this dress did not suit some of the reverend gentlemen, and a deputation called at the office to have it changed. I asked them what they desired. They replied that brass buttons, shoulder-straps, a cap ornament, a sash, and a sword, were necessary to facilitate the performance of their duties, and cause them to be respected. I asked how that dress, especially the sword, would aid them in conducting religious services?

* General Orders, No. 15, dated May 4, 1861, legalized by section 3, act of August 6, 1861.

and how they would use the sword? They said that when they were officiating at service the sword would be laid aside; but now, when they entered a hospital, they were not recognized by the patients, who would pay no heed to them, and they wanted to be known as officers having authority. "Oh," said I, "if you should walk to the bedside of some poor, wounded soldier, arrayed in your shining buttons and sash and sword, would he not suppose that you were the officer of the day coming to carry him off to the guard-house, and be terribly frightened at the idea? I rather think if you are known to the men by your good words, kind offices, and gentle sympathy with them in their trials, the plain black dress will secure you more respect than the showy one." Whether they were satisfied or not, they did not continue the argument. The uniform which had been adopted was actually suggested by a clergyman, well known for his zeal and devotion to the good cause. With the addition of a little black braid, and a cap ornament, it is that now worn by army chaplains.

Two venerable men, whose loyalty to the Union deprived them, in their advanced age, of their only support, were cared for by the fostering hand of the United States Government during their remaining years. One was the Rev. Matthias Harris, post-chaplain at Fort Moultrie, who was with Anderson at Sumter. Having lost his place by the evacuation of that post, he was made post-chaplain at Fort Foote, Maryland. The other was the Rev. Lemuel Wilmer, who, because he "had never in his life drawn a disloyal breath," was forsaken by his congregation. On learning of his straitened circumstances, the Department created Port Tobacco, Maryland, a chaplain post, and appointed him its chaplain.

BOUNTY-JUMPERS.—A great evil connected with the draft and substitute system for recruiting the army arose from the practice, which at one time prevailed to a large extent, of what was called "bounty-jumping." When volunteering began to fail, after nearly every patriotic able-bodied man had entered the service, the draft was resorted to. But, whenever notice of a draft was about to be published, very considerable bounties were first offered, both by the Government and by States, for volunteers. Drafted men were also allowed to procure substitutes, whom they paid. All the men recruited by volunteering and by draft, or substitute, were collected at large depots* preparatory to being sent to regiments in the field. These men often had large sums of money in their pockets, received in the way of bounties, and it became quite a business with sharpers to disguise themselves, pass an examination at a recruiting rendezvous, receive the bounty or substitute money, desert from the depot, and then repeat the operation over and over again, under other names and disguises. Of course their tricks were soon detected, and numbers were arrested and kept in confinement. Photographs were taken of some of the most noted of these criminals, both at the time of their enlistment, when, clean shaved and furbished, they passed

* The guards at these draft rendezvous were composed of "veteran reserve" regiments, made up of men who had been disabled in the army, by wounds or otherwise, so as to be unable to bear the hardships of the field and camp, but all quite equal to duty required in a comfortable garrison. These regiments were at first styled the "Invalid Corps," but an army regulation prescribed that articles of public property condemned by an inspector should be marked with the initials I. C., for "Inspected, Condemned." Therefore, the I. C. (Invalid Corps) regiments had their designation changed to V. R. (Veteran Reserve).

for younger men; and afterward, when the garnishing had faded, and they were exhibited in their true colors.

To put an end to bounty-jumping, I devised a plan, in December, 1864, for taking away their money at the depot, depositing it with an army paymaster stationed there for the purpose, and giving them a check-book in which the amount was entered. They could then draw the amount exhibited on the check-book from a paymaster in the field, at their first payment after joining their regiment. The paymaster who received the money credited the soldier with it on his accounts made to the Treasury, and the one who paid it charged it in his accounts, so that the two accounts were balanced in the settlement at the Treasury. The recruit received his bounty at the recruiting rendezvous, and was never out of sight of a guard till he reached the depot; so that he had no chance to conceal it. Provision was made, under close restrictions, by which he could convey any portion of it to his family if he desired.

When I first submitted this plan to the Secretary of War, he demurred at adopting it. I set forth the advantageous features of it, and told him the Treasury officers assented to it, so far as they were concerned. A man who enlisted in good faith would not object to having his bounty safely kept for him till he wanted it; while a bounty-jumper would not be willing to take the risk of escaping after he had been transported to the army. At last he said, "Well, if you choose to issue the order on your own responsibility, you may, but I will not have any trouble that may arise from it." That was enough; the order was issued. The Secretary told me afterward that the Governor of one of the States, who had been most annoyed by bounty-jumpers, had thanked him for it, and characterized it as "the best order that had emanated from the War Department."

CHAPTER XXIV.

GENERAL FRANK P. BLAIR.

How to legalize an illegal order.

In 1864 General Frank Blair, who had been serving as a major-general of volunteers, was elected to the House of Representatives. He resigned his commission and took his seat. In the month of April the Secretary of War handed me an order from the President, to be issued, assigning Major-General Blair to duty with the army under General Sherman; and directing that some regular officers be ordered to report to him as his staff, and that some civilians be appointed additional aides-de-camp for him. I glanced at the order, and then said:

"Mr. Secretary, General Blair has resigned, and is now a civilian. He is not a major-general, and is not subject to an order."

Secretary. Well, what of that?

General Townsend. Why, such an order can not be legally issued.

Secretary. But the President orders it!

General T. (seeing something peculiar in the Secretary's manner). Shall I issue it, then?

Secretary. I give you no orders about it; there is the President's order.

General T. But what am I to do? It is not a legal order; how can I issue it?

Secretary. I tell you, I have nothing to say about it. You must use your own discretion.

General T. Won't you see the President, and explain the facts to him?

Secretary. No!

General T. What would you advise me to do, then?

Secretary. I give you no advice about it.

General T. You are between the President and me, and I have to come to you in all cases.

Secretary. In this case, I give you full authority to use your own discretion. I have nothing more to say.

General T. (*perceiving that there had probably already been a discussion between the President and Secretary*). Well, may I see the President about it?

Secretary. I tell you I have no orders to give you. You can do what you please.

Accordingly, I took the order and went over to the Executive Mansion. The President was through with the urgent duties of the day, and was seated with his feet on a chair, a towel round his neck, while his servant was shampooing his head.

Having been admitted, I said: "Mr. President, the Secretary has handed me this order, to assign General Blair to a command, and authorized me to come and see you about it. I thought you might not be aware that General Blair's resignation having been accepted, he can not be legally ordered to any military duty. He is now, as a civilian, not subject to orders."

President. Well, I am anxious to have it fixed up some way, so the order can be issued, if you can do it.

General T. There is only one way to do it. If General Blair will apply to have the acceptance of his resignation revoked, I can issue an order revoking it, and then assign him to duty. There have been instances of that sort, and I will do it if you give me authority.

President. I wish you would—I wish you would. Just fix it any way you think best.

I then returned to the department, and wrote a note to General Blair, asking him to call at the adjutant-general's office, on business indicated to me by the President. He came, and I explained the matter to him. He said he was willing to do as the President desired. I then wrote letters for him to sign, asking that his resignation be revoked, and that he be assigned to a command. He signed them, and the order was handed him to report to General William T. Sherman, and to command the Seventeenth Army Corps.

In a few days, when it was known that Frank Blair had gone to take a command in the Army of the South, a resolution was passed in the Senate calling upon the President for information whether any officers whose resignations had been accepted had been put on duty; who such officers were, and under what circumstances they had been so assigned. The Secretary of War then inquired what had been done in General Blair's case. I told him, and said, if he would give me the resolution, I would prepare an answer. So I took it, made copies of the letters General Blair had signed, and of the orders given him, and then cited several instances as precedents where similar action, during many years, had been taken with regular army officers. The Secretary, after examining my report very carefully, forwarded it. No more was heard about it, except that the Senate passed a resolution that, thereafter, no officers whose resignations had been duly accepted should be restored to the service without a new appointment and confirmation by the Senate.

After this General Blair commanded the Seventeenth Army Corps, in Sherman's army, during the famous Southern campaign and "march to the sea," near the close of the war. No one will say that the President had cause to regret having called him to the army. Had he gone through the routine of again nominating him, and waited for his confirmation, too much valuable time would have been lost at that critical period.

CHAPTER XXV.

EARLY'S INVASION.

A false alarm—President Lincoln's narrow escape.

WHILE the Army of the Potomac was closely pressing on Richmond, in July, 1864, General Lee sought to divert some of its strength by sending a considerable force of cavalry and infantry, under Early, to threaten Washington. Intelligence was received of the raid on the 3d of July, and preparations were at once made for defense. There were but few troops around Washington at that time, and they were mostly veteran reserves. But, to meet emergencies, the clerks and employés of the War and some of the civil departments had been for several months organized into regiments, and pretty carefully drilled. These, and all of the large number of men in the hospitals, who were at all able to hold a musket, went to man the forts.

One night, when there were indications that an attack would be made, I was on guard at the War Department. At three o'clock in the morning, I heard loud cries in the street, sounding nearer and nearer to the department. My first impression was that Early's raiders had broken in and were coming to burn and pillage. As I walked rapidly from my room to the door at the other end of the hall, where the noise appeared to be, I had time to consider what had better be done under the circumstances. The pass of Thermopylæ would have been nothing to this occasion. Instead of a pass, there would have been a door; instead of three hundred defenders, there would have been three. A reconnaissance, however, would better indicate the line and measure of defense. On opening the door upon the street, a large herd of beef-cattle was seen wending its way to the commissary's *corral*, and the herders were making the outcry. These cattle had been pastured some miles out in Maryland, and narrowly escaped being captured by Early. Information of his approach was received just in time to save them.

There had been no stampede in Washington. People did not seem to think there was much danger of a catastrophe. The Confederates felt some of the forts; and two or three houses under the guns of Fort Stevens, on the turnpike-road to Brookville, Maryland, were battered down, to dislodge some of the enemy's sharp-shooters who found shelter there while trying to pick off our gunners. It was related of President Lincoln that he rode out to Fort Stevens while the skirmishing was going on, and, heedless of danger, mounted the parapet to get a good view. While standing there, his tall frame presenting a prominent target, a bullet passed between him and a young lady who was standing by his side, and quite near him. He was then induced to descend under cover.

General Grant sent Wright's Sixth Corps up to reenforce the Washington garrison. As soon as it arrived it threw out a line of skirmishers; and, when the Confederates recognized its well-known badge, they drew off and took their departure, probably conceiving that they had effected the relief of Richmond. They afterward received due attention from Sheridan, who entirely destroyed this part of Lee's army in the Shenandoah Valley.

CHAPTER XXVI.

THE SHENANDOAH VALLEY TROPHIES.

Sheridan's black horse—"To Early, in care of Sheridan"—A big scare—Lo, they were gone!

THE 19th of October, 1864, General Sheridan reported:

"My army at Cedar Creek was attacked this morning before daylight, and my left was turned and driven in confusion, with the loss of twenty pieces of artillery. I hastened from Winchester, where I was on my return from Washington, and found the armies between Middletown and Newtown, having been driven back about four miles. I here took the affair in hand and quickly united the corps, formed a compact line of battle just in time to repulse an attack of the enemy, which was handsomely done at 1 P. M.

"At 3 P. M., after some changes of the cavalry from the left to the right flank, I attacked with great vigor, driving and routing the enemy, capturing, according to last report, forty-three pieces of artillery and very many prisoners."

An officer of Massachusetts Volunteers who was present told me he saw General Sheridan when he met his retreating troops. His black horse, by which he was usually recognized, was so completely covered with foam as to appear like an animal with a white skin. This same officer told me that some pieces of artillery were sent from Richmond to the Confederate General Early, each one of which was labeled with his name. After Sheridan's defeat of Early, some wag wrote on the labels to the guns, under Early's name, the words, "Care of General Sheridan."

General Sheridan sent the artillery captured on this occasion by rail to Washington. The Secretary of War determined to make a public display of these trophies, to give an idea of the magnitude of the victory. He accordingly instructed me to have them taken, on their arrival at the railroad depot, to the grounds in front of the War Department, and parked there. The trophies arrived the 29th of October. An excellent volunteer regiment of artillery, stationed at Camp Barry in the outskirts of the city, had been ordered to receive them and put them in position. The officers of the regiment entered into the spirit of the affair, procured a band of music, and marched through the streets with much *éclat*, followed by the usual crowd. Some time was occupied, after the train arrived, in unloading the cars, and putting the carriages together, some of them being much broken; and it was after dark when they reached the department. When all the arrangements were made to receive the guns, I rode on horseback to meet the regiment. Having seen every gun and carriage in place, and posted sentinels around them with orders not to permit any one to go near or touch them, I went home. I had hardly reached there, when a messenger arrived saying the Secretary desired to see me, immediately, at the department. Some one had telegraphed to him at his residence that the ammunition-boxes were filled with powder, and he had hastened down in great alarm lest the whole department should be blown sky-high. He was much excited. He asked me why I had not discovered that the boxes contained powder, and why I had not sent the carriages immediately to the arsenal. I replied that I had taken great precautions, which the result showed were effective, to prevent any one from carelessly opening the boxes; that they were constructed on purpose to carry powder safely on the battle-field, and there was no danger of their exploding unless struck by a shell. I had not anticipated that the boxes would be sent all the way by cars from the place of their capture to Washington, without first having the ammunition removed; but, since they had gone thus far without accident, there did not now seem to be any cause for alarm. The Secretary's mind was so preoccupied with the idea of danger to the public buildings that it put him in a bad humor. He peremptorily ordered that the trophies should be immediately sent down to the Arsenal for safe-keeping, and that I should see it properly done. A messenger was dispatched for the same regiment to transport the things, and I sat in my office with another officer to await its arrival. Presently in came the depot quartermaster, to whom orders had been sent by the Secretary to bring some mules with harness, to do the same work. The quartermaster seemed to be in a quandary about what he was required to do. He said he had plenty of mules and wagon-harness, but he did not see how it could be fitted to haul artillery-carriages. I told him the artillery regiment which brought them up would soon come to take them to the Arsenal; and I did not believe mules and wagon-harness could be of any aid. Meanwhile, the Secretary, having had time to think a little, and recover from his apprehension, since no catastrophe had occurred for two hours, came into my room in an altered mood. I gave him a chair, and he began chatting pleasantly about indifferent matters. I did not join in the conversation. Presently he asked the quartermaster where his dispatch-boat was. "At the wharf, sir, ready to fire up at a moment's warning." "Well," said the Secretary, "you must get her ready for an excursion down the river, and you and Townsend make up a party and go." Then, turning to me, he asked if I would not like to go. I was angry, and had good reason to be, so I replied, curtly, "I have no time for excursions." The Secretary said nothing more, but soon after went home. It was half-past one at night—a cold, drizzling, rainy night—before I saw the last remnant of the procession started on its way to its final resting-place.

114 ANECDOTES OF THE CIVIL WAR.

The next day was Sunday. Quite early in the morning the President walked out to enjoy the promised view of his trophies. His surprise at not finding them in front of the War Department was probably equaled by that of a crowd of citizens who had assembled on the same errand, having heard the evening before that the guns were to be on exhibition.

CHAPTER XXVII.

TRIP TO SAVANNAH.

A Sunday service—A salute at sea—Conference with colored ministers—Fort Fisher—Promoted while asleep.

GENERAL WILLIAM T. SHERMAN'S army occupied Savannah December 21, 1864. "One hundred and fifty heavy guns and plenty of ammunition, and also about twenty-five thousand bales of cotton," were reported captured. The health of the Secretary of War seriously demanded the rest which a sea-voyage could best afford; he therefore determined to go to Savannah to confer with General Sherman, and take measures to secure the large amount of cotton found there. Much of this cotton belonged to the Confederate Government, and was therefore lawful prize to the United States. Arrangements were made for a propeller which had been chartered to convey army supplies from New York to Savannah, to call at Old Point Comfort, Virginia, for the Secretary. Quartermaster-General Meigs, Surgeon-General Barnes, and myself accompanied him;

and Mr. Simeon Draper, of New York, who had held the appointment of Provost-Marshal-General of the War Department,* joined the party in the propeller from New York.

We sailed from Old Point Saturday, January 7, 1865. The next day, Secretary Stanton asked General Meigs to read a portion of the Episcopal Church service to our small party. He joined reverently in the service, and afterward commented on a passage of the Scriptures which had been read.

The next day, as we neared Hilton Head, the steamer James Adger, of the blockading squadron, commanded by Captain (now Rear-Admiral) Thomas H. Patterson, U. S. Navy, made signal for us to hoist our colors. Our captain either did not understand the signal, or at any rate did not heed it, and kept on his course. The Adger then steered for us, and fired a shot across our bow, which of course brought us to, and made us show the Stars and Stripes. Captain Patterson, my relative, having recognized me standing on the deck as I waved my handkerchief to him, sent a boat to ask me aboard his ship. I wrote him a note regretting I could not go, as I was with the Secretary of War, who was aboard of us. Upon this, the Adger stood off, drew her shot, and fired the salute due a Cabinet officer. Probably this is the only instance where a Secretary

---

* Mr. Draper was appointed Provost-Marshal-General October 1, 1862. His office was not the same as that afterward held by General Fry under the act of March 3, 1863, but was created by authority of the War Department to supervise and manage the special provost-marshals employed in States to arrest deserters and disloyal persons, seize stolen property of the Government, detect spies, etc. Mr. Draper's appointment was annulled when General Fry was detailed according to law.

of War was saluted while afloat by a United States ship of war. Mr. Stanton was asleep below when the salute was fired, but when told of it he was much pleased with the incident.

While we were on the voyage, as I was sitting one day in the cabin, alone with the Secretary, he told me he felt much anxiety about the cotton which had been captured at Savannah. He had no doubt attempts would be made to appropriate it. There would be persons who would claim it as their private property, and it would be difficult to discriminate between what was really private and what belonged to the Confederate Government. Then he said he wanted a general officer to command at Savannah, who would see to the safe-keeping and proper disposition of the cotton, and defend the city against military movements to recapture it, which might probably be made after General Sherman's army left. He asked whom I could name for the purpose. I consulted the register, and found plenty of suitable names, but they were either too far off, or in positions where they were much needed. At last I mentioned one general whom I thought suitable, and the most available, though he too had an important command. The Secretary replied: "I can not withdraw him from so critical a command. If I could spare you, I would assign you." I exclaimed, "Me, sir?" "Yes, you, sir!" said he. I replied that nothing could be more agreeable to me than to have the assignment. "But," said he, "I can not do without you where you are."

After personally examining the stores containing the cotton, hearing private claims to certain lots, indicating the marks to be put on the bales, and what disposition should be made of them, the Secretary, on consultation with General Sherman, appointed Mr. Draper to have the charge of the cotton, and General John W. Geary, who belonged to Sherman's army, to be left in military command of Savannah when the army marched northward.

Among the private claimants of cotton was Lamar, notorious as the man who once landed a cargo of negroes, imported direct from Africa, in the yacht Wanderer, on the shores of the United States. This gentleman attempted to give much trouble in the disposal of the captured cotton.

On Thursday, the 12th of January, General Sherman gave the Secretary a grand review of his army. In the evening of that day, by invitation of the Secretary, twenty colored men, chiefly ministers of different churches, assembled in the Secretary's room, to give him their views concerning the present and future of their people. The minutes of this interview, as taken down at the time by the Secretary's own hand, will be found in Appendix F. I offered to act as amanuensis, but he declined, and persisted in writing until after midnight.

We sailed from Savannah Saturday, the 14th, leaving General Meigs and Mr. Draper behind, and spent Sunday at Hilton Head, with General Rufus Saxton, commanding there, leaving for home that same evening.

As we neared Fort Fisher, on the 16th of January, all eyes were strained to discover what had been the result of the combined attack of Admiral Porter and General Terry on that place. At first we could discern only a small flag floating over the fort, with no sign of cannonading. Our joy can be imagined when the Stars and Stripes became distinguishable. The Secretary immediately decided to put in, to learn the particulars of the capture, and congratulate the officers. On our arrival amid the ships, from which the smoke of battle had so recently cleared away, the Secretary communicated with General A. H. Terry, who at once came aboard with his staff. We learned that, at 3 P. M., the 15th of January, the troops assaulted the fort, after heavy cannonading by the fleet. "The fighting for the traverses continued till nearly nine o'clock, two more of them being carried; then a portion of Abbott's brigade drove the enemy from their last remaining strongholds, and the occupation of the work was complete." After a long conversation, the Secretary directed me to make out letters conferring brevets on General Terry and his staff, which were all subsequently submitted to the Senate and confirmed. The general and his officers had scarcely slept for three days. It was now the middle of the evening, and Captain Adrian Terry, assistant adjutant-general, brother to the general, overpowered with fatigue, fell fast asleep. When the general, as he was about to withdraw, aroused Captain Terry, I slipped into his hand a document inclosed in an official envelope. He was yet half asleep, and supposing I was serving a notice of arrest, or something, upon him for falling asleep in the Secretary's presence, he was evidently much troubled. When he opened the letter, however, he said, with a smile of gratification, "I do believe I went to sleep a captain, and have awakened a major!" At this the Secretary and all laughed most heartily.

CHAPTER XXVIII.

AMNESTY.

Proclamation sent through the lines—Good fruits—"Dixie."

On the 8th of December, 1863, President Lincoln issued a proclamation, to make known "to all persons who have, directly or by implication, participated in the existing rebellion, except as hereinafter excepted, that a full pardon is hereby granted to them, and each of them, with restoration of all rights of property, except as to slaves, and in property cases where rights of third parties shall have intervened, and upon the condition that every such person shall take and subscribe an oath, and thenceforward keep and maintain said oath inviolate; and which oath shall be registered for permanent preservation, and shall be of the tenor and effect following, to wit:

"'I, —— ——, do solemnly swear, in presence of Almighty God, that I will henceforth faithfully support, protect, and defend the Constitution of the United States, and the union of the States thereunder; and that I will, in like manner, abide by and faithfully support all acts of Congress passed during the existing rebellion with reference to slaves, so long and so far as not repealed, modified, or held void by Congress or by decision of the Supreme Court; and that I will, in like manner, abide by and faithfully support all proclamations of the President, made during the existing rebellion, having reference to slaves, so long and so far as not modified or declared void by decision of the Supreme Court. So help me God.'"

The classes excepted from the pardon did not include the officers under the rank of general officers, or the rank and file of the Confederate army, unless they had left the United States army to join the rebels, or had committed certain specified offenses.

On the 30th of December a dispatch was received from an officer on the Upper Potomac, saying: "Nine deserters from the Valley just in . . . These deserters heard the President's proclamation and required oath with great surprise, and declared, if it was printed and circulated, thousands would come into our lines."

They were surprised to find the falsity of the statements as to the humane policy and feeling of President Lincoln's administration, which had been from the beginning so persistently impressed upon the Southern people, exposed by this proclamation. In accordance with the suggestion in the dispatch, many thousands of copies of the proclamation were printed in convenient form and sent to commanders along the lines, to be distributed as opportunity offered. Large numbers were conveyed through the pickets, and in other ways. The good effect was announced in a dispatch dated January 23, 1864: "Ninety-seven deserters have reported at this post since the 1st of January. The President's amnesty is having good effect. I am scattering it all through the country."

The following orders were afterward issued, and, together with the proclamation, were printed and folded in such small form that they could be easily concealed, and were profusely distributed:

AMNESTY.

GENERAL ORDERS, No. 64.
WAR DEPARTMENT, ADJUTANT-GENERAL'S OFFICE,
WASHINGTON, *February 18, 1864.*

REFUGEES AND REBEL DESERTERS.

Whenever refugees from within the rebel lines, or deserters from the rebel armies, present themselves at United States camps, or military posts, they will be immediately examined by the provost-marshal, with a view to determine their character and their motive in giving themselves up. If it appear that they are honest in their intention of forever deserting the rebel cause, care will be taken to explain to them that they will not be forced to serve in the United States army against the rebels, nor be kept in confinement. The President's proclamation of December 8, 1863, will be read to them, and, if they so desire, the oath therein prescribed will be administered to them. They will then be questioned as to whether they desire employment from the United States, and, if so, such arrangements as may be expedient will be made by the several army commanders for employing them on Government works within their commands. Those who come to the Army of the Potomac will be forwarded to the military governor of the District of Columbia, at Washington, with reports in their cases, that employment may be given them if desired, or, if not, that they may be sent as far north as Philadelphia.

By order of the Secretary of War:
E. D. TOWNSEND, *Assistant Adjutant-General.*

Among the deserters who surrendered was an entire military band, composed of foreigners, who came within the lines, bringing their instruments with them. They were sent to Washington, and went up to the War Department to pay their respects to the Secretary of War. They played several airs for his amusement, and at last asked if there was any particular one he would like to hear. He called for one after another of our national airs, but they knew none of them! "Well," said he, "let us have '*Dixie*,' then; you probably can play that." So 'Dixie' was rendered with due effect. This band went north, and doubtless found employment as musicians, though they certainly did not seem to possess extraordinary skill in their art.

CHAPTER XXIX.

ILLUMINATION FOR THE CAPTURE OF RICHMOND.

Magic effect—A perverse eagle.

General Weitzel's troops occupied Richmond April 3, 1865. As soon as the news arrived at Washington, the Secretary of War gave orders for a grand illumination of all the buildings occupied by his department. He intrusted to me the arrangements for the War Department proper, for Winder's Building on Seventeenth Street, and the entire row of buildings from that to Pennsylvania Avenue, and two more north of the avenue. The Corcoran Art-Gallery, on the corner of President's Square and Seventeenth Street, then in use by the quartermaster-general, was prepared under his direction. All these formed a group of large buildings in close proximity. Two candles were placed in each pane of glass, and a man provided with matches was stationed at each window. Fire-balls were arranged in a row directly in front of the War Department, and men were near to light them. A military band was seated on the balcony over the north door. At a signal sounded with a trumpet on the corner of the street, the band struck up "The Starspangled Banner," and, as if by magic, the windows of twelve buildings were suddenly ablaze, while columns of red, green, and blue transparent smoke floated over the front of the War Department. So promptly was each match applied, that spectators wondered what mechanical process—like lighting gas-jets by electricity—could have been used in this instance.

Thus far this undertaking was a success. But, after all, there was one failure. The Secretary had conceived the idea of having the word "Richmond" in a scroll, with an eagle clutching it with his talons, in the act of rising on his outspread wings, painted on a transparency which was to be suspended over the top of the front balcony. This was allegorically to represent the American eagle capturing the capital of the Confederacy. The painter employed, not being an artist of high culture, thought he would improve on the instructions given him, and, for the sake of more graceful curves, he represented the eagle soaring away with the end of the scroll in his beak. When the Secretary saw the production he was very much displeased, and would not commend the general effect of the illumination; but there was not time enough, after the transparency was finished, to have another painted. As it was, the public, who remained in ignorance of the intended design, were well satisfied with the entire spectacle.

For my part, anxiety lest an unfortunate spark should turn my illumination into a most expensive bonfire of invaluable records prevented any enjoyment, until, by personally and carefully inspecting every room after the lights were all extinguished, I was assured that everything was safe.

CHAPTER XXX.

AD INTERIM.

Mr. Stanton's suspension—Not sustained—General L. Thomas appointed *ad interim*—Mr. Stanton resists—Colloquy—A lawyer's *ruse*—"Stand firm!"—Neutral ground—Another *ad interim*—A new Secretary.

ON Monday morning, August 5, 1867, President Johnson invited Mr. Stanton to resign as Secretary of War. Under the tenure-of-civil-office law, Mr. Stanton declined. The President, a week after, suspended him, and appointed General Grant, General-in-Chief of the Army, to exercise the functions. This continued until January 13, 1868, when, according to the law, the Senate passed a resolution not sustaining the President's action. The next morning, General Grant came to my office and handed me the key of the Secretary's room, saying: "I am to be found over at my office at army headquarters. I was served with a copy of the Senate resolution last evening." I then went up-stairs and delivered the key of his room to Mr. Stanton.

On Thursday, February 13, 1868, President Johnson addressed to General Grant a letter, saying he desired Major-General L. Thomas to resume his duties as Adjutant-General of the Army. This proved to be a preliminary step to another attempt to remove Mr. Stanton from the department. It was intended to bring the question of the constitutionality of the tenure-of-office law before the Supreme Court of the United States, in the course of the controversy which was expected to arise. General Thomas resumed charge of the adjutant-general's office, February 14th, after an absence of nearly five years. He was very kind, and invited me to continue my desk in his room. On the 19th he asked me to look up certain laws relating to the tenure of civil office, saying that the President desired him to examine them. He then told me, in strict confidence, that the President thought of investing him with the office of Secretary of War *ad interim*, to supersede Mr. Stanton. On Friday, the 21st, the general came to the room where I was sitting with another officer, and, calling him, they went out together. In a short time they returned, and the general threw a letter on my table, which was the one from the President, appointing him Secretary of War *ad interim*. He told me he had delivered the letter to Mr. Stanton, removing him, and had taken the other officer to be a witness to the interview; that, on reading the letter to Mr. Stanton, the latter remarked, "I suppose you will give me time to remove my private papers!" and that he then asked for a copy of the President's letter of appointment. I made this copy, and the general certified it officially as "Secretary of War *ad interim*." When Mr. Stanton received the copy, he said he would consider whether he would recognize it or not. General Thomas seemed to think Mr. Stanton would retire without making any opposition. He said emphatically that he should most certainly, at all hazards, take possession of the war-office on the following Monday, which would give Mr. Stanton ample time to vacate, Saturday (February 22d) being a holiday, and Sunday coming right after. He then sent his letter to the President, accepting the appointment.

On Saturday, February 22d, I went to the War Department, as usual on holidays, merely for my private letters. The rooms were all locked, and the keys were in Mr. Stanton's possession. He had remained in his own office all night. I went to General Schriver's room, which was directly opposite the Secretary's. At about noon General Thomas entered the building unaccompanied. He had been all the night at a masked ball with his family, had just sat down to breakfast without taking off his uniform, when he was arrested and summoned before Chief-Justice Cartter, of the Supreme Court of the District of Columbia. The arrest was made on a warrant issued upon Mr. Stanton's affidavit that, on a pretended appointment of Secretary of War *ad interim*, he had endeavored to exercise the authority of the Secretary of War, contrary to the act "regulating the tenure of certain civil offices," passed March 2, 1867. He gave bail in five thousand dollars to appear on the following Wednesday. From the court he proceeded directly to the President's office, and, after consultation with the President, went to the Secretary's room in the War Department. His arrest had changed his intention of waiting till Monday to demand possession of the office. There were several members of Congress with Mr. Stanton. The general courteously saluted those present, and the following colloquy ensued :

General Thomas (addressing Mr. Stanton). I am Secretary of War *ad interim*, and am ordered by the President of the United States to take charge of this office.

Mr. Stanton. I order you to repair to your room, and exercise your office as adjutant-general.

General T. I am Secretary of War *ad interim*, and I shall not obey your orders; but I shall obey the order of the President to take charge of this office.

Mr. S. As Secretary of War, I order you to repair to your office as adjutant-general.

General T. I shall not do so.

Mr. S. Then you may stand there, if you please; but you will attempt to act as Secretary of War at your peril.

General T. I *shall* act as Secretary of War.

There the *official* interview ended. There was no excitement in language or manner, but each spoke with quiet determination. There was a short-hand writer present who took down every word. Presently, General Thomas crossed the hall to General Schriver's room—both doors had been all the time open. Mr. Stanton, followed only by the stenographer, came in after him. The door of General Schriver's room was then closed. Mr. Stanton, resuming the colloquy, said in a laughing tone to General Thomas, "So you claim to be here as Secretary of War, and refuse to obey my orders, do you?" General Thomas replied, seriously: "I do so claim. I shall require the mails of the War Department to be delivered to me, and shall transact all the business of the department." Seeing that the general looked as if he had had no rest the night before, Mr. Stanton then, playfully running his fingers up through the general's hair, as he wearily leaned back in his chair, said, "Well, old fellow, have you had any breakfast this morning?" "No," said

Thomas, good-naturedly. "Nor anything to drink?" "No." "Then you are as badly off as I am, for I have had neither." Mr. Stanton then sent out for some refreshment; General Thomas related how he had been arrested just after returning with his children from a ball, before he had time to eat his breakfast, and they had a very pleasant conversation for half an hour. Presently, Mr. Stanton asked General Thomas when he was going to give him the report of an inspection of the national cemeteries which he had lately made. Mr. Stanton said if it was not soon rendered it would be too late to have it printed, and he was anxious to have it go forth as a creditable work of the department. There was apparently no special point to this question, and General Thomas evidently saw none, for he answered pleasantly that he would work at it that night and give it to him. It struck me as a lawyer's *ruse* to make Thomas acknowledge Stanton's authority as Secretary of War, and that Thomas was caught by it. I, some time after, asked Mr. Stanton if that was his design. He made no reply, but looked at me with a mock expression of surprise at my conceiving such a thing.

Before General Thomas left the department, Mr. Stanton handed him a letter forbidding him to give any orders as Secretary of War. The general read and indorsed it as received on that date, signing the indorsement as Secretary *ad interim;* which Mr. Stanton seeing, he remarked, laughing, "Here you have committed another offense!" To this the general assented. He soon after went away for the day.

The incidents here related seem to indicate that all the steps taken were to place the whole matter in a form to test, before the highest tribunal, the constitutionality of the tenure-of-office law. There were some persistent reports that it was fully intended that possession of the War Department should be gained by force, if Mr. Stanton would not voluntarily retire. General Thomas told me positively that the story of his intention to "kick Mr. Stanton out of the department" had but slight foundation. He felt no disrespect toward Mr. Stanton, and had too much self-respect to speak of him in such terms. He would not lay a finger on him. He requested me to tell this to Mr. Stanton. The story had its origin in this incident: He was at a reception given one evening by the President, when a man, who said he was from Newcastle, Delaware, the general's old home, took him by the hand, and told him that his State "had its eye upon him, and expected him to stand firm." The general, smiling, straightened himself and replied, "Am I not standing firm?" "But," said the other, "are you not going to kick that man out?" "Oh," said the general, evasively, "some of these days."

As for Mr. Stanton, who had heard some of the reports of intended violence, he gave orders, the evening of the 22d, that, if General Thomas should come to take the department by force, no resistance should be made, but that he should be immediately notified of his approach. This order was kept secret, because, if known, it might lead to the attempt being made. Mr. Stanton, however, declared he would not have blood shed on his account, and, if an assault on the building were attempted, he would not try to repel it.

Monday, February 24th, the House of Representatives passed the resolution impeaching President Johnson, by a vote of 126 yeas to 42 nays. The report about town on Wednesday, the 26th, was, that General Thomas would appear before Judge Cartter, be surrendered by his bail, and, being committed, would sue out a writ of *habeas corpus*, to bring his case before the Supreme Court of the United States. This would test the tenure-of-office law. By this course there might result a conflict of action; for the Senate might impeach the President, while the Supreme Court might sustain General Thomas. When, however, the general appeared before the judge, he was discharged without bail. Thus the attempt to get his case before the Supreme Court was frustrated. If he had afterward been indicted by the grand jury, and tried before the criminal court, and if the President had been adjudged guilty by the Senate, the general would probably have gone to the penitentiary. He came into the office the day after his discharge, and said, "They euchred me again yesterday by discharging me instead of letting me go before the Supreme Court." He was evidently much dejected, and with reason, considering the difficulties in which he was involved.

The state of things which ensued was most remarkable. Of course, the President would have no intercourse with Mr. Stanton. He had also had a serious controversy with General Grant,* the General-in-Chief of the Army, through whom a recently enacted law required that he should issue all orders to the army, and would have noth-

---

* The controversy grew out of the surrender of the office of Secretary of War by General Grant when the Senate passed the resolution not sustaining the President in his first suspension of Mr. Stanton. The President claimed that the general should not have surrendered the office to any one but himself, whereas General Grant had not taken that course.

ing to do with him. General Thomas was asked by the President on the 17th of March to resume his duties as adjutant-general, but declined, lest it should involve the subordinate officers in difficulty, and because he could not recognize Mr. Stanton as Secretary of War. Yet his appointment as Secretary *ad interim* was not formally revoked. It happened, fortunately, that I had not been seriously involved during all these perplexities. A daily paper stated that I had committed myself by replying that I could not recognize any one but Mr. Stanton when General Thomas had asked me if I would acknowledge him as Secretary of War *ad interim*. No such conversation took place between us, and nothing whatever occurred to require me to take side with either of the contending parties. Thus I was as the neutral ground from February to the following May, on which the President, Secretary of War, and General of the Army, conducted the affairs of the army. They each sent directly to me the orders they desired to have executed, and by a little tact I managed to avoid any question of jurisdiction or other difficulty. As the Treasury Department continued to honor requisitions signed by Mr. Stanton, everything ran on smoothly as usual in the army.

On the 16th of May, 1868, the Senate voted on the eleventh of the articles of impeachment. The vote stood 35 for, 19 against. The rules required two thirds for conviction, and so Mr. Johnson was acquitted. On the 26th of May a vote was taken on the second and third articles, with the same result. These three articles contained special reference to the removal of Mr. Stanton, and the appointment of General Thomas, in alleged violation of the tenure-of-office law.

At about a quarter to three o'clock P. M., the same day (26th), Mr. Stanton's son, who was his private secretary, brought me a letter in the following terms:

WAR DEPARTMENT, WASHINGTON CITY,
May 26, 1868.

GENERAL: You will take charge of the War Department, and the books and papers, archives, and public property belonging to the same, subject to the disposal and directions of the President.

EDWIN M. STANTON,
Secretary of War.

Brevet Major-General E. D. TOWNSEND,
Assistant Adjutant-General.

In handing me this letter he said he was to take another letter from Mr. Stanton to the President. I asked at what time he would deliver that letter, remarking that it would be proper for me to see the President immediately after. Mr. Stanton, it seems, changed his first purpose, for in half an hour his son returned, saying his father wished me to deliver the letter to the President. I went over, and was immediately admitted to the President, who was alone, and handed him Mr. Stanton's letter. He invited me to be seated, and conned over the letter for about five minutes, his face wearing an expression of marked displeasure. At last he inquired at what time the War Department had been turned over to me. I replied that the letter was handed me but a few moments before I came to him. Something then prompted me to say: "It is right, Mr. President, that I should say I know nothing of the contents of that letter, except by surmise from the tenor of this one which I received at the same time, directing me to take charge of the

War Department." Upon this, his countenance at once changed. He examined and returned my letter, and in a pleasant voice asked the day of the month, which he noted on Mr. Stanton's communication, and then intimated that he desired nothing further. As I rose to depart, I said, "Have you any orders to give me, sir?" He replied, "None." Thus I concluded that, as he knew I held the charge of the War Department, subject to his "disposal and direction," he intended it should so remain until *he* gave me other instructions; so I put the key of the Secretary's room in my pocket.

In the evening I went to Mr. Stanton's residence and saw him. He said he could not be expected to make any further sacrifice by contending longer for the possession of the office. He had determined to withdraw at any rate, even if the President had been impeached, and had seized on this as an opportune moment to retire. This confirms my impression that he had, contrary to his own inclination, yielded to the arguments* of influential persons in favor of maintaining the contest. His impaired health must have made it peculiarly irksome to him.

The following is a copy of his letter to the President:

WAR DEPARTMENT,
WASHINGTON CITY, *May 26, 1868.*

To the President of the United States.

SIR: The resolution of the Senate of the United States, of the 21st of February last, declaring that the

---

* One of the pressures brought to bear upon him was Senator Sumner's laconic dispatch of February 21st:

"*Hon. E. M. Stanton. Stick.*
"Ever sincerely yours,
"CHARLES SUMNER."

President "has no power to remove the Secretary of War, and designate any other officer to perform the duties of that office *ad interim*," having this day failed to be supported by two thirds of the Senators present and voting on the articles of impeachment preferred against you by the House of Representatives, I have relinquished charge of the War Department, and have left the same, and the books, archives, papers, and property heretofore in my custody, as Secretary of War, in care of brevet Major-General Townsend, the senior assistant adjutant-general, subject to your direction.

EDWIN M. STANTON,
Secretary of War.

The morning after Mr. Stanton's retirement, General Thomas came to my room and asked if I had any keys for him. I replied that I had the keys of the Secretary's room. On his asking for them, I told him I had the day before reported to the President, and he had tacitly confirmed the orders given me to hold the keys subject to *his* direction. The general offered to give me an order in writing, which he would sign, by order of the President, as Secretary *ad interim*, if I desired it. I rather thought that under the circumstances I was as good an *ad interim* as he, so I replied that, to save any possible difficulty, I should prefer to have the President's own sign manual; that I would suggest he had better see the President, and, if the latter gave me such instructions, I would cheerfully give him the keys. The general went to see the President, and at the end of two hours returned, saying the President "would not touch the thing." So it was well I did not.

A singular incident happened that afternoon. A sign about three feet long and six inches wide, which was over the door of the reception-room next the Secretary's, fell to the floor, *face down*, as if to signify that there was now no Secretary of War, not even an *ad interim*.

Things remained *in statu quo* from the 26th to the 29th of May, when I received a visit from the President's military secretary, who sat a little while asking questions as to what was being done. At about three o'clock P. M., he returned, saying the President desired to see me. The President asked in a pleasant manner, "How are you getting on at the War Department?" I said I had not thought it right to attend to any of the business of the War Office, had opened none of the mails, but received them and deposited them in the Secretary's room, the key of which was in my own possession. He said that was right; there might be some business that ought to be transacted, but he hoped something would be done that afternoon or the next morning, and meantime he desired me to continue in the same course. I told him General Thomas had asked me to deliver the keys to him as Secretary *ad interim*, but I had thought it proper to receive the President's own order first. He replied, with evident pleasure, that I was quite right; that circumstances had changed since General Thomas's appointment, and he wished me to keep charge of the department for the present.

General Schofield was confirmed as Secretary of War by the Senate the 30th of May, and on Monday, the 1st of June, the President came to the War Department and installed him. He remarked, laughingly, as he entered the Secretary's room, "It is some time since I was in this room before!"

CHAPTER XXXI.

EDWIN M. STANTON.

"Always tying your shoe"—"Some one had been drinking"—The Secretary obeying orders—Blood enough shed—Malicious reports—Baptism—Kindly notice.

Mr. Stanton entered upon the duties of Secretary of War with a due appreciation of their difficulties and responsibilities. He was beset by persons who had "axes to grind," and some of them were not scrupulous as to the means of gaining their end.

He found that a determined will would often alone enable him to surmount obstacles in the way of the public service. This, added to the nervous irritability which infallibly attends overwork, sometimes made him arbitrary and offensive in his manners. But I always found him ready to make amends when in the wrong—if not directly by apology, yet by some exceedingly kind act which more than atoned for his hasty words. He confirmed this impression, when about to take final leave of the War Department, by saying to me that the only regret he felt in severing official relations with the officers who, under his administration of the War Department, had so faithfully and intelligently served the country, was that, "sometimes when racked in body and mind," he had not been able to control himself, and had addressed language to them which he afterward regretted. Indeed, he had often reminded me of the man who had had a hard time in his domestic circle, where he was forced to restrain himself, but, finding some one tying his shoe-string on the door-step, he vented his pent-up passion upon the poor fellow by knocking him over, saying, "You are always tying your shoe!" This thought often enabled me to refrain from a sharp answer, when it would have done more harm than good. Yet I did not always take an unmerited rebuke quietly. He sent down for me one day to go to his room in the department. I found him alone, pacing the floor. He asked me rather sternly why I had done a certain thing which had but just come to his knowledge. I gave him my reasons. Said he: "You were wrong; you ought not to have done any such thing." As I differed from him, I made no sort of reply. Then he asked why I had not done something else instead. I told him why, briefly explaining the circumstances. He said, in a milder tone, that he didn't agree with me. To this I made no reply. Then he asked, "Don't you think you were wrong?" I said, very deliberately and positively: "No, Mr. Secretary, I do not think I was wrong, and, moreover, I may as well add, once for all, that my best judgment and ability are uniformly exerted to foresee what may require to be done, and to do it as well as possible. If I fail, it is not from want of endeavor; and when you find fault, as you sometimes do, it can not quicken me to greater care and exertion, but only makes me indifferent whether I please you or not." He said, quietly, "I rebuke whom I please." "Yes, sir," said I. Having waited some time, and finding he said nothing more, but continued walking up and down in deep thought, I asked him if he wished anything further. He said, "No," and I withdrew. Half an hour after, the messenger summoned me to his room again. I thought it quite probable he would do as he did with a former chief of a bureau, who got angry at the way Mr. Stanton spoke to him, and resented it by saying he would allow no man to address to him such language. It was at the beginning of his administration, and the Secretary asserted his authority by ordering the refractory chief to a remote city, and never after allowing him to return to duty. But I had taken my stand deliberately, and meant to maintain it. The Secretary was still alone, and standing by his high table. Beckoning to me with his finger in a pleasant way, he put his arm around my shoulder, and drew my head close to his, when he whispered to me a very important secret, which it was not at all necessary I should know. He had weighed all I had said, found I was right, and took this method of showing me extraordinary confidence, by way of acknowledgment. This course, which the Secretary pursued more than once, fully accomplished his generous purpose without subjecting him to a direct confession of wrong, which he thought might weaken his influence. He knew that I well understood it so. In moments of leisure, he would often send for me, and in the most pleasant manner inquire about my business, to inform himself upon what was going on; and then converse generally on topics requiring consideration. In this way he maintained a sufficient knowledge of things he might have to act upon, and broke in upon the headlong current of events which seemed to cause everything to be done in a hurry.

Although Mr. Stanton had the reputation of being very stern, he yet enjoyed a pleasantry as well as other people. He once told me that an attempt had been made on the life of Judge —— by sending him an infernal machine in the form of a daguerreotype-box. I remarked that murderous attempts seemed rife; the papers had stated that a man tried to kill a certain Senator the day before, but that he had drawn a pistol on the fellow, who escaped. "Oh!" said the Secretary, "some one in that company had been drinking." I asked if the Senator was given to such a practice; for I had never then heard of it. "What practice?" said the Secretary, with a quizzical look, as if to say, "I did not say he had been drinking." Not to be caught so, I replied immediately, "Of carrying a pistol!" "Umph!" said the Secretary, laughing.

Nor was Mr. Stanton quick to take offense, when he understood that none was intended. There was one day an alarm that the War Department building was on fire. Smoke was distinctly seen issuing through the roof, and for a time it was thought that the building would soon be in flames. Necessary steps were taken to find the location of the fire and extinguish it. But there was no fire, after all. The old chimney was full of crevices; and, when a larger wood-fire than usual happened to be kindled in one of the rooms, the smoke issued from the holes, and was diffused through the empty space under the roof, finding its way out between the slates. The room of the disbursing clerk was on the floor where the fire was supposed to be, and very near the place from which smoke was issuing. There was a large sum of money in the safe, and the clerk coolly remained at his post to guard it, or, if necessary, be ready to move it. The Secretary, in taking a survey of the operations, opened the door of this room and partly entered. The clerk, not seeing who it was, gruffly ordered him out. "You wish me to go out, do you?" said the Secretary. "Yes, I do," replied the clerk. Without another word, Mr. Stanton withdrew, and closed the door after him. He never alluded to the matter; though, when the clerk ascertained whom he had so peremptorily ordered out, he naturally felt some apprehension of the Secretary's displeasure. The clerk had been faithful to his charge, and that was enough.

Both Messrs. Stanton and Henry Wilson, as soon as the fighting was over, expressed in my presence the strongest desire that peace and hearty good-will should be restored as soon as possible between the two sections. They believed the whole country would rapidly rise to greater prosperity than ever when this was effected. I shall never forget the expression of Mr. Stanton's face when I took to him for the President's action, just after General Lee's surrender, the proceedings of a general court-martial, sentencing a soldier to be shot for some mutinous or other aggravated offense. When he heard the sentence, and was reminded that it required the President's own action, Mr. Stanton turned to me, and said: "Is there no way of avoiding the execution of that sentence? There has been blood enough shed." The man was not executed.

The "absurd and malicious tale" that Judge Stanton took his own life was forever refuted by the letter of Surgeon-General Barnes and affidavits of William S. Dupee and David Jones. (See Appendix G.) If anything more were wanting to confirm me in the persuasion of the falsity of such a story, my own knowledge would suffice. I watched by the body of Edwin M. Stanton the entire night after his death, and could not have failed to know if there had been anything wrong about it. Moreover, I could never be brought to believe that a man who so often gave utterance to religious convictions as he did in friendly conversations with me could have possibly perverted his mind so as to commit such a deed. Only some three or four years preceding his decease, he invited Generals Barnes and Meigs and myself to be present at his baptism. The ceremony was performed in his chamber, by the Rev. Dr. Sparrow, his old-time professor at Kenyon College—no others, except his family, being present.

The estimate of Mr. Stanton's standing with the Northern public was kindly and, I think, justly represented by the following notice of him, clipped from a daily newspaper:

"Mr. Stanton.—Since the assassination of Mr. Lincoln, the public heart has been drawn nearer than ever to the Secretary of War. His bulletins from Washington have been eagerly read and widely praised as models of composition. And it is worthy of mention that the Secretary possesses the full confidence of the nation, no one ever presuming to question any of his statements. During the dark and terrible hours between the firing of the pistol by the assassin and the death of our good President, and while the precious life of Mr. Seward hung suspended by a thread, the announcements of the Secretary were like oil poured upon the troubled waters—

calming public apprehension, and restoring and strengthening confidence. These gentle and kindly offices have given him a place in every good heart."

CHAPTER XXXII.

THE COLORED MESSENGERS.

Datcher—Madison's portrait.

At the outbreak of the war, Francis Datcher was one of the messengers of the Secretary's office. It had been the custom for years to employ colored men, as well as whites, in that capacity. Frank Datcher, of the War Department, Lindley Muse, of the Navy Department, and Brent, of the Second Auditor's office, belong to the list of Uncle Sam's most steady and faithful servants. The veteran Datcher, while very dignified, possessed less of pomposity, and more of learning, than did the usher at the Executive Mansion, of long years ago, who, at a reception, announced a Senator and his daughters as "Senator Foote and the Misses Feet!" Datcher had a parchment on which was engrossed a high testimonial to his character, signed by a long succession of Secretaries on vacating their office. There was but one omission on the list. For some reason Frank had taken a strong dislike to one of the earlier Secretaries, who had so offended him that, like the French cook who dismissed the duke for adding salt to his soup, he would not permit him to affix his signature to the testimonial! Datcher did not serve long in the civil war. The vast increase to the labors of his station proved too severe for the old man, and his efforts to keep up to his work as promptly as usual caused his death.

He was succeeded by another colored man, Frank Madison by name, a good-natured, easy-going personage, who, aided by several active young fellows, did a fair share of running to the Secretary's bell. Frank Datcher was polite and formal in manner; Frank Madison was jovial and always ready for a joke. Secretary Belknap began to make a handsome collection of portraits in oil of his predecessors, to decorate the walls of the War-Office. Much interest was felt in this gallery by all the employés, and when a new picture arrived each one went to take a look at it. The older ones had, perhaps, some reminiscence of the earlier Secretaries to relate for the benefit of later comers. Frank Madison used to come to my room to advise me of each new arrival, and invite me up to see it. One day he came in a great state of excitement, his eyes starting from their sockets, and his head tossed in a manner as lofty as he was capable of. Said he: "General! what do you think? Mr. ———" (one of the clerks, who was a bit of a wag) "says the Secretary is going to have my portrait taken, to hang in his room 'long with all the Secretaries! Won't that be an honor! I don't know yet who is going to paint me, but I'll come down and tell you, soon as I find out. I think, sir, that is doing a handsome thing—don't you, now?" Frank's credulity was perhaps aided by the fact that portraits of some of the generals of the war had been hung beside the Secretaries. It may be imagined that the respondent had a little difficulty in playing his part of a credulous listener. He has been patiently waiting for several years to learn the name of the artist, but is still in ignorance.

CHAPTER XXXIII.

THE RECORDS OF THE ADJUTANT-GENERAL'S OFFICE.

Obstacle to capital-moving—Method of keeping records—Tracing a cotton claim—Tracing a soldier—Confederate archives—The Alabama.

THE infinite number and variety of business matters which have been administered upon by various departments of the United States Government, since the civil war began, can not be appreciated by those not personally conversant with such things. I was once urging before a.Senate committee the want of a fire-proof building to store the records upon which so many millions of dollars depended, where they would be at once safe and easy of access. One of the committee alluded to the efforts at that time made to bring public opinion up to the point of moving the capital westward. I suggested that one fact did not appear to have been brought into view in that connection: It was, that the wheels of government must be nearly brought to a stand-still for at least a year or more, while the process of moving was going on. The innumerable claims arising from contracts, pensions, and every conceivable account against the Treasury, are determined by documentary evidence, which must be carefully preserved for reference in every case. These papers contain the history of claims, and determine their value. Acres of ground are now covered by such records. In order to a change of location, they must all be boxed in parcels that could be handled and transported, and the boxes must be so labeled as to indicate their contents. Meantime, buildings of sufficient capacity must be provided in the new capital to receive them; and when they arrive there they must be unpacked and systematically arranged.

Some little estimate of the time which would be consumed in the packing and transporting, and then unpacking and arranging, can be formed by any one who has passed through the public buildings and observed the towering piles of shelves and pigeon-holes, groaning under the weight of tons of papers. Now, the last estimate for the payment of pensions—only one branch of the public service—was one hundred million dollars, due in sums of from three to thirty dollars a month. Every claimant for portions of this aggregate amount has on file in Washington papers proving the right to the pension. Besides this, thousands of new claims are constantly presented. But, while the Pension-Office is on its journey, almost the entire work upon these cases must be suspended, else wrong payments would be made to a frightful extent, in ignorance of what had been already determined about those same claims.

Nor is this all. The records of the different departments are interlaced, as it were, so that information from one is necessary to intelligent action in another. Thus, if the adjutant-general's muster-rolls are not open to the Pension-Office, the latter is paralyzed in its efforts to detect fraudulent claims.

From this sketch, but a faint conception can be

formed of the unavoidable suspension of public business which must ensue should the location of the capital be changed. This was a new idea to the Senator, and he thought it well worthy of serious consideration.

As must be supposed, a very exact but simple system prevails in the filing of papers, so that they can be easily found when required. In the same way that a book has its index, so has a collection of papers. Each paper is folded and indorsed with the date and place of writing, name of writer, a brief analysis of its contents, and the date of its receipt. The several papers are numbered in the order of their receipt within the year. This entire indorsement is copied in a book, and numbered to correspond with the number on the paper. The history of the subject embraced in the paper, as it progresses, is kept by further indorsements upon the paper, and by filing with it all other documents bearing on the subject. Finally, the date when the decision is communicated to the person concerned is noted on the papers. They are then arranged in pigeon-holes, or on shelves, in the order of their numbers, and according to the years of their dates. If the papers should be referred to any one out of the office, a note is made in the index-book, of the entire reference. Should any paper be required years after its receipt, the first resort is to the index-book which describes it, and the entry there at once reveals the file where it should be, or the reference which was made of it.

This is simply an outline of the system observed, with variations, in all departments of the Government. In illustration of its effectiveness, two incidents may be mentioned: After the close of the war, a gentleman was trying to trace some cotton, for which he had a claim, in the Treasury. He was referred to the adjutant-general, to ascertain what had become of certain papers he had submitted a few years before. An entry was found in the index-book, describing the papers, and showing that they had been sent to the officer commanding a military department, with instructions to him to obtain information and report upon them, and that they had not been returned. The gentleman said he had applied to this department commander, who had sent him to the officer commanding the sub-district where the cotton was taken; he had been to him, and could get no information from either. I asked if they had given him any memoranda, showing that they had ever seen the papers. He replied that both had given him slips, but they afforded him no assistance. He then handed me the slips. The one from the department commander was an exact copy of the entry from the adjutant-general's book, taken from the papers themselves, and showing that they had been received on a certain date, and that they had been referred for a report to the sub-district commander. The slip from the latter exhibited the same data, and that the papers had been given for proper action to a certain agent of the Treasury, appointed for the express purpose of attending to cotton claims. I had only to inform the gentleman that this Treasury agent was the person to whom he should look for his papers, and he departed quite satisfied.

The other instance of the value of such a system was one where some national pride was involved. In March, 1864, an application was made to the Department of State for the discharge of a French citizen, through the

French legation. The minister had gone away temporarily, and left a *chargé* to act for him. The letter inclosed a translation of one from the soldier himself to his father, in Paris, representing that he had been arbitrarily taken from his hotel in New York, told he was a soldier, and, having no one to care for him, had been hurried off to a regiment at Morris Island, in South Carolina, without bounty or pay. He signed himself " A. Cauvet, 3d Regt., V. H. V." The father wrote under the same name —Cauvet. There was no regiment in the Union service designated by the initials V. H. V., but, as the Third Regiment of N. H. (New Hampshire) Volunteers was at Morris Island, the muster-rolls of that regiment were carefully examined. No such man, however, appeared there. The regimental commander and several mustering officers were called upon to investigate the case, but for some time a trace could not be found. At last, after several weeks of patient examination, it was found that one Émile Caulat, a Frenchman, had voluntarily offered as a substitute for a drafted man, and had received from him the usual three hundred dollars; that he had been mustered in at a place in New Hampshire, instead of being kidnapped in New York as was stated, and had been sent to the Third Regiment of New Hampshire Volunteers. The man signed his name on enlistments and receipts very distinctly as Émile Caulat. Owing to the delay in finding him, which was due to difference of name and data, Émile Caulat's regiment had meantime been transferred to Virginia, where he was killed in battle. The French *chargé*, hearing this, addressed another communication to the Department of State, in which he reflected severely on administrative delays through which the

French citizen had found death under the United States flag, when he might have been discharged and saved. He also declared his conviction that statements, of which he had been kept in ignorance, showed the truth of the kidnapping charge.

On receipt of this last communication at the War Department, the Secretary sent to me for the facts. With the file of papers in my hand I gave him from their indorsements the history of the patient investigation that had been made, with the dates when several different officers in New York, New Hampshire, and South Carolina, had been asked to try to find the man, and the statements of their efforts, all in detail. The fact was clearly shown to be, that failure to comply with the request of the legation was due to material errors in the data given by it, and that, instead of being kidnapped in New York, Cauvet, if indeed he were identical with the man Caulat, had voluntarily enlisted as a substitute in New Hampshire. If, however, the identity of the two names were not established, then we had not been able to find Cauvet in the United States service.

Mr. Stanton was much impressed with the pains that had been taken in this investigation, and with the system of record through which its progress had been so accurately preserved. In sending the statement in detail to the Department of State, he expressed the hope that the Secretary would not fail to invite the attention of the French legation to the injustice done by its charges against officers whose fidelity and intelligence could not be surpassed by those of any government. It was a merited compliment to the assistant adjutant-general having immediate charge of that branch of business, for this was only one case out of the thousands from which it had been singled at hap-hazard.

Remembering what large numbers of claims against the Government had arisen from the Mexican War, and what trouble there had been in adjusting them from want of the records made at the time, I asked the Secretary of War to let me issue an order requiring that whenever military posts, departments, etc., were discontinued, all the official record-books and papers belonging to them should be forwarded for file in the adjutant-general's office. Accordingly, such an order was promulgated April 7, 1865.* The third paragraph of the order required that "officers who come in command of places captured from the enemy will collect and forward to this office any papers left behind by the rebels which may be of public use or interest." Struck with the importance of this measure, the Secretary immediately telegraphed the last provision to General Halleck, who commanded in Richmond after its capture. Some of the buildings and records of the Confederate capital had been fired at the time of the evacuation; a large portion, however, were saved. General R. D. Cutts, United States Coast Survey, then an aide-de-camp to General Halleck, collected and arranged all that could be found, and sent them, with invoices, to Washington. The invoices indicated from what public department the records were taken, and, being duly certified, they became of signal value as authentic documents, not only in an historical but in a financial point of view. It would be difficult to estimate the amount actually saved to the United States Treasury by

* In October, 1866, the adjutant-general reported that 3,353 boxes, containing records of 2,165 organizations, had been received.

the use of these archives. In one single case, judgment for a million dollars had been given a certain firm by an inferior court. This judgment, having been appealed to the United States Supreme Court, was reversed upon evidence subsequently discovered among the Confederate archives. In another instance both Houses of Congress passed a bill to pay a claim of about ninety thousand dollars; but the President, having seen indisputable evidence of the claimant's disloyalty, found in the archives, refused to sign the bill, and it was lost.

The most remarkable case of all was that of the Confederate ram Alabama, which was destroyed off Cherbourg, June 19, 1864, by the United States steamer Kearsarge, commanded by Captain John A. Winslow. Claims arising from depredations committed by the Alabama, or "290," as she was sometimes called, were before the High Joint Commission, which assembled in Washington to adjust differences between the United States and Great Britain. Hearing of this, I informed the Secretary of War that there were in the Archive-Office, certified by General Cutts as having been taken from the Confederate Navy Department in Richmond, drawings, plans, specifications, and a contract between the Confederate Navy Department and the Lairds, English ship-builders, for building this identical ram Alabama. Copies of these papers, under the seal of the War Department, were transmitted to the Department of State, and formed an important link in the testimony bearing on the question.

Whereas, at first much discontent was manifested at the South from a misapprehension as to the purpose of the Government concerning these archives, now that it is ascertained that whatever is of merely historical value

152   ANECDOTES OF THE CIVIL WAR.

will be published,* with other documents relating to the war, the Government receives hearty co-operation in its efforts to gather in as many of the same description of papers as it possibly can, in order that the written history of the war may be most complete on both sides.

CHAPTER XXXIV.

A CASE OF CIRCUMSTANTIAL EVIDENCE.

The unknown man—Convincing proofs.

IN the latter part of September, 1866, it was reported to me that an unknown man, laboring under insanity, and without the power of speech, had been found at Tallahassee, Florida, by the United States troops when they occupied that place. He had been there about fifteen months, and no one knew anything about his history. He was supposed, however, to be a Union soldier. A notice of him having appeared in some Northern papers, several persons applied for permission to visit Tallahassee, in hopes of finding in him a missing relative. With the view of bringing him to a more accessible place, and thus increasing the chances of his being identified, and also in the hope that contact with familiar objects might restore him to reason, I sent orders to have him transferred to

* "The War of the Rebellion: A Compilation of the Official Records of the Union and Confederate Armies. Prepared, under the Direction of the Secretary of War, by Brevet Lieutenant-Colonel Robert N. Scott, Third United States Artillery, and published pursuant to Act of Congress, approved June 16, 1880."

the Government Hospital for the Insane, at Washington, under the charge of an intelligent attendant, who might turn to advantage any sign of returning reason. He was admitted there the last of November, 1866. The superintendent of the hospital published personal descriptions of the man in newspapers at the North, and several persons came to see him. In August, 1867, a Mrs. Houghton, from Ontario County, New York, brought me a note from the superintendent of the hospital, stating that Mrs. Houghton had spent some hours with the unknown man, and that she believed him to be her husband. Dr. Nichols thought she was not mistaken, but was not quite so confident of his identity as she was. He recommended that she and the man should be examined together by some medical officers of the army. Accordingly, he was sent to the city, and examined by Surgeon-General Barnes, Assistant Surgeon-General Crane, and Dr. Nichols, superintendent of the hospital, Mrs. Houghton and myself being present. The result was given in a certificate, signed by the medical gentlemen, that they were satisfied the unknown man was Thomas B. Houghton, late a private soldier in the One Hundred and Fortieth Regiment of New York Volunteers; and that Elizabeth E. Houghton had fully identified and proved him to be her husband. The same day, Mrs. Houghton made affidavit that her husband, Thomas B., was a private soldier in Company H, One Hundred and Fortieth Regiment, New York Volunteers; that she had been informed by returned volunteers of the company that he disappeared from his command as the army was advancing to attack Fredericksburg, and that, having been taken sick on the march, he was told to get into the nearest hospital ambulance, and that he had not been heard of afterward. From several marks she had seen on the person of the unknown, she identified him to be her husband. Mrs. Houghton produced testimonials from respectable people in Ontario County, who were known to parties in Washington. The muster-rolls in the adjutant-general's office corroborated Mrs. Houghton's statement. The age and description of Houghton, as given by the muster-rolls, corresponded with the appearance of the unknown man, and with Mrs. Houghton's account of her husband.

Some of the proofs of identity were certainly most remarkable. It was stated in the newspapers that the unknown man had a singular mole upon his back. Mrs. Houghton, having declared that such was the fact as to her husband, was asked by the doctor to describe it and place her finger on it. She gave an accurate account of its size, shape, and appearance, and touched the spot where the "mother-mark," as she called it, was located on her husband. The doctor insisted that this man's mole was much higher up, but she maintained that her husband's was just where her finger indicated. On uncovering the place, she was found to be singularly accurate.

No mention had been made in the public prints of scars, but she described one on the forehead under the hair, and one on the foot, both of which were found as she said. Three remarkable scars of different size were found across the upper part of one shin, which had been erroneously supposed to have been caused by a musket-ball, though it was not easily seen how a ball could have passed through the flesh in such a direction without fracturing the bone. Mrs. Houghton had not seen those scars, but, when asked if she recollected any like them, she said that, some years before her husband left home, he was standing on a stool and reaching up to take a saw down from a beam in the shed, when the stool slipped and the saw fell across his leg below the knee. She did not remember which limb it was, but she knew that scars were left by the wounds. Thus these curious scars on the unknown man were satisfactorily accounted for. The doctors had seen clusters of small scars on the breast and back of the unknown: Mrs. Houghton, when questioned about them, said her husband was once engaged in washing sheep in a river under a hot sun; that he wore a red flannel shirt, and, when he came home, his neck and chest were covered with an eruption; she dressed the places with cream, but without giving relief; and he was under a doctor's care for two months before a cure was effected, leaving deep scars as described. General Barnes had known such cases, where poisonous substances in the dye of the red flannel had caused ulceration of the skin when excited by heat. To show the woman's good faith, when her attention was directed to some scars on the man's arms, she at once said that there were none such on her husband's, except one where he had been vaccinated. Dr. Nichols, however, stated that these scars were evidently of recent origin. It was a common error among medical men, not specially skilled in cases of insanity, to freely bleed the patients; and this vicious practice was apt to produce precisely the kind of dementia under which this man was laboring.

Mrs. Houghton brought with her a lock of her husband's hair, and a daguerreotype of him taken just before he left home. Examination with a microscope failed to detect any difference, in texture or color, between this hair and the man's when they were laid together, except that the latter had a slight sprinkling of gray, which change might easily have occurred in the time he was away from home.

Mrs. Houghton noticed a want of close resemblance between this man and her husband when his picture was taken, but that could be accounted for by lapse of time, and suffering, as well as change of dress. She said that when the man was looking down she could discover no trace of her husband's expression of countenance, but when his attention was attracted, and he looked up as if to speak, his attitude and expression were familiar. The color of the eyes—a singular light blue—was common to this man and to the picture. The daguerreotype showed a remarkable taper to the fingers. The thumbs were long and delicately pointed at the ends—a most unusual thing among laboring-men. This was also a marked peculiarity of the unknown man's hand. He had also a habit of twirling one thumb over the other while sitting, as if in meditation. Mrs. Houghton mentioned this as a notable custom of her husband.

Mrs. Houghton said that, from wearing short shoes, her husband's toes were bent under so that he was sometimes lame in consequence; examination revealed the same formation in this man.

No positive conclusion could be drawn from the effect of Mrs. Houghton's presence upon the man. He had some slight degree of intelligence: when told to stand up he comprehended with difficulty, but obeyed; and he seemed excited by the presence of persons to whom he was unaccustomed. Mrs. Houghton, in conversing with him, had endeavored to elicit some sign of recognition, by telling in brief sentences of his family and friends. He sat by her side passively, but several times looked up quickly and seemed to make an effort to speak. She said that in the morning, after the first night which she passed in the ward, she sat by him, and talked for some little time, and then, wishing him good-by, arose and went toward the door. He promptly got up and followed her, a thing quite unusual. Stopping at the door, she turned, put out her hand, and said, "Come, Thomas, won't you go with me?" He turned back with his face toward the wall, and trembled violently. She related this circumstance with great emotion, which she exerted herself to suppress, and seemed to think it a proof that he recognized her. In her subsequent meetings with him he showed less excitement than at first.

In view of all this remarkable chain of circumstances, it was not a surprise to me, but rather a peculiar gratification, when General Barnes sent me, rather more than a year after, the following copy of a letter from Dr. Nichols, indicating, as it seemed, beyond a possibility of doubt, that the last link of the chain had been forged:

GOVERNMENT HOSPITAL FOR THE INSANE,
NEAR WASHINGTON, D. C., *January 29, 1869.*

Brevet Major-General J. K. BARNES, *Surgeon-General U. S. Army.*

GENERAL: From the deep interest you have manifested in the case, I feel sure that you will derive as much pleasure from the intelligence as I do in being able to communicate it, that Thomas B. Houghton, late a private in the One Hundred and Fortieth Regiment New York

Volunteers, *spoke* on Saturday last, saying, in a distinct but low tone of voice, " *Yes, sir*," in reply to a leading question in respect to his health, by Dr. Eastman, the physician in immediate charge of him. He spoke somewhat more freely than he did at first, but still hesitatingly and timidly, and only in brief reply to direct questions. His answers are intelligent, however, and his intelligence appears to be increasing every day. When asked his name this morning he distinctly replied that it is "Thomas B. Houghton"; when asked the name of his wife, he shook his head and said, "I don't know, sir"; and, when asked where he is from, replied, "*New York*."

You will recollect the case of late private Houghton as that of the unknown man who was admitted to this hospital November 28, 1866, from the general army hospital at Tallahassee, Florida, in which he had been under treatment for about fifteen months, having been received as a destitute sick person, and under the supposition that he had been a Union prisoner among the rebels, and who was identified in your office on the 23d of August, 1867, as *Thomas B. Houghton*, late, etc., husband of Elizabeth E. Houghton, of Ontario County, New York.

Houghton did not speak while in the Tallahassee hospital, and has not spoken since he has been under the care of this institution till last Saturday; and it thus appears that he was *entirely dumb* for a period of *three and one half years*, and, as he was in a feeble, passive condition, and did not speak when admitted to general hospital, the disuse of his voice probably antedated that period many months. I now intend to address another communication to you in relation to this case when its history and result are more fully developed.

As the identification of late private Houghton was primarily due to brevet Major-General E. D. Townsend, assistant adjutant-general, who ordered his transfer from Tallahassee to this hospital, where he would be more accessible to those in pursuit of lost friends, and who, as you are aware, displayed a deep personal interest in this extraordinary case, I respectfully suggest that he be apprised of Houghton's improvement, and of the interesting event of his having found his long-lost voice.

I am, general, very respectfully,
Your obedient servant,
C. H. NICHOLS, *Superintendent, etc.*

Time wore on, and I occasionally heard that our patient was progressing favorably. His wife had gone home, preferring to leave him in the Government Hospital, where he could have far better attendance than she could otherwise procure. He steadily improved, and began to converse a little. He was employed at light labor, and grew robust in health. Suddenly, one day, when some one addressed him by the name of Houghton, he laughed and said that was not his name. He gave another name, and, when asked if he did not belong to the One Hundred and Fortieth New York Regiment, he said "No." A few days after, he said, with a peculiar chuckle, that he had never been a Yankee soldier, but had been overseer of a plantation in Georgia, or, as he called it, "a negro-driver." When Dr. Nichols heard this, he questioned him at different times, until the man stated that he was a native of Georgia. He gave the town where he lived, and the names of persons residing there and elsewhere in the State. He said he had gone into Florida on business, and had been drafted into a company of Florida conscripts; that he lost his mind soon after, and did not remember anything that had since occurred. Dr. Nichols wrote to the persons he named, and from their replies became convinced that the story was true.

Thus all our circumstantial evidence was completely overturned. When he was quite restored, the man expressed a desire to go home to the South, and he was sent accordingly. His answering at first to the name of Houghton may be accounted for by his having been called by that name, and hearing himself spoken of as from New York, for some time after his intelligence began to return.

CHAPTER XXXV.

ORIGIN OF MILITARY COMMISSIONS.

General Scott in Mexico—Martial law —Lieber's instructions.

BEFORE General Scott went to Mexico to assume command of the army, he endeavored to procure some provision by the War Department for trying a class of offenses which he foresaw must arise in the progress of his arms. There was no article of war, or other act of Congress, which would, in the ordinary practice, cover crimes committed by soldiers against Mexican citizens, or by citizens against soldiers of the United States army. The general submitted a *projet* of his plan in October, 1846, but, for some reason, no action was taken upon it. At the very outset of military operations, the general was

ORIGIN OF MILITARY COMMISSIONS. 161

met at Vera Cruz by just such a necessity as he had anticipated. To dispose of these cases, he first issued his General Orders, No. 20, dated February 19, 1847, and afterward republished it, with additions, the 17th of September, 1847, in his General Orders, No. 287 (see Appendix II).

A regiment of volunteers was raised in the District of Columbia, the command of which was given to an officer of the army by President Polk. When the army moved on toward the city of Mexico, this regiment was left to garrison Jalapa. Its colonel, as the senior officer, commanded the district around that town. The colonel was much embarrassed by the absence of any tribunal, civil or military, to enforce police regulations in the town. For want of a legal mode of punishment, he caused one of the enlisted men of his regiment to be flogged for some injury done a citizen of the place. This example seemed to have the desired effect, and he had little trouble in his command afterward. When the regiment had returned to Washington and been disbanded, a civil suit for damages was brought against the colonel in the name of the soldier whom he had punished with stripes. As I had mustered the regiment into service, I was called as a witness to prove that this soldier had been regularly mustered, and that he was stationed at Jalapa at the time of the alleged assault. Messrs. Bradley and Carlisle were the counsel on opposite sides. They questioned me as to the nature of the service in that foreign city, and the laws relating to military discipline in force there. In reply to these questions I stated in substance that the city had been captured from the enemy by United States forces, and was garrisoned by this colonel's regiment; that the colonel had been appointed military governor, and was responsible for the good order and police of the town; that there were no courts of the country or of the United States there; that the colonel had not power to assemble a general court-martial to try his men; and, even if he had, the offense committed by this soldier was not covered by the rules and articles of war; that the commanding general of the army alone had power to institute a military commission which could have tried the soldier for this civil offense, but he was so far off in the enemy's country that it was impracticable to communicate with him. Under these circumstances, the colonel had probably judged this summary punishment to be the only and necessary way to make an example which would prevent the prevalence of lawlessness and disorder. On hearing this, the judge said: "I perceive, sir, that you use a term not familiar to this court; will you please explain to the court what you mean by a military commission?" To this I replied: "As I understand the matter, when the United States forces landed and took possession of Vera Cruz and the surrounding country, all the civil magistrates fled, and the civil courts of Mexico were suspended. Hence arose, from the existing status of war, the necessity for a tribunal which could adjudicate and punish offenses committed by United States soldiers against citizens or each other, or by citizens against soldiers, or even by Mexican citizens against each other. This class of cases could not be lawfully tried by any military court constituted under the rules and articles of war. The foreign territory occupied by the United States forces being, then, practically and of necessity under martial law, General Scott conceived the plan of assembling what he designated 'military commissions,' which were composed of a number of officers of the army acting as jurors, and governed by the common law of the United States, which followed its armies in their camps, and by this tribunal all such cases, not strictly military in nature, were disposed of."

When I had finished, Mr. Carlisle arose and said, "Your Honor may thank the witness for a lucid explanation of a question which has puzzled the most acute lawyers for two hundred years past." I knew how much controversy there had been over the rights and powers of "martial law," and supposed Mr. Carlisle meant to make a point for his side, by a little sarcasm on the witness. I said then, "I am no lawyer, your Honor, but have endeavored to give you, to the best of my ability, what I suppose to be the true explanation of the matter."

Since the war of the rebellion, Mr. Bradley, and other lawyers of high authority, have told me I did give the true explanation. Upon this principle, then, which it seems I had rightly apprehended, and which General Scott's General Orders, No. 287, had elucidated, Congress enacted several laws during the civil war, making military commissions a legal tribunal. They were made use of in many exceedingly important instances, notably for the trial of the conspirators in the murder of President Lincoln. Washington was a garrisoned town, having in and around it several thousand soldiers, to protect the public officials and the public property. The President was commander-in-chief of the army, and his murder was adjudged to be clearly within the statutes.

In the codification of the military laws, the only trace left of military commissions is in section 1,343 of the

Revised Statutes, which provides for the trial of spies before them. A much larger scope of offenses, however, such as murder, robbery, etc., has been added to the list which a general court-martial may try; and orders No. 100, of the year 1863, prepared by Dr. Francis Lieber, LL. D., with much wisdom and learning, containing "Instructions for the Government of Armies of the United States in the Field," supplied a great gap in the codes of the world. It is now ingrafted upon the regulations for the army.

CHAPTER XXXVI.

MEDALS AND CORPS-BADGES.

Medals of honor—Recommendations—"Kearny patch"—Red, white and blue—Legal recognition—Legends—Devices.

MEDALS.—As soon as news of the civil war in the United States became known in Europe, many persons who had been officers in foreign armies came to offer their services to the Government. It frequently happened that these gentlemen brought letters of introduction and testimonials of their military career. Sometimes they came accredited to our Department of State. They usually paid their respects to General Scott, and not unfrequently, on such an occasion, wore their uniform, with all their decorations—medals or orders. There were many men in our volunteer service who had served abroad, and it was quite the habit among them to display on their uniforms such marks of distinction if they possessed them.

It is no wonder if they were objects of envy to many of our young aspirants for military glory.

The experience of the Mexican War, when the honor of a brevet was so often persistently sought for through political influence, sometimes without any special military merit to sustain it, early suggested to me the probability that the same evil in magnified form would arise during the civil war. It was very desirable, therefore, if possible, to prevent what afterward actually happened, the destruction of the practical benefit arising from the brevet system. Instead of tardy and sometimes indiscriminate recommendations for brevets, why should not our generals, when in command of armies in time of war, be clothed with the power of rewarding distinguished acts of bravery, *on the instant*, by issuing orders conferring a medal for them, such orders to be as soon as possible confirmed and executed by the War Department? Mistakes would rarely, if ever, be made;* and the excellent effect of a prompt recognition of gallantry in battle is no new thing in history.

---

* On one occasion, a commanding general, after a successful battle, sent a number of men, who had captured flags, to present them in person to the Secretary of War. The Secretary received them publicly at the department, and, as each one delivered his trophy, the Secretary pronounced his name, and ordered a medal of honor to be conferred on him. He then gave them collectively the thanks of the department for their distinguished bravery. Among them was a foreigner who bore a small, dirty, torn flag. When he produced it, I observed something in his manner that struck me unfavorably. His truly brave comrades, appreciating the high honor they had fairly won and ashamed of such companionship, exposed his imposture. His flag was originally found in an abandoned camp of the enemy, and had been borne in derision on the bayonets of our men, tossed from one to another, until, weary of the sport, they had cast it into the bushes. This fellow had picked it up, and had the effrontery to come forward as its captor in battle, and to claim a medal for it. He did not get one.

Impressed with these ideas, I, early in 1861, urged their adoption upon General Scott, and upon the chairman of the Senate Military Committee, the Secretary of War, and others in influence. They objected that it was contrary to the spirit of our institutions to wear decorations, and therefore the measure would not be popular. I instanced the pride which children feel in wearing medals won at school, and the pains taken by parents to foster it; and suggested that, if those who won medals did not choose to wear them, they would none the less value them, and so would their descendants after them. Nothing was done in that direction, however, until the 12th of July, 1862, when Congress passed a resolution to award medals of honor to enlisted men, which, by the act of March 3, 1863, was extended to officers also. These medals, although intrinsically of but little value, have been eagerly sought for and highly prized. The main objection to them is the mode of conferring, under which years have sometimes elapsed before sufficiently reliable testimony could be obtained that the claimant was justly entitled to one, according to the terms of the law.

In my annual report of October 31, 1864, the matter was presented to the notice of the Secretary of War, and of Congress, in these words:

"The medal of honor is of bronze, of neat device, and is highly prized by those on whom it has been bestowed. Hitherto no medals have been conferred upon commissioned officers, apparently under the idea that at some future day their acts of distinguished bravery would be recognized by brevets. It is believed that, in the majority of cases, the award of a gold or a silver medal would be quite as acceptable as the brevet, and of more substantial value, especially in the volunteer service. . . . If an act were passed to authorize it, a prompt and gratifying acknowledgment of distinguished services could be made, by publishing a general order awarding to the officer 'the gold medal' or the 'silver medal,' with the privilege of engraving thereon the name and date of the battle in which his gallantry was conspicuous. In case of his again winning distinction, he would be authorized in general orders to add to the inscription upon his medal the name and date of his new exploit. If both gold and silver medals were authorized, there would be no objection to the same officer being the recipient of both, if won by meritorious conduct at different times, and different in degree. The system of medals need in no wise interfere with the conferring of brevet rank in cases where such rank might be actually exercised in high commands, or at the discretion of the President; but it would relieve the pressure for brevets on the part of the many officers who justly believe they have won a title to some mark of honor, and would avoid the many vexed questions likely to arise from the possession of brevet rank by so large a number of officers as can reasonably prefer a claim to reward."

Corps-Badges.—As a sort of substitute for medals, the corps-badges have come to be regarded as a proud mark of distinction, and memorial of service in the war. It would be difficult to describe the true sentiment connected with them in more eloquent language than that used by the commander of the Twenty-fifth Corps, in his

168   ANECDOTES OF THE CIVIL WAR.

order announcing the device for his command.* So highly are they valued, that large sums have often been expended on presentation gold and jeweled badges. Yet there seems to be one objection to these badges: there is nothing to prevent their being worn by any man who served, whether meritoriously or not, during the war. Once only, so far as is known, was an attempt made to restrict their use, and that was by resolutions passed at a meeting of officers and enlisted men belonging to the Army of the Cumberland. †

The adoption of badges appears to have originated in the "Kearny patch." One day, when his brigade was on the march, General Philip Kearny, who was a strict disciplinarian, saw some officers standing under a tree by the road-side. Supposing them to be stragglers from his command, he administered to them a rebuke, emphasized by a few expletives. The officers listened in silence, respectfully standing in the "position of a soldier," until he had finished, when one of them, raising his hand to his cap, quietly suggested that the general had possibly made a mistake, as they none of them belonged to his command. With his usual courtesy Kearny exclaimed: "Pardon me; I will take steps to know how to recognize my own men hereafter." Immediately on reaching camp, he issued orders that all officers and men of his brigade should wear conspicuously on the front of their caps a round piece of red cloth, to designate them. This became generally known as the "Kearny patch." After the battle of Fair Oaks, or Seven Pines, it was observed that the Confederate prisoners universally wore strips of red, blue,

* See "Badge of the Twenty-fifth Corps," p. 188.
† See "Badge of the Army of the Cumberland," p. 195.

or white cloth on their caps, which they said were to designate the commands to which they belonged. General Kearny, in conversation with General Hooker, enthusiastically instanced this as illustrating the utility of his " patch."

General D. B. Birney, in his General Orders No. 49, dated September 4, 1862, from the headquarters of Kearny's division, announced the death of General Philip Kearny. After the usual requirement to wear crape on the left arm for thirty days, the order says : " To still further show our regard for him, and to distinguish his officers as he wished, each officer will continue to wear on his cap a piece of scarlet cloth, or have the *top or crown-piece of cap made of scarlet cloth.*"

After the "Kearny patch," several army corps, one by one, adopted distinctive badges. The divisions of each corps were indicated by one of the colors red, white, blue, and green and orange, if there were more than three divisions, upon some part of the badges. They were either suspended by the tricolored ribbon, or fastened with a pin. As there were usually three divisions in a corps, the national colors were the ones sure to be represented. For the headquarters, some slight modifications were made in the form worn by the divisions. When several army corps were consolidated into an " army," the badge of that army headquarters consisted of a combination in one of all those of the corps. But it is believed that, with the exception of the Army of the Cumberland, the " army-badges " were adopted by societies of the several armies subsequent to the war. The badges were painted on the wagons of the corps, and stenciled on all its articles of public property.

Corps-badges have now a legal recognition in the Revised Statutes of the United States:

"SECTION 1,227.—All persons who have served as officers, non-commissioned officers, privates, or other enlisted men, in the regular army, volunteer, or militia forces of the United States, during the war of the rebellion, and have been honorably discharged from the service, or still remain in the same, shall be entitled to wear, on occasions of ceremony, the distinctive army-badge ordered for or adopted by the army corps and division respectively in which they served."

LEGEND AND DESCRIPTION OF BADGES.—To Major-General Joseph Hooker probably belongs the credit of first having issued orders for the adoption of regular corps-badges, to be worn by officers and enlisted men of all the regiments of various corps through the entire Army of the Potomac. Just before the Chancellorsville campaign, on the 21st of March, 1863, he issued a circular prescribing the device for a badge for each corps, "for the purpose of ready recognition of corps and divisions of this army, and to prevent injustice by reports of straggling and misconduct, through mistake as to their organizations."* They were to be "fastened on the center of the top of the cap." The devices seem to have been arbitrarily chosen, without particular significance.

In obedience to orders from the War Department, Major-General Meade, in his General Orders, No. 10, of

---

* This same phraseology was used in the Orders No. 62, April 26, 1864, announcing the badges of corps in the Department of the Cumberland.

MEDALS AND CORPS-BADGES.   171

March 24, 1864, consolidated the Second, Fifth, and Sixth Army Corps into two divisions, transferred two divisions of the Third Corps to the Second Corps, and the third Division to the Sixth Corps. In this order he directed that the troops transferred should preserve "their badges and distinctive marks." This was done by combining their old badges with their new ones.

FIRST CORPS.

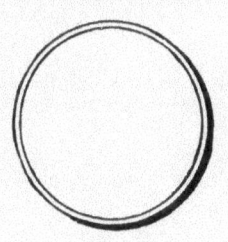

A SPHERE.

[Circular, Headquarters, Army of the Potomac, March 23, 1861.]

SECOND CORPS.

A TREFOIL.

[Circular, Headquarters, Army of the Potomac, March 23, 1861.]

THIRD CORPS.

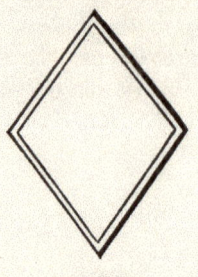

A LOZENGE.

[Circular, Headquarters, Army of the Potomac, March 21, 1863.]

FOURTH CORPS.

AN EQUILATERAL TRIANGLE.

[General Orders, No. 62, Headquarters, Department of the Cumberland, April 26, 1864.]

The Fourth Corps, which was commanded by General E. D. Keyes, was discontinued August 1, 1863, before the adoption of this badge.

MEDALS AND CORPS-BADGES. 173

FIFTH CORPS.

A MALTESE CROSS.

[Circular, Headquarters, Army of the Potomac, March 21, 1863.]

When the Army of the Potomac was reorganized, in March, 1864, and the First Corps was consolidated with the Fifth, the men who were transferred from the old First then combined the badges of the two corps, thus:*

[General Orders, No. 10, Headquarters, Army of the Potomac, March 24, 1864.]

---

* The author is indebted to Mr. J. W. Kirkley, of the Adjutant-General's Office, for this and other interesting items.

174   ANECDOTES OF THE CIVIL WAR.

SIXTH CORPS.

A GREEK CROSS.
[Circular, Headquarters, Army of the Potomac, March 21, 1863.]

The men transferred from the old Third Corps to the Sixth combined the lozenge and cross of the two corps, thus: *

[General Orders, No. 10, Headquarters, Army of the Potomac, March 24, 1864.]

SEVENTH CORPS.

A CRESCENT ENCIRCLING A STAR.
[Circular, Headquarters, Department of Arkansas, June 1, 1865.]

* The author is indebted to Mr. J. W. Kirkley, of the Adjutant-General's Office, for this and other interesting items.

The Seventh Corps, which served in the Department of Virginia, and was commanded by Major-General John A. Dix, was discontinued August 1, 1863, and was quite different from the Seventh which served in the Department of Arkansas.

EIGHTH CORPS.

A STAR WITH SIX RAYS.

[No order issued.]

NINTH CORPS.

A SHIELD WITH THE FIGURE 9 IN THE CENTER, CROSSED WITH A FOUL ANCHOR AND CANNON.

[General Orders, No. 6, Headquarters, Ninth Corps, April 10, 1864, and General Orders, No. 49, December 23, 1864.]

This corps served afloat for some time.

TENTH CORPS.

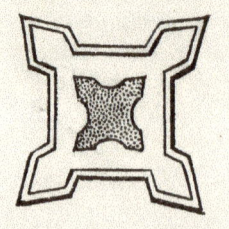

THE TRACÉ OF A FOUR-BASTIONED FORT.

[General Orders, No. 18, Headquarters, Tenth Corps, July 25, 1864.]

This corps was employed in the reduction of forts on the seaboard, and was under General Terry at the capture of Fort Fisher, North Carolina. This service suggested the device.

ELEVENTH CORPS.

A CRESCENT.

[Circular, Headquarters, Army of the Potomac, March 21, 1863.]

TWELFTH CORPS.

A STAR WITH FIVE RAYS.

[Circular, Headquarters, Army of the Potomac, March 21, 1863.]

This corps was consolidated with the Eleventh Corps, to form the Twentieth, April 18, 1864. The Twentieth adopted its badge.

THIRTEENTH CORPS.
(No badge adopted.)

FOURTEENTH CORPS.

AN ACORN.

[General Orders, No. 62, Headquarters, Department of the Cumberland, Chattanooga, Tennessee, April 26, 1864.]

From General Jefferson C. Davis this legend of the Acorn-Badge was received: After the battle of Chickamauga, Roser's army made a stand at and around Chattanooga. Rosecrans's army, owing to exceedingly muddy roads, and the cutting of its lines of communication by the Confederates, had great difficulty in getting supplies. The Fourteenth Corps was encamped near a wood of oak-trees, which were at that time covered with acorns. As the rations fell short, many of the men gathered the acorns and ate them roasted, till at length it was observed that they had become quite an important part of the ration, and the men of the corps jestingly called themselves "The Acorn-Boys." Receiving an order about that time which required the adoption of a corps-badge, the acorn was selected by acclamation.

FIFTEENTH CORPS.

A MINIATURE CARTRIDGE-BOX, BLACK, SET TRANSVERSELY ON A SQUARE. ABOVE THE CARTRIDGE-BOX PLATE THE MOTTO, "FORTY ROUNDS."

[General Orders, No. 10, Headquarters, Fifteenth Army Corps, February 14, 1865.]

In announcing this badge, Major-General John A. Logan, commanding the Fifteenth Corps, says: "If any corps in the army has a right to take pride in its badge, surely that has which looks back through the long and glorious line [enumerating thirty-five engagements and battles, 'and scores of minor struggles']; the corps which had its birth under Grant and Sherman in the darker days of our struggle; the corps which will keep on struggling until the death of rebellion."

The device of the badge of the Fifteenth Corps was suggested by the following incident: The Eleventh and Twelfth Corps were transferred from the Army of the Potomac to the Department of the Cumberland. They were better dressed than the other troops of that department, and a little rivalry sprang up between these Eastern boys and those who came from the West. The latter spoke of the former as "the men who wore paper shirt-collars, and crescents and stars." Before the Fifteenth Corps had any badge, an Irishman belonging to it went to the river near camp to fill his canteen. There he met a soldier of one of the newly arrived corps, whose badges were the subject of ridicule by his comrades. The latter saluted the Irishman with the query, "What corps do you belong to?" "The Fifteenth, sure." "Well, then, where is your badge?" "My badge, is it? Well" (clapping his hand on his cartridge-box), "here's my badge! Forty rounds! It's the orders to always have forty rounds in our cartridge-box, and we always do."

SIXTEENTH CORPS.

The badge of this corps is sometimes *erroneously* represented as follows:

[No order issued.]

From Colonel J. J. Lyon, Assistant Inspector-General, Sixteenth Corps, the following correct description of the badge is derived:

"The device is, A CIRCLE, WITH FOUR MINIÉ-BALLS, THE POINTS TOWARD THE CENTER CUT OUT OF IT. The bare spaces represent the shape of the balls cut out, and the remainder forms a cross resembling the Maltese, with the lines curved."

The badge was suspended from a ring attached to the points of two arms of the cross, instead of the center of one arm, to distinguish the device more clearly from the Maltese cross, previously adopted by the Nineteenth Corps.

It having been determined to assume a badge for the Sixteenth Corps, several of the officers made designs, which, by common consent, were put in a hat, and the one drawn out was accepted. The design contrived by brevet Brigadier-General John Hough, assistant adjutant-general of the corps, was drawn out, and received the approval of the corps commander, Major-General A. J. Smith. "The new badge was then and there duly consecrated, adopted, baptized, by the usual ceremonies practiced in the army on such momentous occasions,* . . . and named the A. J. Smith Cross," in honor of the first commander of the corps after a badge was adopted by it.

General Hough, the author of the design, has given the following account of the rule by which it was constructed :

"In any circle draw two diameters perpendicular to each other, dividing the circle into four quarters ; bisect the arc of each quarter, and, with the bisecting points as a center, and a radius five sixths of the radius of the original circle, inscribe segments of a circle ; cut out the parts

* We are not informed what these ceremonies were. Did the spirit of the Widow Cliquot inspire them ?

inclosed between any two of these segments, and the remainder will be the badge of the Sixteenth Army Corps."

SEVENTEENTH CORPS.

AN ARROW.

[General Orders, No. 1, Headquarters, Seventeenth Corps, March 25, 1865.]

Major-General Francis P. Blair says in his order: "The badge now used by the corps being similar to one formerly adopted by another corps, the major-general commanding has concluded to adopt, as a distinguishing badge for the command, an arrow.

"In its swiftness, in its surety of striking where wanted, and in its destructive powers when so intended, it is probably as emblematical of this corps as any design that could be adopted."

EIGHTEENTH CORPS.

A CROSS, WITH FOLIATE SIDES.

[Circular, June 7, 1864, and General Orders, No. 108, of August 25, 1864, Headquarters, Eighteenth Corps.]

MEDALS AND CORPS-BADGES. 183

NINETEENTH CORPS.

A FAN-LEAVED CROSS, WITH OCTAGONAL CENTER.

[General Orders, No. 11, Headquarters, Nineteenth Corps, November 17, 1864.]

TWENTIETH CORPS.

A STAR WITH FIVE RAYS, as heretofore worn by the Twelfth Corps.

[General Orders, No. 62, Headquarters, Department of the Cumberland, April 26, 1864.]

This corps was formed by consolidating the Eleventh and Twelfth Corps, April 18, 1864. For some time after the consolidation the men of the old Eleventh combined the two badges thus:

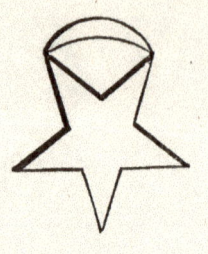

TWENTY-FIRST CORPS.

[No badge was ever adopted.]

TWENTY-SECOND CORPS.

QUINQUEFOLIATE IN SHAPE, WITH A CIRCLE INSCRIBED IN THE CENTER.

[No order issued.]

The signification of this design seems to be a building inside defensive works, in allusion to the continued service of the corps in and around Washington.

MEDALS AND CORPS-BADGES.

TWENTY-THIRD CORPS.

A PLAIN SHIELD.

[No order issued for its adoption; but Special Orders, No. 21, Headquarters, First Division, Twenty-third Army Corps, near Raleigh, North Carolina, April 15, 1865, directs that "the badges which have just been issued to this command will be worn upon the top of the cap, or left side of the hat."]

General J. D. Cox has kindly furnished the following information concerning this badge :

"It was adopted at the beginning of the Atlanta campaign (spring of 1864). There was no legend connected with it.

"The Twenty-third Corps had been intimately associated with the Ninth (under Burnside) in the campaign in East Tennessee in 1863, being organized in that year for the purpose of becoming part of Burnside's Army of the Ohio.

"This association led to our adopting a shield somewhat similar in form to the badge of the Ninth Corps, but with sufficient marks of distinction.

"To secure uniformity in the shape and proportions of the badge, the following rules were established for constructing or drawing it, which I draughted, and am therefore able to reproduce :

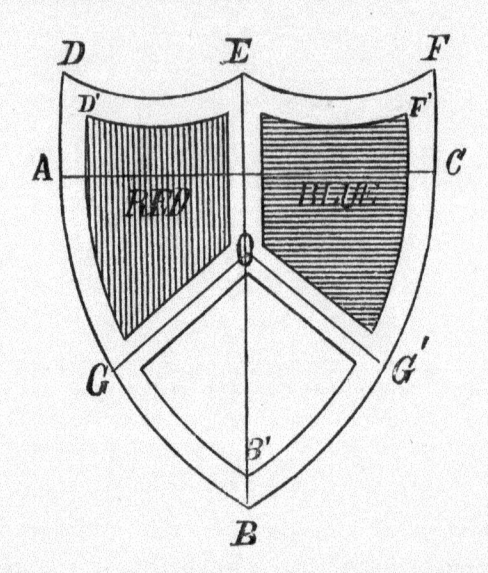

"With the radius A C, strike the curves C B and A B, from the centers A and C respectively. Make A D and C F *perpendicular*, and one fourth A C in length. Strike the curves D E and E F with radius of one half A C. Make the inner curves parallel to the outer ones. From G, *the middle of* A B, draw G O in the direction of F', and draw G' O in like manner in the direction of D'. Complete the radiating bars, and tint the panels red, white, and blue. The border and divisions between the panels are gilt.

"The above is for *corps headquarters*, and was displayed on a blue silk banner, with fringed edge.

"For *divisions*, all the panels were of one tint: first division, red; second division, white; third division, blue.

MEDALS AND CORPS-BADGES. 187

"For *brigades*, the flags were of bunting, the shield smaller, of same color as division to which the brigade belonged; one small shield in upper corner next the staff for first brigade, two small shields for second brigade, and three for third.

"The same badge was painted on the covers of all wagons and ambulances, etc., substituting yellow for the gilt border."

TWENTY-FOURTH CORPS.

A HEART.

[General Orders, No. 32, Headquarters, Twenty-fourth Corps, March 18, 1865.]

This corps was organized late in the war, and was for the most part composed of veterans who had served in other corps. Major-General John Gibbon, in his orders adopting the badge, says: "The symbol selected is one which testifies our affectionate regard for all our brave comrades—alike the living and the dead—who have braved the perils of this mighty conflict, and our devotion to the sacred cause—a cause which entitles us to the sympathy of every brave and true heart, and the support of every strong and determined hand.'

"The major-general commanding the corps does not doubt that soldiers who have given their strength and blood to the fame of their former badges will unite in rendering the present one even more renowned than those under which they have heretofore marched to battle."

TWENTY-FIFTH CORPS.

A SQUARE.

[Orders, February 20, 1865, Headquarters, Twenty-fifth Corps, Army of the James, Virginia.]

This corps was composed entirely of colored soldiers. It was the first to occupy Richmond, Virginia, April 3, 1865. The following is Major-General Godfrey Weitzel's order:

"In view of the circumstances under which this corps was raised and filled, the peculiar claims of its individual members upon the justice and fair dealing of the prejudiced, and the regularity of the conduct of the troops which *deserve* those *equal rights* that have hitherto been denied the majority, the commanding general has been induced to adopt the *square* as the distinctive badge of the Twenty-fifth Army Corps.

"Wherever danger has been found and glory to be

won, the heroes who have fought for immortality have been distinguished by some emblem to which every victory added a new luster. They looked upon their badge with pride, for to it they had given its fame. In the homes of smiling peace it recalled the days of courageous endurance and the hours of deadly strife, and it solaced the moment of death, for it was a symbol of a life of heroism and self-denial. The poets still sing of the 'Templar's cross,' the 'crescent' of the Turk, the 'chalice' of the hunted Christian, and the 'white plume' of Murat, that crested the wave of valor, sweeping resistlessly to victory.

"Soldiers! to you is given a chance, in this Spring campaign, of making this badge immortal. Let history record that, on the banks of the James, thirty thousand freemen not only gained their own liberty, but shattered the prejudice of the world, and gave to the land of their birth peace, union, and glory."

HANCOCK'S FIRST CORPS—VETERAN VOLUNTEERS.

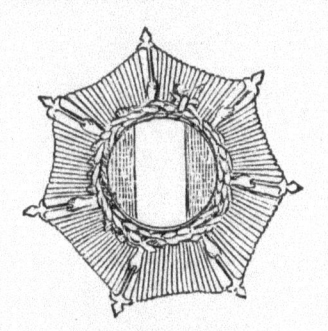

[No order issued.]
(This corps was organized in 1864.)

To Major-General Hancock's courtesy is due the information that this badge was designed by his "chief of staff, General C. H. Morgan, and had no special legend or significance attached to it, the object being to have it as distinct and different as possible from other corps badges, so that it might be easily distinguished and recognized when worn by troops in campaign."

It may be thus described: A circle is surrounded by a double wreath of laurel. A wide red band passes vertically through the center of the circle. Outside the laurel-wreath, rays form a figure with seven sides of concave curves. Seven hands, springing from the circumference of the laurel-wreath, grasp spears, the heads of which form the seven points of the external radiated figure.

SHERIDAN'S CAVALRY CORPS.

Design: "GOLD CROSSED-SABERS, ON A BLUE FIELD, SURROUNDED BY A GLORY IN SILVER.

[No order issued.]

(This badge was only worn by commissioned officers.)

Concerning this badge, Colonel Gerrard Irvine Whitehead, who served on the staff of the corps, kindly gives the information that, while General Pleasanton commanded the corps, he (Colonel Whitehead) was charged with procuring a badge. He accordingly caused a number to be made, but they were not ready for delivery until the summer of 1864. Meanwhile, General Sheridan came in command, and the corps was "entirely too busy to think about badges." It thus happened that few, if any, were ever worn by the enlisted men.

WILSON'S CAVALRY CORPS.

A RIFLE, OR CARBINE, FROM WHICH IS SUSPENDED, BY CHAINS, THE RED SWALLOW-TAIL GUIDON OF THE CAVALRY, WITH GILT CROSSED-SABERS UPON IT.

[No order issued.]

From Generals J. H. Wilson and Edward Hatch the following facts are derived: The rifle was the badge of the Fifth Division of this corps (formerly First Division of the Army of the Tennessee). The red swallow-tail guidon, with sabers crossed upon it, was the flag of the corps headquarters. The corps badge, a combination of the rifle (or the Spencer carbine, "which was found to be a most efficacious arm") and the guidon, was adopted by a committee of officers belonging to the corps.

FRONTIER CAVALRY.

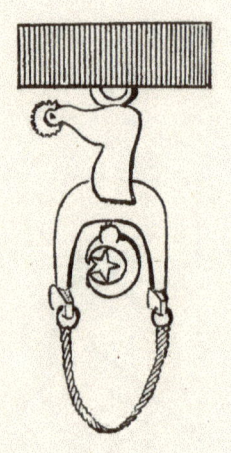

A SPUR, WITH CURB-CHAIN, AND CRESCENT AND STAR SUSPENDED.

[No order issued.]

This cavalry served in the Seventh Corps in Arkansas. The crescent and star were the badge of Moonlight's division. The shank of the spur was bent, to represent the figure 7 of the corps.

MEDALS AND CORPS-BADGES.   193

CUSTER'S CAVALRY CORPS.

[No order issued.]

Mr. Thomas Haslam, of the Adjutant-General's office, gives the following interesting statement:

Custer's dashing style, as he rode at the head of his command, whether in the act of charging in real, earnest war, or peacefully marching in review, is as well known as his name. He wore his hair long, and flowing in careless curls about his neck. His collar was open at the front, only loosely confined by a bright-red scarf tied with a sailor-knot. His men, in this, as in their conduct, caught the spirit of their commander, and all wore the red scarf. They could be distinguished at a long distance by this their only badge.

ENGINEER AND PONTONIER CORPS.

TWO OARS CROSSED OVER AN ANCHOR, THE TOP OF WHICH IS ENCIRCLED BY A SCROLL SURMOUNTED BY A CASTLE; THE CASTLE BEING THE BADGE OF THE U. S. CORPS OF ENGINEERS.

[No order issued.]

194   ANECDOTES OF THE CIVIL WAR.

SIGNAL CORPS.

TWO FLAGS CROSSED, WITH A FLAMING TORCH BETWEEN THEM. Indicating the implements used in signaling, the flags by day and the torch by night. The star on the left flag is red; the scroll in the right one is blue; the flame of the torch is red and gilt.

DEPARTMENT OF WEST VIRGINIA.

A SPREAD EAGLE.

[General Orders, No. 2, Headquarters, Department of West Virginia, January 3, 1865.]

MEDALS AND CORPS-BADGES.

DEPARTMENT OF THE CUMBERLAND.

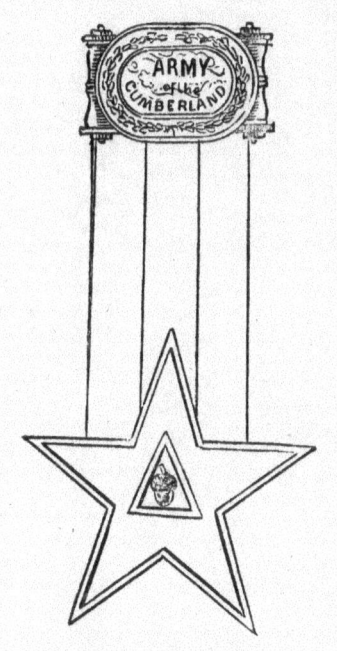

COMBINATION OF THE FOURTH, FOURTEENTH, AND TWENTIETH CORPS.

[General Orders, No. 41, Headquarters, Department of the Cumberland, Nashville, Tennessee, June 19, 1865.]

Major-General George H. Thomas published the proceedings of a meeting of the officers and enlisted men of the Army of the Cumberland, held "for the purpose of considering the propriety of adopting a badge to signalize and perpetuate the history of the Army of the Cumberland."

"It was unanimously agreed to adopt such a badge";

and, "on motion, the following preamble and resolutions were adopted:

"*Whereas*, Many of the soldiers of the Army of the Cumberland are about to abandon the profession of arms, and again mingle in the peaceful pursuits of home:

"*Resolved*, That, in parting with each other, we do so with mingled feelings of sorrow, sadness, and pride: sorrow, because friends, bound together by ties formed on many battle-fields, must part; sadness at turning our backs upon the thousand fresh-made graves of our brave comrades; and pride, because it has been our good fortune to be numbered among the members of the Army of the Cumberland, and have each done his part in proving to the world that republics have the ability to maintain and perpetuate themselves.

"*Resolved*, That, in parting, we do, as we have many times done in the face of the enemy, renew our pledges of unending fidelity to each other; and that, in whatever position of life we may happen to be, we will never permit our affections to be estranged from those who continue to fight our battles, but that we will sustain and defend them at all times and in all proper places.

"*Resolved*, That the following-named persons, and none others, are authorized to wear the badge of the Army of the Cumberland:

"1. All soldiers of that army now in service and in good standing.

"2. All soldiers who formerly belonged to that army, and have received honorable discharges from the same.

"*Resolved*, That any soldier of the Army of the Cumberland who is now entitled to wear the badge of the army, who may hereafter be dishonorably dismissed the service, shall, by such discharge, forfeit the right to wear such badge.

"*Resolved*, That we exhort all members of the Army of the Cumberland to discountenance any attempt on the part of unauthorized persons to arrogate to themselves honor to which they are not entitled, by wearing our badge."

CHAPTER XXXVII.

CONFEDERATE FLAGS.

Inevitable Stars and Stripes—The Southern Cross—The Stars and Bars—The battle-flag—The white flag—Its surrender to the Monitor—The black flag.

DURING the war a large number of Confederate flags, captured in battle, were sent to Washington, where they were kept in a room, a few being displayed as samples. They were an object of great interest, constantly visited by sight-seers. Many of these flags also found their way to Capitols of the loyal States, where they were preserved among the mementos of volunteer regiments. It was once suggested that the captured Confederate flags should be deposited at the West Point Military Academy among similar trophies of other wars; but this was not done, because, while the Government insisted on loyalty to it, it deemed it not proper to perpetuate in the minds of its young soldiers any feeling of exultation on the one side, or of regret on the other, in connection with such objects after the war was all over.

Doubtless many flags captured from Union troops

were also preserved by the Confederates. Indeed, some were found at Richmond at the time of its occupation by the Union forces, and sent with the rebel archives to Washington. There was also found at Richmond a collection of designs proposed by many persons for the Confederate national flag. Over two hundred devices were submitted, accompanied by letters explaining their symbolic meaning. It is noticeable that in a very large proportion of the plans there is some combination of stars, or of stripes, or of both. At first sight it would appear that this showed only an accidental association of ideas, and a want of originality in the designers. This view would naturally be strengthened by the tone of hostility to the Union seen in their newspapers. But the correspondence on the subject betrays much warm affection for the old flag, and gives undoubted proof that the emblems were intentionally retained, the main object of the authors being to form such a combination of colors, or arrangements of the stars, or stripes, or both, as to avoid fatal mistakes in battle.

One gentleman wrote, in February, 1861: "Those stars and stripes which have been so honorably borne to every accessible sea, and have so proudly fluttered to every breeze of the habitable globe, will ever be cherished and admired by true American hearts. May they ever be the flag of all American republics formed out of the once confederated States—the United States of America—without marring the beauty of that proud flag as it is, or that chaste blending of the 'red, white, and blue,' which makes it the grandest in the world!

"If your convention, looking to the formation of a Southern republic, and the adoption of the stars and stripes for its flag, has not already devised one, I would respectfully and modestly suggest the substitution of a renowned constellation, 'the Southern Cross' (both emblematic and suggestive) for the union of stars now in the blue field of the present flag of the United States, and that a star for each State be placed on one of the central stripes, so the stars and stripes may yet be the flag of your new as they were of the old republic."

In the same month another wrote in relation to a flag for the Southern Confederacy: "I would respectfully suggest that we have one not only plain and of striking contrast in color, but approximating to, yet differing essentially from, the flag of the United States. This flag we can not but regard as one under which our common country has risen to unexampled prosperity, and under which also some of the most noble achievements of the present age have been accomplished, lifting our national reputation into a truly high and commanding position, and to which proud elevation none certainly have contributed more than our own native brethren of the sunny South."

Another, in sending a design, says: "We still have a 'star-spangled banner,' which is dear to the people from old associations, and we can afford to let the Yankees keep the stripes. We are entitled to a 'star-spangled banner,' because the best poetry in honor of it was composed by a Southern man, and the incident which occasioned its composition occurred on Southern soil, and reflected honor on Southern soldiers."

One says: "I have taken the liberty to recommend to your attention the manifest propriety of adopting the 'star-spangled banner' as the flag of the Southern Confederacy, changing only the color of the red stripes to blue. That flag is as dear to every true Southern heart as a babe to its mother's affections."

Another said: "Do retain the 'stars and stripes.' It belongs to the South as much as to the North. It is not an abolition flag. Colonel Jefferson Davis (now President Davis) won glory under it in Mexico; so did the Palmetto Regiment."

And another: "Let the Yankees keep their ridiculous tune of 'Yankee Doodle,' * but, by all that is sacred, do not let them monopolize the stars and stripes. You have fought well under our glorious banner; could you fight as well under another? Never! Change it, improve it, alter it as you will, but, for Heaven's sake, keep the stars and stripes!"

Another says: "I refer to the important feature that your flag, though sufficiently peculiar to give *national individuality* to the emblem, still possesses the attribute of retaining all the hallowed associations which, both at home and abroad, have for years, in every American breast, clustered around the 'stars and stripes' of a nation once the most glorious the world ever beheld; and of that nation we ourselves and all the world can not fail to remember that the Southern States were but lately its *proudest element*, blest in its privileges, blest in its widespread fraternal love, and equal in the possession of all its common glories, past, present, and prospective."

Another: "Pray do not give up the stars and stripes

---

* The Yankees did keep it; but Mr. Lincoln, when he was serenaded on a certain occasion, being asked what tune he would like to have, called for the Confederate tune, "Dixie," saying, "I believe we have captured that tune, and have a right to it now."

to the North. It is ours as fully as it is theirs. It is hallowed by associations and memories, and is dear to every military and naval officer, every soldier and tar, and every citizen who has seen it float in a foreign land. Keep the stripes, keep the azure field and a star for each sovereignty in the constellation, and then distinguish it by a red cross (the Southern Cross), cutting the stripes at right angles. This is a very important matter. The songs of a nation and its flag have a prodigious moral influence."

One says: "I don't like the cross. It is significant of Catholic rule, and, besides, had too much to do with the machinery of the dark ages. The old stars must, I think, be abandoned. They belong to night, and, besides, the North will keep them. It is morning with us. The stripes are distinctive, and ought to be preserved; but let there be seven stripes, one for each of the original States, as the thirteen were for the original States of the old Confederacy. Suppose these stripes be vertical instead of horizontal?"

At the first session of the Provisional Congress, the committee on a flag and seal made its report, which was more or less shaped by the many expressions of feeling on the subject. The report said: "Whatever attachment may be felt from association for the stars and stripes (an attachment which your committee may be permitted to say they do not all share), it is manifest that, in inaugurating a new government, we can not with any propriety or without encountering obvious difficulties, retain the flag of the Government from which we have withdrawn. . . . As to the 'glories of the old flag,' we must bear in mind that the battles of the Revolution, about which our fondest and proudest memories cluster, were not fought beneath its folds; and, although in more recent times—in the War of 1812 and in the war with Mexico—the South did win her fair share of glory and shed her full measure of blood under its guidance and in its defense, we think the impartial page of history will preserve and commemorate the fact more imperishably than a mere piece of stupid bunting."

The design recommended by this committee, and which was adopted by the Provisional Government, was known as the "Stars and Bars." It was thus described:

"To consist of a red field, with a white space extending horizontally through the center, and equal in width to one third the width of the flag; the red spaces, above and below, to be of the same width as the white; the union blue extending down through the white space, and stopping at the lower red space; in the center of the union a circle of white stars corresponding in number with the States in the Confederacy."

THE STARS AND BARS.

Blue	Red
	White
Red	

This was the "stars and stripes," with the same colors, only the stripes were wider, and but three in number; and the stars were arranged in a circle, as in the old United States national flag before the States of the Union became so numerous.

Immediately after the Confederate Government took the place of the Southern Provisional Government, the question of adopting another flag was agitated. The joint committee appointed for the purpose offered, in April, 1862, a device, with a report, in which it said: "Nearly all the designs submitted to the committee contained a combination of stars. This heraldic emblem, however, has been discarded, as a manifestation of our entire and absolute severance from the United States, and a complete annihilation of every sentiment indicating the faintest hope of reconstruction." The chairman of the committee said that " it might be a matter of surprise to those who had always been so enthusiastic on the subject of the beauty of the stars and stripes, that there never was a single star emblazoned on any flag of the old United States. They were nothing but mullets, or imitations of the rowels of the spurs of the knight, and five-pointed. But the committee had fallen upon those heraldic emblems, and had adopted the device of the great luminary of day before which all stars shall pale and fade into obscurity."

The "Richmond Examiner" described this device as " a red field, bestraddled with a long-legged white cross, in the center of which (the cross) there is a blue Norman shield, and in the center of that again a Lord Rosse's telescope may discover a star of the fifth magnitude, which is intended to represent a sun." The committee intended the rays of the sun to correspond in number with the States composing the Confederacy.

This device was not adopted. Verily, it was hard to get away from the stars and stripes—the red, white, and blue.

Since the first battle of Bull Run, the Confederate armies had been using a battle-flag the origin of which was thus given by a Southern paper, in March, 1863: "We have always thought that General Joseph E. Johnston settled the question of a national flag when he selected the blue-spangled saltier upon a red field as his battle-ensign. It may be recollected that the choice was made in consequence of the difficulty that had been seriously felt, in the first battle of Manassas, in distinguishing between the Yankee colors and our own, and at a time when the two hostile armies were confronting each other on the plains of Fairfax, with a prospect of a renewal of the bloody fight at any moment. Haste was necessary in the preparation of the flags, and secrecy was also desirable, lest the enemy should discover our change of colors, and provide themselves with counterfeits to be basely used for our own destruction. General Johnston's pattern was thereupon sent to Richmond, and seventy-five ladies from each one of four or five churches were set to work making the battle-flags. Their fair fingers wrought silk and bunting into the prescribed shape and arrangement of colors; but, despite the injunction of inviolable confidence, the device was known the subsequent day all over the capital. How could General Johnston expect four or five hundred female tongues to be silent on the subject? No harm was done by the disclosure, however, and, when next the brave troops of the

Confederacy went into the fight, those flags were seen dancing in the breeze, the symbol of hope to the defenders of our country, wherever the fire was the deadliest over the crimson field, borne always aloft where follower and foe might behold it, ever the chosen perch of victory ere the fight was done. Could these gay little pieces of the handiwork of the women of Richmond be collected now, what emotions would not the sight of them awaken, blackened as they are with the smoke of powder, riddled with bullets, many of them stained with the blood, the last drops, that welled up from the heart of a patriot hero!"

BATTLE-FLAG.

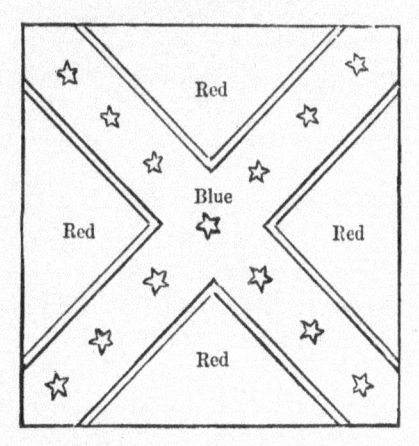

A member of the Confederate army wrote: "I was originally in favor of retaining the old flag, that 'star-spangled banner' at whose very name our hearts were wont to thrill. . . . Then the 'stars and bars' became our flag, and waved over the heads of our regiments when we first marched to guard the borders of Virginia. It retained most of the distinctive features of the old flag, but was thought to differ from it sufficiently; but the first field of Manassas proved that it was a mistake. The union was the same, the colors were all the same, and when the flags drooped around the staff on that sultry day it was impossible to distinguish them. There was no difficulty, however, when the flags were spread by the breeze, and I see no reason why the 'stars and bars' should not still float above all forts, ships, and arsenals of the Confederacy. But we needed another battle-flag. Glorious 'Old Joe' willed it, and the Southern Cross rose brightly in the bloody field among the constellations of war. It fulfilled all the desiderata of a battle-flag. . . . Since that time it has become historic. Displayed on a hundred stricken fields, it has never been dishonored. . . . Certainly, no soldier desires that Congress should do what the Yankees have never been able to do—take that flag from us."

A general sentiment had by this time arisen in favor of the battle-flag, the only objection made to it being that it could not be reversed as a signal of distress. General Beauregard wrote, in April, 1863: "Why change our battle-flag, consecrated by the best blood of our country on so many battle-fields? A good design for the national flag would be the present battle-flag as union-jack, and the rest all white, or all blue."

This was the design eventually chosen by the Confederate Congress in May, 1863, and was thus described:

"The field to be white; the length double the width of the flag, with the union (now used in the battle-flag) to be a square of two thirds the width of the flag, having the ground red, thereon a saltier of blue, bordered with white, and emblazoned with mullets, or five-pointed stars, corresponding in number to that of the Confederate States."

Still the red, white, and blue, and the inevitable mullets!

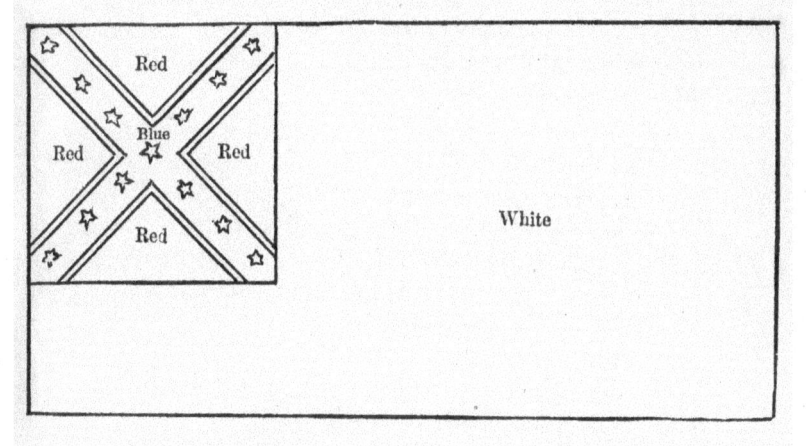

Great satisfaction was expressed on all sides at the adoption of this new flag. An Atlanta (Georgia) paper said: "The design for a flag for the Confederate States . . . is at last decided, and the whole South is satisfied. In the new flag is preserved the battle-flag—the invention of Beauregard and Johnston—an invention which necessity forced upon these Confederate commanders soon after the battle of Manassas. In addition to this, there is nothing but the white flag.

"Our old flag always awakens unpleasant reminiscences; it bears too striking a resemblance to the emblem of tyranny, the 'stars and stripes.' As it was this resemblance which caused it at first to be adopted, so also it was this that caused it to be rejected. . . . We, therefore, hail our new flag with joy. Every star, every color, is sacred and endeared to our hearts and to the hearts of our whole people. . . . The large predominance of the color, white, can never be mistaken, as alluding to the Christian leniency with which we have treated our enemies at all times; the red battle-flag will tell a tale of the heroism of our soldiers on which the nations of the earth will hang with breathless attention."

In November, 1861, an English blockade runner, called the Fingal, succeeded in getting into Savannah with a valuable cargo of arms and ammunition. She was prevented by the United States vessels from going out again with a cargo of cotton, as was intended; and finally was changed to an iron-clad vessel of war under the name of the Atlanta. She was deemed by the Confederates to be their strongest iron-clad.

On the 17th of June, 1863, accompanied by two other steamers, she ran down to Warsaw Sound, to capture the United States monitors Weehawken, Captain John Rodgers, and Nahant, Commander John Downes. The two steamers took on board a gay company of ladies from Savannah to witness the combat. These vessels were to tow the monitors, in the event of their capture, in triumph up to Savannah. The new flag was to have been hoisted everywhere in the Confederacy on the coming 4th of July; but authority was given for its use the first time by the Atlanta in her contest with the two United States monitors. The iron-clad was not proof against the tremendous shot of the monitors, and in less than half an hour she surrendered to the Weehawken, which had alone engaged her, the Nahant not even having had time to come into action. The new Confederate flag which she was to inaugurate was sent to Washington and hung as a trophy in the Navy Department at about the same time the law of the Confederate Congress adopting it went into operation.

At the time of Mr. Jefferson Davis's capture a fresh, handsome silk regimental flag—a veritable star-spangled banner—was found among his effects. Why he had taken it with him in his flight it is not easy to say; but he, too, evidently found it very difficult to get away from the stars and stripes!

A Union picket one day discovered two Confederates having a black flag, with a white disk in the center. He watched them until he saw one go for some water a short distance off, and the flag resting against a tree. With a sudden dash he overpowered the Confederate and carried off the flag. This flag was exhibited among the trophies at Washington, and it was amusing to see the horror with which visitors regarded it, accompanied by such exclamations as "A black flag! So they really did give no quarter! Here is actual proof of it!" After enjoying their indignation a little while, the attendant would explain that this was one of the system of signal-flags, and was used against a light-tinted sky so as to be distinctly seen, by contrast, at a long distance.

The smoke of battle is now all cleared away. Again "hallowed associations, . . . both at home and abroad, . . . in every American breast, cluster around the stars and stripes" of this nation. And "the Southern States

... are blest in its privileges, blest in its wide-spread fraternal love, and equal in the possession of all its common glories, past, present, and prospective." *

CHAPTER XXXVIII.

FORT SUMTER.

A pleasure-trip—The programme—Fac-simile of Anderson's dispatch—The flag-raising—Festivities—News of the President's death.

WHEN it became certain that the end of the Confederacy was near at hand, the United States Government determined to celebrate the anniversary of the fall of Fort Sumter, Charleston Harbor, by hoisting the Stars and Stripes, with imposing ceremonies, over the ruins of the fort. Major Robert Anderson, United States Army, had evacuated the fort, April 14, 1861, after firing a salute to his flag. His Confederate adversary, Brigadier-General Beauregard, had agreed to this in these courteous terms: " Apprised that you desire the privilege of saluting your flag on retiring, I cheerfully concede it, in consideration of the gallantry with which you have defended the place under your charge." And now, on the 14th of April, 1865, Brigadier-General Robert Anderson was to have the honor of raising that identical flag over the ruins of the recaptured fort.

Secretary Stanton issued orders to that effect, as follows:

* See letter, page 200.

FORT SUMTER.

GENERAL ORDERS, No. 50.
WAR DEPARTMENT, ADJUTANT-GENERAL'S OFFICE,
WASHINGTON, *March 27, 1865.*

Ordered: First. That at the hour of noon, on the 14th day of April, 1865, brevet Major-General Anderson will raise and plant upon the ruins of Fort Sumter, in Charleston Harbor, the same United States flag which floated over the battlements of that fort during the rebel assault, and which was lowered and saluted by him and the small force of his command when the works were evacuated on the 14th day of April, 1861.

Second. That the flag, when raised, be saluted by one hundred guns from Fort Sumter, and by a national salute from every fort and rebel battery that fired upon Fort Sumter.

Third. That suitable ceremonies be had upon the occasion, under the direction of Major-General William T. Sherman, whose military operations compelled the rebels to evacuate Charleston,* or, in his absence, under the charge of Major-General Q. A. Gillmore, commanding the department. Among the ceremonies will be the delivery of a public address by the Rev. Henry Ward Beecher.

Fourth. That the naval forces at Charleston, and their commander on that station, be invited to participate in the ceremonies of the occasion.

By order of the President of the United States:

EDWIN M. STANTON, *Secretary of War.*

Official:
E. D. TOWNSEND, *Assistant Adjutant-General.*

* General Sherman did not stop, in his march north from Savannah, to make any demonstration against Charleston; but, as Anderson remarked, "conquered Charleston by turning his back on it." Sherman's march compelled its evacuation by the Confederates.

Invitations were sent to such persons as the Secretary of War designated; and the splendid steamer Arago, formerly of the line of Havre packets, but chartered by the United States as a transport-ship, was employed to convey the party to Charleston Harbor. She was commanded by that courteous and able seaman, Captain Gadsden. Among the guests were, besides Mr. Beecher and Rev. Dr. Storrs, of Brooklyn, some of the noted orators and prominent abolitionists of the time.

The Arago sailed from New York April 8th, with such of the company as were there, and touched at Fort Monroe, Old Point Comfort, Virginia, for others who went down from Washington to meet her. The Secretary sent me in charge of the excursion, leaving to my discretion all details necessary to make it successful. I was much gratified at the notice in one of the newspapers of New York, by a correspondent aboard, that among those who joined the ship at Fort Monroe was General E. D. Townsend, and, "as the representative of the Secretary of War, General Townsend thenceforth, and with entire acceptance, occupied the position of our host."

The ship arrived at Hilton Head, South Carolina, on the 12th of April. As there were some days to spare, trips were made to Savannah, Beaufort, and Fort Pulaski. A number of the party went to Mitchelville, where a sort of impromptu town had been established for the "freedmen," as they began to be styled. At this last place there was abundance of speech-making. Mr. Beecher preferred to remain in quiet at Hilton Head, and employed himself in preparing his address. Finding that there were numerous pieces of poetry and other effusions offered for a part of the ceremonies, and that many persons were desirous of actively participating in them, among whom were some who went down in the steamer Oceanus, which they chartered for the trip, I conceived it necessary to form a programme which should strictly limit the performances. General Anderson was greatly in favor of excluding all but the religious feature, but we at last agreed upon one which apparently proved satisfactory to the entire assemblage. While the principal parts were taken by a few, every one had the opportunity of swelling the grand chorus to the "Star-spangled Banner," and joining in the doxology, to the tune of "Old Hundred."

Mr. Joseph H. Sears, the editor of "The New South," a paper published at Hilton Head, printed enough copies of the programme for distribution among the company; and also several copies of Mr. Beecher's address for the representatives of the press. When I asked him for his bill, he replied, in a note: "I regret that our type and presses can do no better work. My excuse is, that the sand, which frequently rises in clouds here and penetrates even to the sacred precincts of our *sanctum sanctorum*,' pays no regard to types or presses, and they soon wear out.

"Allow me to present this job (excuse a printer's term) to the United States."

This was Mr. Sears's acceptable contribution to the grand occasion.

The programme consisted of—

1. A prayer by Rev. Matthias Harris, Chaplain of the United States Army, who, being at the time chaplain at Fort Moultrie, accompanied Major Anderson's command over to Fort Sumter, and made a prayer at the raising of the flag over that fort, December 27, 1860.

214   ANECDOTES OF THE CIVIL WAR.

2. Reading of several Psalms, antiphonally, by the Rev. Dr. Storrs and the people.

3. Reading of the following dispatch from Major Anderson, by brevet Brigadier-General E. D. Townsend :*

S. S. BALTIC. OFF SANDY HOOK APR. EIGHTEENTH. TEN THIRTY A.M. VIA NEW YORK. HON. S. CAMERON, SECY WAR. WASHN. HAVING DEFENDED FORT SUMTER FOR THIRTY FOUR HOURS UNTIL THE QUARTERS WERE ENTIRELY BURNED THE MAIN GATES DESTROYED BY FIRE. THE GORGE WALLS SERIOUSLY INJURED. THE MAGAZINE SURROUNDED BY FLAMES AND ITS DOOR CLOSED FROM THE EFFECTS OF HEAT. FOUR BARRELLS AND THREE CARTRIDGES OF POWDER ONLY BEING AVAILABLE AND NO PROVISIONS REMAINING BUT PORK. I ACCEPTED TERMS OF EVACUATION OFFERED BY GENERAL BEAUREGARD BEING ON SAME OFFERED BY HIM ON THE ELEVENTH INST. PRIOR TO THE COMMENCEMENT OF HOSTILITIES AND MARCHED OUT OF THE FORT SUNDAY AFTERNOON THE FOURTEENTH INST. WITH COLORS FLYING AND DRUMS BEATING. BRINGING AWAY COMPANY AND PRIVATE PROPERTY AND SALUTING MY FLAG WITH FIFTY GUNS. ROBERT ANDERSON. MAJOR FIRST ARTILLERY. COMMANDING.

* I well remember the feeling which came over me while reading this dispatch aloud to General Scott, on its first receipt. It conveyed intelli-

4. Raising the flag, with salutes, and bands playing national airs.

5. Singing the "Star-spangled Banner."

6. Address by the Rev. Henry Ward Beecher.

7. Singing the doxology, to the tune "Old Hundred."

8. Closing prayer and benediction by Rev. Dr. R. S. Storrs, Jr.

All things being ready, the company again assembled on board the Arago, and Thursday evening, the 13th of April, she left Hilton Head for Charleston Bar. The next day, Friday (Good Friday!), was so windy, and the sea was so high, that Captain Gadsden was afraid to venture on the bar, so he came to anchor outside, and transferred his passengers to the small steamer Delaware. The rolling of both vessels made it a hazardous undertaking for the ladies; but, being safely accomplished, it rather added to the interest of the occasion.

The fort was found to be a perfect mass of ruins. Hardly any trace of its character, except broken gabions and shattered casemates, was to be seen. "A large platform, diamond-shaped, covered with myrtle, evergreens, and flowers, had been erected in the center of the parade-ground, with an arched canopy overhead, draped with the American flag, and intermingled with beautiful wreaths

gence of the first note of war sounded by the South. They had made their choice—they could have as much of it as they wished. It was noticed by my friend Governor Clifford, of Massachusetts, who was present at the ceremonies in 1865, that my voice assumed a tone of quiet defiance—entirely unpremeditated—as I read the dispatch again on this occasion, and the association of ideas returned to me.

The original dispatch was printed by Morse's telegraph, and the ribbon-like strips were pasted on a sheet of paper for better preservation and convenience. This copy is made from a photograph of the original.

of evergreens and flowers. This platform was for General Anderson, the orator of the day, and other distinguished visitors, and was the combined taste of six Union ladies of Charleston. On the stage, beside the speaker's stand, was a golden eagle holding a handsome wreath of flowers and evergreens. The flag-staff, about one hundred and fifty feet high, had been erected immediately in the center of the parade-ground, and the halyards adjusted by three of the crew of the Juniata, who took part in the assault on Fort Sumter, ordered by Admiral Dahlgren, September 9, 1863." *

Those who could not find room on the platform had a fine view from the parapet, and could distinctly hear, from their more elevated position.

At the proper time, Major Anderson received the old flag, packed in the Fort Sumter mail-bag, from Sergeant Hart, the soldier of Anderson's command who hauled down the flag. Together, they opened the flag and adjusted the halyards. At this moment some one handed to Anderson a bright wreath of roses, which he fastened to the top of the flag. When all was ready, as soon as he could control his emotion, Anderson said:

"My friends, and fellow-citizens, and brother soldiers: By the considerate appointment of the Honorable Secretary of War, I am here to fulfill the cherished wish of my heart through four long, long years of bloody war, to restore to its proper place this dear flag, which floated here during peace, before the first act of this cruel rebellion.

"I thank God that I have lived to see this day, and to be here to perform this duty to my country. My heart

* Correspondence of the "Baltimore American."

is filled with gratitude to that God who has so signally blessed us; who has given us blessings beyond measure.

"May all the world proclaim, 'Glory to God in the highest; and on earth peace, good-will toward men.'"

At the close of these remarks a hearty "Amen!" was uttered by many persons standing around.

Anderson then seized the halyards, Sergeant Hart also passing them through his own hands, while the general's young son, Robert, held on to the end of them. The flag was sent up to the peak by Anderson's own hand. He refused the proffered aid of every one, and seemed determined that his own strength alone should restore "this dear flag" to its old place, if it were to be the last effort of his life. The shout which arose, when the halyards were made fast, must be imagined; it can scarcely be described. Then came the booming of the guns from the fleet, and from half a dozen batteries, and the playing of several bands vying with each other in rendering the national airs.

Mr. Beecher's address, which followed, was very able and eloquent. As might have been expected, it denounced the rebellion in strong terms, and exulted in the fruits of liberty to the slave which the contest had secured. But it breathed a spirit of conciliation, which his sermon before his congregation, just prior to his departure from Brooklyn, had foreshadowed. He held the leaders of secession responsible, yet had no vengeance to execute upon them; while, for the mass of the people, he had naught but fraternal greeting. At Brooklyn he had said: "If I had my way after the close of fighting, I would not let one drop of blood be spilled, and then I could say to the world that this great civil war has been ended as none other ever was. 'Ought there not to be a terrible spectacle of retribution?' say some. In Mercy's name, has there not been suffering enough? Is not the penalty already paid? God's vengeance patent enough? We don't want any more vengeance. I would not expatriate any leaders on the ground of vengeance, for, as they have once misled the people, they might do so again. I would not expatriate and disfranchise them. . . . And more: we wish now to show the South their total misapprehension of our former sentiments. Their cunning politicians have made them believe that we hate them; but we don't. . . . There are no antagonistic interests between the North and the South. Religion, blood, business, are the same; and, if there are no social or political reasons for hatred, why should we not be the best of friends?"

At Sumter he said: "But for the people misled, for the multitudes drafted and driven into this civil war, let not a trace of animosity remain. The moment their willing hand drops the musket, and they return to their allegiance, then stretch out your honest right hand to greet them. Recall to them the old days of kindness. Our hearts wait for their redemption. All the resources of a renovated nation shall be applied to rebuild their prosperity and smooth down the furrows of war. . . . We are not seeking our own aggrandizement by impoverishing the South. Its prosperity is an indispensable element of our own. We have shown, by all that we have suffered in war, how great is our estimate of the importance of the Southern States of this Union; and we will measure that estimate now, in peace, by still greater exertions for their rebuilding."

After the ceremonies at the fort, the company went

up to Charleston, where two or three days were spent in visiting the various parts of the city, and viewing with mournful interest the ravages of fires and of cannonading. In the evening of the 14th the fleet was brilliantly illuminated, and fire-works were displayed from the ships and monitors. An entertainment was given by General Gillmore at the Charleston Hotel, at which eloquent speeches were made by General Holt, Hon. W. D. Kelly, of Pennsylvania, Daniel Dougherty, George Thompson, William Lloyd Garrison, and others. Tributes were paid by all to him who, at about that hour, fell before the hand of an assassin in the nation's capital.

The Arago sailed for New York Saturday evening, April 15th, Mr. Beecher and some of his immediate party remaining behind. As the ship neared the Capes, several gentlemen requested me to telegraph to the Secretary of War for permission to wind up our delightful excursion by making a trip to Richmond. Richmond was in possession of United States troops when we left, and we had heard of Lee's surrender just as we were about to land at Fort Sumter. I went below, and was in the act of writing the telegram, to be sent from Old Point Comfort, when some one rushed down the gangway, exclaiming, "The President has been shot by an assassin!" The news had been received from a vessel which passed us as we were going in between the Capes. Of course, this put an end to all thought of further pleasure excursions, and we made the best of our way back to Washington.

Mr. Beecher had said in his address on that fatal Good Friday, "We offer to the President of these United States our solemn congratulations that God has sustained his life and health under the unparalleled burdens and sufferings of four bloody years, and permitted him to behold this auspicious consummation of that national unity for which he has waited with so much patience and fortitude, and for which he has labored with so much disinterested wisdom."

And, probably within the same hour in which the awful deed was committed, General Anderson had offered in the festive hall this sentiment: "I beg you, now, that you will join me in drinking the health of another man, whom we all love to honor—the man who, when elected President of the United States, was compelled to reach the seat of government without an escort, but a man who now could travel all over our country with millions of hands and hearts to sustain him. I give you the good, the great, the honest man, Abraham Lincoln."

And this was the sequel: "The President has been shot by an assassin!"

CHAPTER XXXIX.

THE FUNERAL OF PRESIDENT LINCOLN.

Unparalleled grief—Guard of honor—Funeral-train—Lying in state—Mottoes and floral tributes—Imposing demonstrations—The veteran Scott—"Come home"—At the tomb—A long farewell.

THE funeral of Abraham Lincoln! How can justice be done to the theme? The obsequies, continued through sixteen days and sixteen nights, of the man whose ruthless taking off called forth the sympathies of people and their rulers in every clime! The official expressions of horror and grief, received by the United States Government

THE FUNERAL OF PRESIDENT LINCOLN. 221

from every known country in the world, alone fill a quarto volume of nine hundred and thirty pages.

As soon as news of the President's death was received, places of business and amusement were closed, houses were draped in mourning, and meetings were held at which resolutions were passed, everywhere. Of all the events of the war, none had produced such general and intense excitement.

History has no parallel to the outpouring of sorrow which followed the funeral *cortége* on its route from Washington to Springfield, Illinois. Hundreds of thousands of men, women, and children, crowded the highways and streets, by day and by night, to do reverence to those mortal remains; and not a smile or sign of levity was seen among them all. Often would they kneel, as the funeral-car passed them, with heads bowed as if in silent prayer. Many wept in quiet, but none betrayed the slightest mark of unconcern. The shocking deed by which the President had been taken from his people seemed to intensify their love and veneration for his memory.

The President died at about half-past seven, the morning of April 15, 1865.* His remains lay in state in the East-Room of the Executive Mansion from Tuesday the 18th till two o'clock Wednesday the 19th, and were viewed by a very large number of citizens. On Wednesday a civic and military procession conducted them to the Capitol, where they reposed in state in the Rotunda during that day, and till late at night the next. The ceremonies

* Most of the incidents in this account were recalled to memory by a scrap-book made up of slips from the newspapers of the day, which accurately described the scenes at each place by which the *cortége* passed.

at the Mansion and at the Capitol were of the most imposing character.

The Secretary of War detailed as a guard of honor to accompany the remains to Springfield—

Brevet Brigadier-General E. D. TOWNSEND, Assistant Adjutant-General, to represent the Secretary of War.

Brigadier-General A. B. EATON, Commissary-General of Subsistence.

Brevet Major-General J. G. BARNARD, Lieutenant-Colonel of Engineers.

Brigadier-General G. D. RAMSAY, Ordnance Department.

Brigadier-General A. P. HOWE, Chief of Artillery.

Brevet Brigadier-General JAMES A. EKIN, Quartermaster's Department.

Brevet Brigadier-General D. C. McCALLUM, Superintendent of Military Railroads.

Major-General DAVID HUNTER, U. S. Volunteers.

Brigadier-General J. C. CALDWELL, U. S. Volunteers, and twenty-five picked men, sergeants of the Veteran Reserve Corps, who acted, always, as bearers.

The Secretary of the Navy completed the list of twelve officers by detailing—

Rear-Admiral CHARLES HENRY DAVIS, Chief of the Bureau of Navigation.

Captain WILLIAM ROGERS TAYLOR, U. S. Navy, and Major THOMAS Y. FIELD, U. S. Marine Corps.

At the request of the Secretary of War, Governor John Brough, of Ohio, and John W. Garrett, Esq., President of the Baltimore and Ohio Railroad, arranged a time-table and prepared regulations for the movements of the funeral-train. The time for arriving at and departure from each city was thereby fixed. General McCallum was given military control of the train; Captain C. B. Penrose was detailed as commissary; Captain J. P. Dukehart, the veteran and efficient conductor, accompanied the train to Springfield. Invitations to take seats in the passenger cars of the train were issued to a few persons, among them the late President's pastor, Rev. Dr. Gurley. Some of these gentlemen accompanied it the whole way; others joined, and left it, at points along the route. The proper preservation of the body, which had been embalmed, was intrusted to the embalmer and undertaker.

Two elegant cars were provided, one for the funeral-car, the other for the guard of honor, and six others were attached to the train for the mourners. The funeral-car was heavily draped, within and without, with black, while silver stars and tassels relieved the somber festoons. This car was divided into three parts, a sleeping-apartment in the center, and a sitting room at each end. The coffin containing the President's remains rested on a bier covered with black drapery, in the room at the rear. The body of his little son Willie, who died in Washington in 1862, was placed in the front room, that it might be interred with his father's in Springfield.

The President's remains, escorted by a military command, and followed by the Cabinet and other distinguished personages, were moved to the Baltimore and Ohio depot, where they were received by the guard of honor. The train started on its mournful journey at eight o'clock A. M., Friday, April 21, 1865, preceded by a pilot-engine to guard against accident.

The depots everywhere were draped in mourning, and

many had mottoes conspicuously displayed. In more than one the motto was "Washington the Father, Lincoln the Saviour of the Country." * The cities vied with each other in the elegance with which their buildings, public and private, were draped. Crowds thronged the depots and streets, but there was no jostling, no noise; all was solemn and sad.

In every city where the remains were exposed to view, a guard of honor was selected to be present while the crowd passed through the hall. This was a relief to the regular guard, as only two of them at a time had to be present. But there was never a moment throughout the whole journey when at least two of this guard were not by the side of the coffin. No bearers, except the veteran guard, were ever suffered to handle the President's coffin.

At the Relay House the train was detained a few minutes to permit a party of ladies to lay some beautiful floral tributes upon the bier. This was the first of those tender exhibitions of feeling which were afterward so frequently repeated.

At Baltimore, where the train arrived at ten o'clock A. M., the Governor, Lieutenant-Governor, State and city officials were in waiting. An imposing procession was formed. The President's coffin, borne by the guard of Veteran Reserve sergeants, was placed in a beautiful hearse, and taken to the Rotunda of the Exchange, where a catafalque had been erected immediately under the dome. All around the catafalque were tastefully ar-

* An elegant medallion, bearing the bust of Washington on one side and of Lincoln on the other, was struck off in gold and in silver, at the Mint in Philadelphia. This was worn as a badge by several of the guard of honor.

ranged evergreens, wreaths, calla-lilies, and other choice flowers. The coffin was opened so as to display the face and bust to view, and arrangements were made so that the crowd of citizens, eager for one parting look, could pass through without confusion.

The schedule required a departure from Baltimore at three o'clock P. M. The procession was accordingly re-formed in time, and moved to the Northern Central Depot, *en route* to Harrisburg, Pennsylvania.

At York a beautiful wreath was placed on the coffin by some ladies.

At Harrisburg, which was reached at a little past eight o'clock P. M., a driving rain and the darkness of the evening prevented the reception which had been arranged. Slowly through the muddy streets, followed by two of the guard of honor and the faithful sergeants, the hearse wended its way to the Capitol. There the remains were exposed to view until eleven o'clock A. M., Saturday the 21st, when a very large procession escorted them to the depot. Guns were fired and bells tolled through the morning, and trains came in from the surrounding country, laden with people who sought to do honor to the occasion.

Leaving Harrisburg at noon, the train soon reached Middletown, where a large crowd was gathered. The cars passed into the depot under an arch of evergreens, while national flags draped in mourning were fluttering all around.

At Elizabethtown a large flag was suspended from the depot, to which was affixed the motto, "We mourn a nation's loss." At Mount Joy, and all along the road, large numbers of people were congregated, the country people flocking to neighboring towns, or to the line of the railroad.

At Lancaster the crowd was enormous. The depot was decorated with flags and crape; and in large letters was the motto: "Abraham Lincoln, the illustrious martyr of liberty. The nation mourns his loss. Though dead, he still lives."

The "Philadelphia Inquirer" said: "At the outskirts we found the force of the Lancaster Iron-Works in line along the road, with uplifted hats, and their buildings draped. They paid their last tribute to the patriot and statesman. Near the track, in many places, we found old men had been carried down in their chairs, and women with infants held out to see the *cortége* pass, formed at times groups seldom if ever witnessed."

And so it was with all the towns and villages. Business was stopped, and all the people crowded to see the funeral pass.

Arriving at Philadelphia at half-past six P. M., a dense crowd received us with every manifestation of grief. With a magnificent escort and procession, the hearse was conducted through Independence Square— which was illuminated with calcium-lights — to Independence Hall. In that spot, on the 22d of February, 1861, Abraham Lincoln had uttered these words: "It was something in the 'Declaration of Independence,' giving liberty, not only to the people of this country, but hope to the world for all future time. . . . Now, my friends, can the country be saved upon that basis? If it can, I will consider myself one of the happiest men in the world if I can help to save it. But, if this country can not be saved without giving up that principle, I was about to say, I would rather be assassinated upon this spot than to surrender it."

And now his lifeless body had come to make that utterance prophecy.

Words can but faintly portray the elegant taste with which the historic old hall was draped and decorated with floral offerings—that hall to whose legends another of intense interest was now added. The skilled pen of the "Inquirer" shall again lend us its aid:

"A magnificent floral device,* composed of a large wreath of brilliant-colored flowers, and containing a beautiful shield in the center, also composed of choice flowers, occupied a prominent position on the lid of the coffin. This wreath bore the following inscription:

"'Presented by the ladies of York, Pennsylvania, to be laid on the body of our lamented President if possible.'

"At the head of the coffin was suspended a highly wrought cross, composed of japonicas, with a center consisting of jet-black exotics. The device contained the following inscription:

"'To the memory of our beloved President, from a few ladies of the United States Sanitary Commission.'

"On the old Independence bell, and near the head of the coffin, rested a large and beautifully made floral anchor, composed of the choicest exotics. This beautiful offering came from the ladies of St. Clement's Church. Four stands, two at the head and two at the foot of the coffin, were draped in black cloth, and contained rich candelabra, with lighted wax-candles. Directly to the

* Most of the decorations were deposited in the rooms of the Historical Society after the ceremonies were over.

rear of these were placed three additional stands, also containing candelabras with burning tapers; and again, another row of four stands, containing candelabras also, brought up the rear, making in all eighteen candelabras and one hundred and eight burning wax-tapers.

"Between this flood of light, shelving was erected, on which were placed rare vases filled with japonicas, heliotropes, and other rare flowers. These vases were about twenty-five in number.

"A most delicious perfume stole through every part of the hall, which, added to the soft yet brilliant light of the wax-tapers, the elegant uniforms of the officers on duty, etc., constituted a scene of Oriental magnificence but seldom witnessed.

"The hall at large was completely shrouded with black cloth, arranged in a very graceful and appropriate manner. The old chandelier that hangs from the center of the room, and which was directly over the coffin of the deceased, was entirely covered, and from it radiated in every direction festoons of black cloth, forming a sort of canopy over the entire room. The walls of the room presented the appearance of having been papered with black. . . . The statue of Washington, at the east end of the room, stood out in bold relief against the background. Wreaths of immortelles were hung on the black drapery that covered the walls, and were placed about midway between the floor and ceiling.

"One of the wreaths that lay near the head of the coffin contained a card bearing the following inscription:

"'Before any great national event I have always had the same dream. I had it the other night. It is of *a ship sailing rapidly.*'

"These words were used by Mr. Lincoln in conversation not long since.

"A beautiful wreath was presented on Saturday evening, containing the following:

"'A lady's gift. Can you find a place?'

"A balustrade was erected on either side of the coffin, which acted as a barrier to the throng that pressed in to see the remains, and prevented them from approaching too closely to the coffin.*

"An incident, humble in its character, yet not without its due effect, took place while the hall was being placed in readiness for the reception of the remains. An old negro woman managed by some means to effect an entrance into the sacred inclosure, and approached the committee of arrangements with a rudely made wreath in her hand, which she requested, with tears in her eyes, might be placed on the coffin of the deceased. The wreath contained the motto:

"'The nation mourns his loss. He still lives in the hearts of the people.'

"The old woman's heart beat with delight when she was informed that her offering should be placed in an appropriate position.

"A beautiful full-length portrait of Mr. Lincoln was placed in front of the State-House, and covered with black cloth so closely that the figure alone was exposed to view. A curtain was drawn over the painting, which was thrown aside just as the body was about being taken into Independence Hall, when it was brilliantly illumi-

---

* There was a desire not unfrequently expressed, and in some cases amounting almost to insanity, to touch the face, as if virtue would flow from the contact.

nated. A motto composed of gas-jets, surmounted the portrait, containing the words—

"'Rest in peace.'"

It was estimated that over two hundred thousand people passed through Independence Hall between ten o'clock Saturday evening and one o'clock A. M. Monday. Double lines, extending three miles, were formed of persons waiting their turn to enter the hall. The entrances were through windows facing Independence Square. In the crowd were hundreds of colored people. One aged colored woman, after gazing a moment at the silent features, threw up her hands, the tears coursing down her cheeks, and exclaimed in audible tones: "O Abraham Lincoln! he is dead! he is dead!" Precisely at midnight, Saturday, three ladies entered the hall and deposited on the coffin a cross of perfectly white flowers, to which a card was fastened with a white ribbon, bearing this inscription:

"A tribute to our great and good President, who has fallen a martyr to the cause of human freedom.

'In my hand no price I bring,
Simply to thy cross I cling.'"

Although the hour of departure from Philadelphia was so early, the crowd was in no wise diminished. Many mothers held their infants above the heads of the multitude, as if to place it in their power to say in after-life, "I saw President Lincoln's funeral."

At four o'clock A. M., the train was on its way for New York.

At Jersey City admirable arrangements had been made; and the Secretary of State of New York there received the remains, on behalf of the State. As the hearse moved out of the depot to go on board the ferry-boat, a dirge was sung by a chorus of two hundred voices. As the boat entered the dock at New York, guns were fired and bells tolled. The flags of the shipping hung at half-staff. The New York Seventh Regiment—that regiment which had given President Lincoln so much relief by its arrival in Washington in April, 1861—now formed the escort for his remains to the City Hall.

The locality chosen for the body to repose, in the City Hall, was the most convenient for the purpose of any on the whole route. The ascent from the ground-floor to the room of the City Council was by two flights of stone stairs, on one side of the large circular rotunda. There was but one step from the platform at the top of the stairs to the passage, or entry, leading to the Council-chamber. By placing a dais, slightly inclined from head to foot, just within the entry, persons ascending one flight of steps would have a perfect view of the features while crossing the platform to descend by the other flight. Thus, a constant stream of people entered one door, viewed the body without stopping, and left the rotunda by another door.

The interior of the rotunda was draped from the ground to the cupola; and an arch of black cloth was formed over the entrance to the Council-room passage, beneath which the dais lay.

Probably more than half a million souls passed across that platform while the doors remained open. Among them, all classes and conditions of men, women, and children were represented. Of them all, none paid a more sincere homage than did the poor Irishwoman, who, as she hastily passed, laid a small cross of evergreen at the foot of the coffin, fervently ejaculating, "God preserve your soul!"

A grand feature of the New York ceremonies was the procession which followed the funeral-car to the depot on its way to Albany, on the afternoon of Tuesday, the 25th. It was composed of from fifty to seventy thousand persons on foot. The "Herald" said:

"The procession included not only the military, the firemen, the trades' societies, and the benevolent and other associations, but also many citizens who never marched through our streets before in honor of any man, or any occasion. Remarkable upon this account, it was no less remarkable on account of its unanimity—all classes, conditions, creeds, and politics joining in it with a common, sympathetic impulse.

"Certainly New York city eclipsed herself upon this occasion, and appropriately represented the universal sentiment of the country. In solemn silence, unbroken by the slightest expression of applause at the drill of the soldiery or by the appearance of various popular men and societies, the mournful pageant moved through miles of magnificent dwellings hung with black; and, when the impressive ceremonies were over, the vast assemblage dispersed so quickly and quietly that in a couple of hours no trace of its existence remained."

And so the grand procession passed on, minute-guns firing, bells tolling, chimes sounding dirges. There was no standing-place left on the sidewalks, heads were uncovered, and not so much as a smile was seen. At the windows of the draped dwellings stood hosts of ladies with handkerchiefs to their eyes; and not even the children seemed tempted by curiosity to strain for a better view.

When not far from the Hudson River Depot, the *coupé* of General Scott was descried drawn up by the sidewalk. I immediately alighted, and, after greeting my old commander, conducted his vehicle to a place in the procession. Though pale and feeble, he insisted on walking into the depot, and paying his parting respects to the deceased President.

The line of the Hudson River road seemed alive with people. At each of the towns by which it passes, the darkness of night was relieved by torches, which revealed the crowds there assembled. At Hudson, where the train arrived at midnight, elaborate preparations had been made. Beneath an arch hung with black and white drapery and evergreen wreaths, was a tableau representing a coffin resting upon a dais; a female figure in white, mourning over the coffin; a soldier standing at one end and a sailor at the other. While a band of young women dressed in white sang a dirge, two others in black entered the funeral-car, placed a beautiful floral device on the President's coffin, then knelt for a moment in silence, and quietly withdrew. This whole scene was one of the most weird ever witnessed, its solemnity being intensified by the somber lights of torches, at that dead hour of night.

It was long after midnight when the coffin was placed in the State Capitol at Albany. Yet the stream of visitors began the instant the doors could be thrown open. Governor Fenton and staff received the remains at the depot and escorted them to the Capitol. The city was profusely decorated with mourning. Among the many mottoes displayed from the buildings was an extract from one of Mr. Lincoln's addresses:

"Let us resolve that our martyred dead shall not have died in vain."

At four o'clock P. M., Wednesday the 26th, the train again started on its journey, and wended its way in the night toward Buffalo, passing through Rochester at about a quarter past three o'clock A. M. Ten thousand people were out to receive it. The mayor, common council, military and civic organizations, were in line at the depot. The sounds of martial music and of bells tolling were heard till we were far beyond the depot.

At Batavia, at a quarter past five A. M., a concourse had assembled, and, during the short stay in the depot there, a choir of male and female voices chanted a requiem, while minute-guns were firing and bells tolling.

At Herkimer, among the numerous assemblage was a large band of ladies dressed in white, with black sashes, each holding a draped miniature national flag.

At Little Falls, some ladies laid upon the coffin a large cross and wreath of flowers.

At Utica, bands played dirges, bells were tolled, and minute-guns fired.

Arriving at Syracuse near midnight, a hard rain did not deter over thirty thousand people from turning out to witness the passing of the train, with torches and bonfires, bells and cannon.

At Batavia, ex-President Fillmore and several other distinguished citizens from Buffalo came to join the mourners. Arriving at Buffalo at seven o'clock A. M., the 27th, an imposing procession escorted the remains to St. James Hall. At this city every arrangement was of the most perfect character. In the hall, a canopy of crape, extending from the floor to the ceiling, was ar-

THE FUNERAL OF PRESIDENT LINCOLN. 235

ranged for the reception of the coffin. A brilliant light was thrown upon it from a large chandelier, whose rays dimly lighted the rest of the hall. Just before the coffin was opened, the St. Cecilia Society sang a dirge, while all others present stood around in solemn silence. The Mayor and Council of Rochester came to offer their tribute of respect. The crowd of visitors, though immense, was perfectly orderly, and cheerfully yielded to the efforts of officers who volunteered for the occasion, and the city police, in preventing undue pressure and confusion. Thus everything passed off without the least accident. Here we first received intelligence of the capture and death of Booth, the assassin.

As the President's remains went farther westward, where the people more especially claimed him as their own, the intensity of feeling seemed if possible to grow deeper. The night journey of the 27th and 28th was all through torches, bonfires, mourning drapery, mottoes, and solemn music. Leaving Buffalo at ten o'clock in the evening of the 27th, Cleveland was reached at seven o'clock the next morning.

At Cleveland, committees were formed to make every possible arrangement in the most elaborate manner. There being no building thought suitable for the purpose, a superb canopy, thirty-six feet long, twenty-four broad, and fourteen high, was erected in the Public Square. The roof was supported by pillars, and the ends were open, so as to admit of a large crowd passing in at one end and emerging at the other. No device that skill and good taste could conceive was omitted in the construction of this temporary resting-place for the revered remains. It was surmounted by a scroll between two poles, bearing the inscription,

"*Extinctus amabitur idem.*" For the evening, the structure was lighted by gas-jets. The dais was higher at the head than at the foot, so that the remains were in view from the moment of entering the canopy. So great was the influx of persons from the neighboring towns and country, that hundreds were unable to find a resting-place for the night.*

Solemn religious services, including the singing of hymns, were conducted at the canopy by the Right Rev. C. P. McIlvaine, Bishop of Ohio. Except that a rain prevailed through the day, nothing occurred to interfere with the melancholy interest of this most solemn scene. An immense procession conducted the remains, at midnight, between two lines of torch-lights to the depot.

There was an interesting "special feature about the running of the train from Erie to Cleveland," which was recorded in one of the daily papers. "As far as possible, everything connected with the train was the same as on the occasion of Mr. Lincoln's going East over that road in 1861. The locomotive—the 'William Case'—was the same. The engineer, William Congden, was dead, and the engine was run by John Benjamin. The fireman, in 1861, George Martin, was an engineer, but asked and obtained the privilege of again acting as fireman on that train. The same conductor, E. D. Page, had control of the train. Superintendent Henry Nottingham, as before, had the complete management."

The next resting-place was at Columbus, Ohio, where for twelve hours, Saturday, the 29th, streams of people

* To a gentleman, a stranger to me, who kindly lent me his room at a hotel, I was indebted for fifteen hours' unbroken sleep, to bring up arrears.

viewed the body lying in state.* Here the rear of the escorting procession was brought up by colored Masons.

Another night was spent on the way from Columbus to Indianapolis, Indiana, which was reached at seven o'clock Sunday morning, the 30th. Of course, every other pursuit was set aside for this great occasion. It was the first Sunday we had spent on the way since leaving Philadelphia, and never was a Sabbath more hallowed by a universal consent of the people in their demonstration of sincere mourning.

At midnight the route was resumed for Chicago. While the darkness prevailed, the approach to every town was made apparent by bonfires, torches, and music, while crowds of people formed an almost unbroken line. One of the most effective scenes was at Michigan City, where the train stopped for a few minutes, at half-past eight o'clock A. M., the first day of May. A succession of arches, beautifully trimmed with white and black, with evergreens and flowers, and with numerous flags and portraits of the President, was formed over the railway-track. Many mottoes were displayed from different parts of the structure; among them—

"Abraham Lincoln, the noblest martyr of freedom, sacred thy dust; hallowed thy resting-place."
And—
"The purposes of the Almighty are perfect, and must prevail."

* While at Columbus I received a note from a lady, wife of one of the principal citizens, accompanying a little cross made of wild violets. The note said that the writer's little girls had gone to the woods in the early morning and gathered the flowers with which they had wrought the cross. They desired it might be laid on little Willie's coffin, "they felt so sorry for him."

Near the arches was a group of sixteen maidens dressed in white and black, who sweetly sang "Old Hundred." Another group, in white, surrounded a central figure representing America. They stood upon a platform decorated with flowers, and each held in her hand a small flag. This was a striking tableau. A party of sixteen ladies, headed by a niece of Speaker Colfax, entered the car and placed flowers on the coffin.

The train arrived at Chicago at eleven o'clock A. M., May 1st. Here the most elaborate preparations had been made. The decorations were profuse and of the most costly description. A magnificent arch spanned the street where the coffin was taken from the car, and under this the body rested while a dirge was sung by a numerous band of ladies dressed in white, with black scarfs. Meantime the grand procession was formed in line, and the march commenced. Nearly every dwelling on Michigan Avenue, which was on the route, was dressed with mourning, and many displayed touching mottoes. One gentleman, who had accompanied the train from Washington, telegraphed to have conspicuously placed on the front of his residence—

"Mournfully, tenderly bear him to his rest."

He told me these words were suggested by the really tender care with which the Veteran sergeants—always the bearers—lifted and carried their charge.

The rotunda of the court-house was the place chosen for the remains to lie in state. It was decorated without and within with every possible tasteful combination of black velvet, white muslin, silver stars and fringe, wreaths of white flowers, and mottoes, such as these:

"The beauty of Israel is slain upon thy high places."
And—
"Illinois clasps to her bosom her slain but glorified son."

A canopy supported by four pillars was raised over the catafalque, which lay directly under the dome. Numerous lights were so distributed as to throw their concentrated rays through the drapery upon the coffin. A marble eagle, with flags gracefully festooned around it, stood on a velvet pedestal at the head of the coffin.

The remains were here displayed from early afternoon, all through the night, and until eight o'clock the following evening. At intervals a choir sang selections from oratorios, and other choice solemn music. It seemed as if Milwaukee and all the country within many miles of Chicago must have been quite deserted, so great was the concourse at the latter city.

The *cortége* left Chicago, the last stopping-place before Springfield, at half-past nine o'clock P. M. As usual, night was forgotten by the people in their anxiety to show all possible respect for him whom they expected; and bonfires and torches threw their uncertain light upon mourning emblems which were destined to stand in their places as memorials for weeks to come. At Lockport the motto was seen on one house—

"Come home."

It rained at Joliet, and it was midnight; but, just the same, ten thousand persons were gathered at the depot. Here was an illuminated portrait, with the motto:

"Champion, defender, and martyr of liberty."

The train passed under an arch, while sweet voices sang, "There is rest for thee in heaven."

At Lincoln, a place named for the President, and in which he had felt much interest, an arch was erected over the track, on which was a portrait with the motto:

"With malice for none, with charity for all."

There was not a single place on the whole route where some touching demonstration was not made.

At last, at nine o'clock A. M., Wednesday, May 3d, we reached Springfield, the home of Abraham Lincoln at the time he was elected President of the United States. Those who claimed him as their own would naturally exhaust their powers of contrivance to make this last reception worthy of the deep affection and pride which they entertained for him more than for any other man who ever lived. A large procession, in which were many of the most distinguished men in the land, escorted the body, which was conveyed in a splendid hearse, brought for the purpose from St. Louis, drawn by six black horses.

In the Representative Hall of the Capitol the catafalque was erected. The handsome building was uniquely draped on the outside, and the decoration of the hall was very handsome. Conspicuous on the walls were seen the mottoes:

"Sooner than surrender this principle,
I would be assassinated on the spot."

And—

"Washington the Father, Lincoln the Saviour."

Perhaps a more than usual display of grief was apparent among the multitudes who here visited the remains. It was truly the hall of mourning. It seemed hard for these, his old-time neighbors and friends, to realize the dreadful fact that he had come back to them in this guise; and still harder that all that was left of him must, in a few brief hours, be closed from their view forever. Springfield had become classic ground. The President's law-office, his old residence, and the one he occupied until his departure for Washington, were freely thrown open to the thousands eager to see the places which had known him, and should know him no more.

In the morning of Thursday, the 4th of May, the doors of the hall were closed to all save the guard of honor, who stood around while the undertaker and embalmer renewed some of the trimmings of the coffin, cleansed the dress and face, and reverently sealed the coffin-lid. At this moment a little rose-bud attached to a geranium-leaf, which a woman had dropped upon the body at Buffalo, was found nestling directly over the heart.

The procession moved at about noon for the beautiful Oak Ridge Cemetery, just outside the city. A fine horse which had belonged to Mr. Lincoln was led immediately behind the hearse. Military and civic organizations had arrived since the morning of the 3d, to swell the pageant. The ceremonies at the tomb were surpassingly grand and impressive. The vault, of Joliet limestone, was at the foot of a knoll, surrounded by noble trees. The interior of the vault was lined with black velvet, covered with green sprigs of cedar. In the center was a brick foundation, with white-marble top, for the coffin. Little Willie's coffin was deposited near by. A chorus of male voices sang the "Dead March in Saul," as the President's remains were laid to rest. Then began the religious services. First, singing a dirge; next, reading selections from Scripture, and prayer; then, singing a hymn; then, reading of the President's last inaugural, in which occurs that oft-quoted passage, "With malice toward none, with charity for all, with firmness in the right, as God gives us to see the right, let us strive on to finish the work we are in." The choir then sang a dirge; after which Bishop Simpson, of the Methodist Episcopal Church, delivered a funeral address. The ceremonies were concluded with another dirge, and then prayer and benediction, by the President's Washington pastor, Rev. Dr. Gurley.

The door of the vault was then locked and the key confided to Mr. Stuart, of Springfield, who was designated by Captain Robert Lincoln to receive it. The guard of honor having thus surrendered their trust, began to realize how closely their interest had centered upon this object which, for twelve days and twelve nights, had scarcely for one moment been out of their sight.

Thus closed this marvelous exhibition of a great nation's deep grief. It seemed as though for once the spirit of hospitality and of all Christian graces had taken possession of every heart in every place. Not one untoward event can be recalled. Every citizen rivaled his neighbor in making kindly provision for the comfort of the funeral company while in their midst. Unstinted hospitality was not forgotten in the exceeding pains taken with the public displays. Mr. Lincoln, on his way from Springfield to Washington in 1861, had passed through all the cities where now his mortal remains had rested for a few hours on their way home. At the principal places he had had enthusiastic public receptions. There could not now be wanting many sad contrasts in the memories of those who had participated in the first ovations to the new President, and who now remained to behold the last of him on earth. Can there be imagined one item wanting to perfect this grandest of human dramas? It is entire; it is sublime!

On the 11th of February, 1861, on departing from Springfield, Mr. Lincoln said to his neighbors, gathered to take leave of him:

"My friends, no one not in my position can appreciate the sadness I feel at this parting. To this people I owe all that I am. Here I have lived more than a quarter of a century; here my children were born, and here one of them lies buried. I know not how soon I shall see you again. A duty devolves upon me which is, perhaps, greater than that which has devolved upon any other man since the days of Washington. He never would have succeeded except for the aid of Divine Providence, upon which he at all times relied. I feel that I can not succeed without the same aid which sustained him, and on the same Almighty Being I place my reliance for support; and I hope you, my friends, will all pray that I may receive that Divine assistance without which I can not succeed, but with which success is certain. Again I bid you all an affectionate farewell."

It was a long—a last farewell. Let the world's verdict say, were those prayers answered?

CHAPTER XL.

THE GRAND REVIEWS.

A vast camp—War-worn veterans—The Bummer Brigade—Final discharge.

THE war was over. The nation was in mourning for its President. The soldiers who had triumphed under him as commander-in-chief were to disperse to their homes and resume the avocations of peace. Following the precedents set by other nations, the United States Government decreed that its armies should pass in review in the capital they had defended, before the rulers and the distinguished men of the land, that all might unite in lavishing honors upon their heroes of so many hard-fought battles.

All the corps, as fast as they could be assembled there, were encamped within a radius of four miles from Washington, and the whole country became a vast camp of veterans, still maintaining their discipline, though no note of war would now sound to alarm their sentries, or turn them out to the long roll of the drum.

A central stand was erected on the broad sidewalk in front of the Executive Mansion. Here were congregated the President and Cabinet, high military officers, and the diplomatic corps. One of the three other stands received Governors of States, members of Congress, and United States judges. The rest were for any persons who could secure places upon them. Pennsylvania Avenue and other streets along which the processions passed were densely packed, and every window and balcony was occupied by residents and visitors. It was a sight never before witnessed in this country, and perhaps to be never again. Reviews of large numbers of troops, up to as high as one hundred thousand at a time, had been held as part of the preparatory discipline for battle. But here were the war-worn and generally shabbily-clad veterans, whose battles were finished. Before, on their way to the field, their new and fresh-looking banners were borne with the air of men determined to stand by them to the last. Now, they were brought back torn in shreds by bullets, and dingy with the smoke of war, vastly more prized than ever, and sending to the hearts of spectators a strange thrill of admiration for those men who had fulfilled their silent pledge, and brought back what was left of their colors, enveloped in glorious histories.

First in the order of reviews, May 23, 1865, came the "Army of the Potomac," headed by Major-General GEORGE G. MEADE,* consisting of MERRITT's cavalry corps, PARKE's Ninth Corps, GRIFFIN's Fifth Corps, and HUMPHREY's Second Corps.

The appearance of this army was never finer. The horses of the principal officers had been decorated with garlands by admiring hands. As each general passed, he bowed acknowledgments to the crowds who shouted and waved their handkerchiefs; and scarcely did a regiment fail to receive at some point a signal token of recognition.

General WILLIAM T. SHERMAN's army was reviewed May 24th.

First came General SHERMAN, upon a superb blooded horse, with a heavy wreath about his neck. Then the

* General GRANT, as General-in-Chief of all the Armies of the United States, occupied a seat on the President's stand.

right wing, under Major-General LOGAN,* composed of HAZEN's Fifteenth and FRANK BLAIR's Seventeenth Army Corps, constituting the "Army of the Tennessee." Next, the left wing, under Major-General SLOCUM, consisting of MOWER's Twentieth and J. C. DAVIS's Fourteenth Army Corps, constituting the "Army of Georgia."

The rear of Sherman's army was brought up by the "Bummer Brigade," a humorous yet vivid and truthful representation of one of its characteristics. It consisted of a lot of the smallest donkeys ever seen, mingled with others of larger sizes, led by regular specimens of Southern field-hands, and laden with the spoils of war in the foraging line. There were pots and pans, chickens and grain. On the back of one mule stood a goat, on another a raccoon, and several roosters on others. These seemed to have been preserved as pets from the slaughter, but might fall victims in some woful hour of short rations.

A marked difference was observed between the men of this and of the "Army of the Potomac." These were Western men, generally quite young, and taken from farms. The others were older, as a general rule, and of the city type of levies. There had been an impression that Sherman's men, though excellent fighters, were without much discipline or drill. Agreeable surprise was expressed, then, on seeing them march and manœuvre with as much precision as the best. They probably received a rather more enthusiastic greeting, if possible, than Meade's men, because they were a novelty at the seat of government—stranger-guests, as it were.

Major-General H. G. WRIGHT's Sixth Army Corps

* General HOWARD had already been detached to become chief of the Freedmen's Bureau.

had been detached on a service which prevented its appearing with the "Army of the Potomac," to which it belonged. It was therefore reviewed on the 7th of June. This was the corps sent by General Grant from before Richmond to the relief of Washington when threatened by Early in 1864. Its three divisions, under Generals Frank Wheaton, Getty, and Ricketts, were therefore objects of special interest on this occasion. The Second Brigade of the Third Division was commanded by brevet Brigadier-General J. WARREN KEIFER, Speaker of the House of Representatives in the Forty-seventh Congress.

General Sheridan was not with his cavalry corps in the review. He had been detached with re-enforcements to take command of the army in the Southwest, for the purpose of operating against Kirby Smith. The surrender of that Confederate general, however, took place before any serious movements were made against him. He had a well-appointed army, and might have made a good fight; but the capture of Mr. Davis, and of the forces attempting to cover his escape, put an end to the scheme of moving the capital of the slave confederacy to Texas, and perhaps eventually annexing the upper provinces of Mexico to that and such other States as could be saved. Kirby Smith maintained his forces in hopes that his President might succeed in joining him with some remnant of the Army of Northern Virginia. This having failed, he could have no object in prolonging the contest.

Sheridan's new army was too far off to be brought to Washington for review.

After the armies had been reviewed in Washington, they were transported by the Government to fifty depots near their homes. They had been mustered out of service by officers appointed for the purpose, before they left the field. Their final muster-rolls were boxed up and transported with them, their final payment being made contingent upon their remaining in their ranks, and conducting themselves in an orderly manner until released. At the depots paymasters awaited them; and, having been transported and subsisted up to the last moment, they were paid in full, and discharged almost at their very homes. Thus it was that 800,963 men in arms were all released from military restraint and returned to the walks of civil life, within the space of two months, without a single act of lawlessness being reported.

It would seem to be superfluous to make any comment on this grand *finale* to the civil war in the United States— a war grand in its proportions, grand in its displays of heroism and endurance, grand in its results. If that war shall, as now seems most probable, prove to have been the cause of a better cemented strength to the Union, future ages will rank it foremost in the great struggles for principles and liberty.

APPENDIX A.

GENERAL SCOTT'S "VIEWS."

"*Views suggested by the Imminent Danger (October 29, 1860) of a Disruption of the Union by the Secession of one or more of the Southern States.*

"To save time, the right of secession may be conceded, and instantly balanced by the correlative right, on the part of the Federal Government, against an *interior* State or States, to re-establish by force, if necessary, its former continuity of territory.—(Paley's Moral and Political Philosophy, last chapter.)

"But, break this glorious Union by whatever line or lines that political madness may contrive, and there would be no hope of reuniting the fragments except by the laceration and despotism of the sword. To effect such result the intestine wars of our Mexican neighbors would, in comparison with ours, sink into mere child's play.

"A smaller evil would be to allow the fragments of the great republic to form themselves into new confederacies, probably four.

"All the lines of demarkation between the new Unions can not be accurately drawn in advance, but many of them approximately may. Thus, looking to natural boundaries and commercial affinities, some of the following frontiers, after many waverings and conflicts, might perhaps become acknowledged and fixed:

"1. The Potomac River and the Chesapeake Bay to the Atlantic. 2. From Maryland, along the crest of the Alleghany (perhaps the Blue Ridge) range of mountains, to some point in the coast of Florida. 3. The line from, say, the head of the Potomac to the west or northwest, which it will be most difficult to settle. 4. The crest of the Rocky Mountains.

"The Southeast Confederacy would, in all human probability, in less than five years after the rupture, find itself bounded by the first and second lines indicated above—the Atlantic and the Gulf of Mexico—with its capital at, say, Columbia, South Carolina. The country between the second, third, and fourth of those lines would, beyond a doubt, in about the same time, constitute the Northeast Confederacy, with its capital at Albany.

"It, at the first thought, will be considered strange that seven slaveholding States and parts of Virginia and Florida should be placed (above) in a new confederacy with Ohio, Indiana, Illinois, etc. But when the overwhelming weight of the great Northwest is taken in connection with the laws of trade, contiguity of territory, and the comparative indifference to free-soil doctrines on the part of Western Virginia, Kentucky, Tennessee, and Missouri, it is evident that but little if any coercion, beyond moral force, would be needed to embrace them; and I have omitted the temptation of the unwasted public lands which would fall entire to this confederacy—an appanage (well husbanded) sufficient for many generations. As to Missouri, Arkansas, and Mississippi, they would not stand out a month. Louisiana would coalesce without much solicitation; and Alabama, with West Florida, would be conquered the first winter, from the absolute need of Pensacola for a naval depot.

"If I might presume to address the South, and particularly dear Virginia—'being native here and to the manor born'—I would affectionately ask: Will not your slaves be less secure, and their labor less profitable, under the new order of things than under the old? Could you employ profitably two hundred slaves in all Nebraska, or five hundred in all New Mexico?* The right, then, to take them thither would be a barren right. And is it not wise to

'Rather bear the ills we have,
Than fly to others that we know not of?'

"The Declaration of Independence proclaims and consecrates the same maxim: 'Prudence, indeed, will dictate that governments long established should not be changed for light and transient causes.' And Paley, too, lays down as a fundamental maxim of statesmanship, 'Never to pursue national *honor* as distinct from national *interest*'; but adds, 'This rule acknowledges that it is often necessary to assert the honor of a nation for the sake of its interests.'

"The excitement that threatens secession is caused by the near prospect of a Republican's election to the presidency. From a sense of propriety, as a soldier, I have taken no part in the pending canvass, and, as always heretofore, mean to stay away from the polls. My sympathies, however, are with the Bell and Everett ticket. With Mr.

* In relation to the practical use of slavery in New Mexico, a singular incident occurred in the spring of 1850, while the compromise measures were under discussion. My old friend Major K—— was stationed in New Mexico, and had traveled much through such parts of the Territory as were then accessible. He wrote me to this effect: "I imagine that they are now wrangling in Congress over the question of admitting slaves to this Territory. If the truth were known, there are not many square miles where they could exist, in the whole Territory. Its natural conformation easily settles that question." This letter was received near the 7th of March, 1850, when Mr. Webster, in his famous speech on the subject, said in effect, "I fancy that, while we are discussing the question of admitting slavery to New Mexico, if the facts were known, the face of the country would, of itself, preclude all possibility of their being employed there."

I handed to Mr. Seaton an extract from Major K——'s letter, with its date, and called his attention to Mr. Webster's speech. In a day or two, an interesting article on the subject appeared in the "National Intelligencer."

Lincoln I have had no communication whatever, direct or indirect, and have no recollection of ever having seen his person; but can not believe any unconstitutional violence, or breach of law, is to be apprehended from his administration of the Federal Government.

"From a knowledge of our Southern population, it is my solemn conviction that there is some danger of an early act of rashness preliminary to secession, viz., the seizure of some or all of the following posts: Forts Jackson and St. Philip, in the Mississippi, below New Orleans, both without garrisons; Fort Morgan, below Mobile, without a garrison; Forts Pickens and McRee, Pensacola Harbor, with an insufficient garrison for one; Fort Pulaski, below Savannah, without a garrison; Forts Moultrie and Sumter, Charleston Harbor, the former with an insufficient garrison, and the latter without any; and Fort Monroe, Hampton Roads, without a sufficient garrison. In my opinion, all these works should be immediately so garrisoned as to make any attempt to take any one of them by surprise or *coup de main* ridiculous.

"With the army faithful to its allegiance and the navy probably equally so, and with a Federal Executive, for the next twelve months, of firmness and moderation, which the country has a right to expect—*moderation* being an element of power not less than *firmness*—there is good reason to hope that the danger of secession may be made to pass away without one conflict of arms, one execution, or one arrest for treason.

"In the mean time it is suggested that exports should remain as free as at present; all duties, however, on imports collected (outside of the cities*), as such receipts would be needed for the national debt, invalid pensions,

* "In forts, or on board ships of war. The great aim and object of this plan was to gain time—say eight or ten months—to await expected

etc., and only articles contraband of war be refused admittance. But even this refusal would be unnecessary, as the foregoing views eschew the idea of invading a seceding State.

"WINFIELD SCOTT."

"*October 29, 1860.*"

"Lieutenant-General Scott's respects to the Secretary of War, to say:

"That a copy of his 'Views, etc.,' was dispatched to the President yesterday, in great haste; but the copy intended for the Secretary, better transcribed (herewith), was not in time for the mail. General S. would be happy if the latter could be substituted for the former.

"It will be seen that the 'Views' only apply to a case of secession that makes a *gap* in the present Union. The falling off (say) of Texas, or of all the Atlantic States, from the Potomac south, was not within the scope of General S.'s provisional remedies.

"It is his opinion that instructions should be given at once to the commanders of the Barrancas, Forts Moultrie and Monroe, to be on their guard against surprises and *coups de main*. As to *regular approaches*, nothing can be said or done, at this time, without volunteers.

"There is one (regular) company at Boston, one here (at the Narrows), one at Pittsburg, one at Augusta, Georgia, and one at Baton Rouge—in all five companies only, within reach,* to garrison or re-enforce the forts mentioned in the 'Views.'

measures of conciliation on the part of the North, and the subsidence of angry feelings in the opposite quarter."

* "Within reach"—that is to say, so near that they can be reached immediately. There were other "regular" companies that with a little more time could be reached for the purpose indicated, while, for a greater emergency, the idea of "volunteers," for "regular approaches," was plainly hinted at.

"General Scott is all solicitude for the safety of the Union. He is, however, not without hope that all dangers and difficulties will pass away, without leaving a scar or painful recollection behind.

"The Secretary's most obedient servant,

"W. S."

"*October 30, 1860.*"

RE-ENFORCING AND HOLDING FORTS.

"HEADQUARTERS OF THE ARMY,
"WASHINGTON, *December 28*, 1860.

"Lieutenant-General Scott (who has had a bad night, and can scarcely hold up his head this morning) begs to express the hopes to the Secretary of War—1. That orders may not be given for the evacuation of Fort Sumter; 2. That one hundred and fifty recruits may instantly be sent from Governor's Island to re-enforce that garrison, with ample supplies of ammunition and subsistence, including fresh vegetables, as potatoes, onions, turnips; and, 3. That one or two armed vessels be sent to support the said fort.

"Lieutenant-General Scott avails himself of this opportunity also to express the hope that the recommendations heretofore made by him to the Secretary of War respecting Forts Jackson,* St. Philip,* Morgan,† and Pulaski,‡ and particularly in respect to Forts Pickens # and McRee # and the Pensacola Navy-Yard, in connection with the two last-named works, may be reconsidered by the Secretary.

"Lieutenant-General Scott will further ask the attention of the Secretary to Forts Jefferson ‖ and Taylor,△ which

---

* At mouth of Mississippi River.   # Pensacola Harbor, Florida.
† Mobile Bay, Alabama.   ‖ Dry Tortugas, Florida.
‡ Savannah River, Georgia.   △ Key West, Florida.

are wholly national, being of far greater value even to the most distant points of the Atlantic coast, and to the people on the upper waters of the Missouri, Mississippi, and Ohio Rivers, than to the State of Florida. There is only a feeble company at Key West for the defense of Fort Taylor, and not a soldier in Fort Jefferson to resist a handful of filibusters or a row-boat of pirates; and the Gulf, soon after the beginning of secession or revolutionary troubles in the adjacent States, will swarm with such nuisances.

"Respectfully submitted to the Secretary of War,
"WINFIELD SCOTT."

THE "WAYWARD SISTERS."

"WASHINGTON, *March 3, 1861.*

"DEAR SIR: Hoping that in a day or two the new President will have happily passed through all personal dangers, and find himself installed an honored successor of the great Washington, with you as the chief of his Cabinet, I beg leave to repeat, in writing, what I have before said to you orally, this supplement to my printed 'Views' (dated in October last) on the highly disordered condition of our (so late) happy and glorious Union.

"To meet the extraordinary exigencies of the times, it seems to me that I am guilty of no arrogance in limiting the President's field of selection to one of the four plans of procedure subjoined:

"I. Throw off the old and assume the new designation—the Union party; adopt the conciliatory measures proposed by Mr. Crittenden, or the Peace Convention, and, my life upon it, we shall have no new case of secession; but, on the contrary, an early return of many, if not of all the States which have already broken off from the Union. Without some equally benign measure, the remaining slaveholding States will probably join the Montgomery Confederacy in less than sixty days; when this city, being included in a foreign country, would require a permanent garrison of at least thirty-five thousand troops to protect the Government within it.

"II. Collect the duties on foreign goods outside the ports of which the Government has lost the command, or close such ports by act of Congress, and blockade them.

"III. Conquer the seceded States by invading armies. No doubt this might be done in two or three years by a young and able general—a Wolfe, a Desaix, a Hoche—with three hundred thousand disciplined men, estimating a third for garrisons, and the loss of a yet greater number by skirmishes, sieges, battles, and Southern fevers. The destruction of life and property on the other side would be frightful, however perfect the moral discipline of the invaders.

"The conquest completed, at the enormous waste of human life to the North and Northwest, with at least $250,000,000 added thereto, and *cui bono?* Fifteen devastated provinces! not to be brought into harmony with their conquerors, but to be held for generations by heavy garrisons, at an expense quadruple the net duties or taxes which it would be possible to extort from them, followed by a protector or an emperor.

"IV. Say to the seceded States, Wayward sisters, depart in peace.

"In haste, I remain, very truly yours,

"WINFIELD SCOTT."

"Hon. WILLIAM H. SEWARD, etc., etc."

APPENDIX B.

PRECAUTIONS AGAINST ATTACK.

GENERAL ORDERS, NO. 4.
>HEADQUARTERS OF THE ARMY,
>WASHINGTON, *April 26, 1861.*

I. FROM the known assemblage near this city of numerous hostile bodies of troops, it is evident that an attack upon it may soon be expected. In such an event, to meet and repel the enemy, it is necessary that some plan of harmonious co-operation should be adopted on the part of all the forces, regular and volunteer, present for the defense of the capital—that is, for the defense of the Government, the peaceable inhabitants of the city, their property, the public buildings and public archives.

II. At the first moment of an attack, every regiment, battalion, squadron, and independent company, will promptly assemble at its established rendezvous (in or out of the public buildings), ready for battle, and wait for orders.

III. The pickets (or advanced guards) will stand fast till driven in by overwhelming forces; but it is expected that those stationed to defend bridges—having every advantage of position—will not give way till actually pushed by the bayonet. Such obstinacy on the part of pickets so stationed is absolutely necessary, to give time for the troops, in the rear, to assemble at their places of rendezvous.

IV. All advanced guards and pickets, driven in, will fall back slowly, to delay the advance of the enemy as much as possible, before repairing to their proper rendezvous.

V. On the happening of an attack, the troops, lodged in the public buildings, and in the navy-yard, will remain for their defense, respectively, unless specially ordered elsewhere; with the exceptions that the Seventh New York

Regiment and the Massachusetts Regiment will march rapidly towards the President's Square for its defense; and the Rhode Island Regiment (in the Department of the Interior). when full, will make a diversion by detachment, to assist in the defense of the General Post-Office Building, if necessary. WINFIELD SCOTT.

By command:

E. D. TOWNSEND, *Assistant Adjutant-General.*

APPENDIX C.

EXTRACT FROM SECRETARY OF WAR'S REPORT TO THE PRESIDENT, DECEMBER 1, 1862.

A CHIEF hope of those who set the rebellion on foot was for aid and comfort from disloyal sympathizers in the Northern States, whose efforts were relied upon to divide and distract the people of the North, and prevent them from putting forth their whole strength to preserve the national existence. The call for volunteers and a draft of the militia afforded an occasion for disloyal persons to accomplish their evil purpose by discouraging enlistments, and encouraging opposition to the war and the draft of soldiers to carry it on.

Anxiety was felt in some States at the probable success of these disloyal practices, and the Government was urged to adopt measures of protection by temporary restraint of those engaged in these hostile acts. To that end provost-marshals were appointed in some of the States, upon the nomination of their Governors, to act under the direction of the State Executive, and the writ of *habeas corpus* was suspended by your order. By the order of the department arrests were forbidden unless authorized by the State Executive or by the judge-advocate. Some instances of unauthorized arrests have occurred, but when brought to the notice of the department the parties have been immediately discharged. By a recent order, all persons arrested for discouraging enlistments or for disloyal practices, in States where the quotas of volunteers and militia are filled up, have been released. Other persons, arrested by military commanders and sent from departments where their presence was deemed dangerous to the public safety, have been discharged upon parole to be of good behavior and do no act of hostility against the Government of the United States. While military arrests of disloyal persons form the subject of complaint in some States, the discharge of such persons is complained of in other States. It has been the aim of the department to avoid any encroachment upon individual rights, as far as might be consistent with public safety and the preservation of the Government. But reflecting minds will perceive that no greater encouragement can be given to the enemy, no more dangerous act of hostility can be perpetrated in this war, than efforts to prevent recruiting and enlistments for the armies, upon whose strength national existence depends. The expectations of the rebel leaders and their sympathizers in loyal States, that the call for volunteers would not be answered and that the draft could not be enforced, have failed, and nothing is left but to clamor at the means by which their hopes were frustrated, and to strive to disarm the Government in future, if, in the chances of war, another occasion for increasing the military force should arise.

APPENDIX D.

PLAN OF CAMPAIGN.

NOTE.—The words in the original draft erased by General Scott are here inserted in brackets, and the words substituted or added by him are printed in italics. (See page 56.)

[*Confidential.*]

HEADQUARTERS OF THE ARMY,
WASHINGTON, *May 3, 1861.*

Major-General G. B. McCLELLAN, *commanding, etc.*

SIR: I have read and carefully considered your plan for a campaign, and now send you, confidentially, my own views, supported by certain facts of which you should be advised :

1. It is the design of the Government to [call for] *raise* 25,000 additional regular troops, and 60,000 volunteers for [two] *three* years. It will be inexpedient either to rely on the three months' volunteers for extensive [military] operations, or to put in their hands the best class of arms we have in store. The term of service would expire [before the] *by the* commencement of a regular campaign, and the arms [would] *not lost* be returned [many of them] *mostly* in a damaged condition. Hence, I must strongly urge upon you to confine yourself strictly to the quota of three months' men called for by the War Department.

2. [I] *We* rely greatly on the sure operation of a complete blockade of the Atlantic and Gulf ports [such as it is designed to enforce] *soon to commence.* In connection with such blockade, [I] *we* propose a [strong] *powerful* movement down the [Western Rivers] *Mississippi* to [New Orleans] *the ocean*, with a cordon of posts at proper points, and [a reoccupation] *the capture* of Forts Jackson and St.

PLAN OF CAMPAIGN. 261

Philip; the object being to clear out and keep open th[e]*is* great line[s] of [water] communication[s, and] in connection with *the strict* blockade [above adverted to] *of the seaboard, so as* to envelope the insurgent States, and bring them to terms *with less blood-shed than by any other plan.* For this end I [say] *suppose* there will be needed from twelve to twenty steam-gunboats, and a sufficient number of steam-transports (*say 40*) to carry all the personnel* (*say 60,000 men*) and materiel* of th[is]*e* expedition. [A part] *Most* of the gunboats to [go in] *be in* advance to open the way, and [others] *the remainder* to follow [and prevent the recapture of posts of the proposed cordon, after the head column has advanced beyond supporting distance] *and protect the rear of the expedition.* Th[e]*is* army, *in* which it is not improbable you may [command] *be invited to take an important part,* should be composed of [the] *our* best regulars [we can find] for the advance, and of [two] *3 years*' volunteers, all well [appointed] *officered,* and with [a sufficient supply of subsistence and munitions] *4½ months' of instruction in camps, prior to* (*say*) *Nov. 10.* In the progress down the River all *the enemy's* batteries [which may have been planted] on its banks [must be] *we of course would* turn[ed] and capture[d], [and] *leaving* a sufficient number of posts [must be left] with competent garrisons to keep the River open [to its mouth] *behind the expedition.* Finally, *it will be necessary that* New Orleans [must be] *should be strongly* occupied and securely held until the present difficulties are composed.

3. [I come] *A word* now *as* to the *greatest* obstacle[s to be encountered in carrying out] *in the way of* this plan— the great danger now pressing upon us—[is] the impatience of our patriotic and loyal Union friends, [Northern

---

* Underlined by the general.

men, which is forcing them on to] *They will urge* instant and vigorous action, regardless, I fear, of consequences [We must not now despise the stern lessons of experience. It is more glorious to win a sure success, without a single reverse, by waiting until our plans are matured and our preparations are perfected, than to plunge into the midst of dangers arising from climate, want of discipline, etc., etc., intending by indomitable courage and energy to rise above them all. Impress this]; *that is, unwilling to wait for the slow instruction of (say) 12 or 15 camps; for the rise of rivers and the return of frosts to kill the virus of malignant fevers, below Memphis. I fear this; but impress right* views, on every proper occasion, upon the brave men who are hastening to the support of their Government. Lose no time, while necessary preparations [are making for an expedition] *for the great expedition are in progress*, in organizing, drilling, and disciplining your [men] *3 months' men*, many of whom, it is hoped, will be ultimately found enrolled under the call for [two] *3 years'* volunteers. Should an urgent and immediate occasion arise, meantime, for their services, they will be the more effective.

I commend these views to your [calm and serious deliberation] *consideration*, and shall be happy to hear the result [when your opinion is fully made up].

With great respect, yours truly,
WINFIELD SCOTT.

Major-General GEORGE B. MCCLELLAN,
  Commanding Ohio Volunteers,
    Cincinnati, Ohio.

APPENDIX E.

RETIREMENT OF GENERAL SCOTT.

Act approved August 3, 1861.

SECTION 15. *And be it further enacted,* That any commissioned officer of the army, or of the marine corps, who shall have served as such for forty consecutive years, may, upon his own application to the President of the United States, be placed upon the list of retired officers, with the pay and emoluments allowed by this act.

SEC. 16. . . . *Provided,* That should the brevet lieutenant-general be retired under this act, it shall be without reduction in his current pay, subsistence, or allowances.

"HEADQUARTERS OF THE ARMY,
"WASHINGTON, *October 31, 1861.*

"*The Hon.* S. CAMERON, *Secretary of War.*

"SIR: For more than three years I have been unable, from a hurt, to mount a horse or to walk more than a few paces at a time, and that with much pain. Other and new infirmities, dropsy and vertigo, admonish me that repose of mind and body, with the appliances of surgery and medicine, are necessary to add a little more to a life already protracted much beyond the usual space of man. It is under such circumstances, made doubly painful by the unnatural and unjust rebellion now raging in the Southern States of our so lately prosperous and happy Union, that I am compelled to request that my name be placed on the list of army officers retired from active service. As this request is founded on an absolute right, granted by a recent act of Congress, I am entirely at liberty to say that it is with deep regret that I withdraw myself in these momentous times from the orders of a President who has treated me with much distinguished kindness and courtesy, whom I know upon much personal intercourse to be patriotic, without sectional prejudices; to be highly conscientious in the performance of every duty, and of unrivaled activity and perseverance; and to you, Mr. Secretary, whom I now officially address for the last time, I beg to acknowledge my many obligations for the uniform high consideration I have received at your hands, and have the honor to remain, sir, with the highest respect,

"Your obedient servant,
"WINFIELD SCOTT."

A special Cabinet council was convened this morning (November 1st) at nine o'clock, to take the subject into consideration. It was decided that General Scott's request, under the circumstances of his advanced age and infirmities, could not be declined. General McClellan was, therefore, with the unanimous agreement of the Cabinet, notified that the command of the army would be devolved upon him.*

"At four o'clock in the afternoon the Cabinet again waited upon the President and attended him to the residence of General Scott. Being seated, the President read to the general the following order:

"On the first day of November, A. D. 1861, upon his own application to the President of the United States, brevet Lieutenant-General Winfield Scott is ordered to be placed, and hereby is placed, upon the list of retired officers of the Army of the United States, without reduction in his current pay, subsistence, or allowance. The American people will hear with sadness and deep emotion that General Scott has withdrawn from the active control of the army, while the President and unanimous Cabinet express

* The following account was taken from a daily newspaper.

their own and the nation's sympathy in his personal affliction, and their profound sense of the important public services rendered by him to his country during his long and brilliant career, among which will ever be gratefully distinguished his faithful devotion to the Constitution, the Union, and the flag, when assailed by parricidal rebellion.
(Signed) "ABRAHAM LINCOLN."

"General Scott thereupon arose and addressed the Cabinet, who had also risen, as follows :

"President, this honor overwhelms me. It overpays all the services I have attempted to render to my country. If I had any claims before, they are all obliterated by this expression of approval by the President, with the remaining support of his Cabinet. I know the President and his Cabinet well. I know that the country has placed its interests in this trying crisis in safe keeping. Their counsels are wise, their labors as untiring as they are loyal, and their course is the right one.

"President, you must excuse me. I am unable to stand longer to give utterance to the feelings of gratitude which oppress me. In my retirement I shall offer up my prayers to God for this Administration and for my country. I shall pray for it with confidence in its success over all enemies, and that speedily."

"The President then took leave of General Scott, giving him his hand, and saying that he hoped soon to write him a private letter expressive of his gratitude and affection. The President added :

"General, you will naturally feel a solicitude about the gentlemen of your staff, who have rendered you and their country such faithful service. I have taken that subject into consideration. I understand that they go with you to New York. I shall desire them at their earliest convenience after their return to make their wishes known to me. I desire you now, however, to be satisfied that except the unavoidable privation of your counsel and society, which they have so long enjoyed, the provision which will be made for them will be such as to render their situation as agreeable hereafter as it has been heretofore.

"Each member of the Administration then gave his hand to the veteran, and retired in profound silence.

"The Secretary of the Treasury and the Secretary of War accompanied General Scott to New York on the following morning by the early train.

"The following was the response of the Secretary of War to the letter of General Scott:

"War Department, Washington, *November 1, 1861.*

"General: It was my duty to lay before the President your letter of yesterday, asking to be relieved on the recent act of Congress. In separating from you I can not refrain from expressing my deep regret that your health, shattered by long service and repeated wounds, received in your country's defense, should render it necessary for you to retire from your high position at this momentous period of our history. Although you are not to remain in active service, I yet hope that, while I continue in charge of the department over which I now preside, I shall at times be permitted to avail myself of the benefits of your wise counsels and sage experience. It has been my good fortune to enjoy a personal acquaintance with you for over thirty years, and the pleasant relations of that long time have been greatly strengthened by your cordial and entire co-operation in all the great questions which have occupied the Department and convulsed the country for the last six months. In parting from you I can only express the hope that a merciful Providence that has protected you amid so many trials will improve your health and continue your life long after the people of the country shall have been restored to their former happiness and prosperity.

"I am, general, very sincerely,
"Your friend and servant,
"SIMON CAMERON, *Secretary of War*
"Lieutenant-General WINFIELD SCOTT, present."

APPENDIX F.

COLLOQUY WITH COLORED MINISTERS.

ON the evening of Thursday, the 12th day of January, 1865, the following persons of African descent met, by appointment, to hold an interview with EDWIN M. STANTON, Secretary of War, and Major-General SHERMAN, to have a conference upon matters relating to the freedmen of the State of Georgia, to wit:

1. *William J. Campbell,* aged fifty-one years, born in Savannah; slave until 1849, and then liberated by will of his mistress, Mrs. Mary Maxwell; for ten years pastor of the First Baptist Church of Savannah, numbering about eighteen hundred members; average congregation nineteen hundred; the church property belonging to the congregation (trustees white) worth eighteen thousand dollars.

2. *John Cox,* aged fifty-eight years, born in Savannah; slave until 1849, when he bought his freedom for eleven hundred dollars; pastor of the Second African Baptist Church; in the ministry fifteen years; congregation twelve hundred and twenty-two persons; church property worth ten thousand dollars, belonging to the congregation.

3. *Ulysses L. Houston,* aged forty-one years, born in Grahamsville, South Carolina; slave "until the Union

army entered Savannah"; owned by Moses Henderson, Savannah; and pastor of Third African Baptist Church, congregation numbering four hundred; church property worth five thousand dollars, belongs to congregation; in the ministry about eight years.

4. *William Bentley*, aged seventy-two years, born in Savannah; slave until twenty-five years of age, when his master, John Waters, emancipated him by will; pastor of Andrew's Chapel, Methodist Episcopal Church (only one of that denomination in Savannah), congregation numbering three hundred and sixty members; church property worth about twenty thousand dollars, and is owned by the congregation; been in the ministry about twenty years; a member of Georgia Conference.

5. *Charles Bradwell*, aged forty years, born in Liberty County, Georgia; slave until 1851; emancipated by will of his master, J. L. Bradwell; local preacher, in charge of the Methodist Episcopal congregation (Andrew's Chapel) in the absence of the minister; in the ministry ten years.

6. *William Gaines*, aged forty-one years, born in Wills County, Georgia; slave "until the Union forces freed me"; owned by Robert Toombs, formerly United States Senator, and his brother, Gabriel Toombs; local preacher of the Methodist Episcopal Church (Andrew's Chapel); in the ministry sixteen years.

7. *James Hill*, aged fifty-two years, born in Bryan County, Georgia; slave "up to the time the Union army come in"; owned by H. F. Willings, of Savannah; in the ministry sixteen years.

8. *Glasgow Taylor*, aged seventy-two years, born in Wilkes County, Georgia; slave "until the Union army come"; owned by A. P. Wetter; is a local preacher of the Methodist Episcopal Church (Andrew's Chapel); in the ministry thirty-five years.

COLLOQUY WITH COLORED MINISTERS. 269

9. *Garrison Frazier*, aged sixty-seven years, born in Granville County, North Carolina; slave until eight years ago, when he bought himself and wife, paying one thousand dollars in gold and silver; is an ordained minister in the Baptist Church, but, his health failing, has now charge of no congregation; has been in the ministry thirty-five years.

10. *James Mills*, aged fifty-six years, born in Savannah; free-born, and is a licensed preacher of the First Baptist Church; has been eight years in the ministry.

11. *Abraham Burke*, aged forty-eight years, born in Bryan County, Georgia; slave until twenty years ago, when he bought himself for eight hundred dollars; has been in the ministry about ten years.

12. *Arthur Wardell*, aged forty-four years, born in Liberty County, Georgia; slave until "freed by the Union army"; owned by A. A. Solomons, Savannah, and is a licensed minister in the Baptist Church; has been in the ministry six years.

13. *Alexander Harris*, aged forty-seven years, born in Savannah; free-born; licensed minister of Third African Baptist Church; licensed about one month ago.

14. *Andrew Neal*, aged sixty-one years, born in Savannah; slave "until the Union army liberated me"; owned by Mr. William Gibbons, and has been deacon in the Third Baptist Church for ten years.

15. *James Porter*, aged thirty-nine years, born in Charleston, South Carolina; free-born, his mother having purchased her freedom; is lay-reader and president of the board of wardens and vestry of St. Stephen's Protestant Episcopal Colored Church in Savannah; has been in communion nine years; the congregation numbers about two hundred persons; the church property is worth about ten thousand dollars, and is owned by the congregation.

16. *Adolphus Delmotte*, aged twenty-eight years, born in Savannah; free-born; is a licensed minister of the Missionary Baptist Church of Milledgeville, congregation numbering about three or four hundred persons; has been in the ministry about two years.

17. *Jacob Godfrey*, aged fifty-seven years, born in Marion, South Carolina; slave "until the Union army freed me"; owned by James E. Godfrey, Methodist preacher, now in the rebel army; is a class-leader, and steward of Andrew's Chapel since 1836.

18. *John Johnson*, aged fifty-one years, born in Bryan County, Georgia; slave "up to the time the Union army came here;" owned by W. W. Lincoln, of Savannah; is class-leader, and treasurer of Andrew's Chapel for sixteen years.

19. *Robert N. Taylor*, aged fifty-one years, born in Wilkes County, Georgia; slave "to the time the Union army come"; was owned by Augustus P. Wetter, Savannah, and is class-leader in Andrew's Chapel—for nine years.

20. *James Lynch*, aged twenty-six years, born in Baltimore, Maryland; free-born; is presiding elder of the Methodist Episcopal Church, and missionary to the Department of the South; has been seven years in the ministry, and two years in the South.

Garrison Frazier being chosen by the persons present to express their common sentiments upon the matters of inquiry, makes answers to inquiries as follows:

1. State what your understanding is in regard to the acts of Congress, and President Lincoln's proclamation, touching the condition of the colored people in the rebel States.

Answer. So far as I understand President Lincoln's proclamation to the rebellious States, it is, that if they would lay down their arms and submit to the laws of the United States before the 1st of January, 1863, all should be well; but if they did not, then all the slaves in the rebel States should be free, henceforth and forever : that is what I understood.

2. State what you understand by slavery, and the freedom that was to be given by the President's Proclamation.

Answer. Slavery is receiving by irresistible power the work of another man, and not by his consent. The freedom, as I understand it, promised by the proclamation, is taking us from under the yoke of bondage and placing us where we could reap the fruit of our own labor, and take care of ourselves, and assist the Government in maintaining our freedom.

3. State in what manner you think you can take care of yourselves, and how can you best assist the Government in maintaining your freedom.

Answer. The way we can best take care of ourselves is to have land, and turn in and till it by our labor—that is, by the labor of the women, and children, and old men—and we can soon maintain ourselves and have something to spare; and to assist the Government, the young men should enlist in the service of the Government, and serve in such manner as they may be wanted (the rebels told us that they piled them up and made batteries of them, and sold them to Cuba, but we don't believe that). We want to be placed on land until we are able to buy it and make it our own.

4. State in what manner you would rather live, whether scattered among the whites, or in colonies by yourselves.

Answer. I would prefer to live by ourselves, for there is a prejudice against us in the South that will take years to get over; but I do not know that I can answer for my brethren.

[*Mr. Lynch* says he thinks they should not be separated, but live together. All the other persons present being questioned, one by one, answer that they agree with "brother *Frazier*."]

5. Do you think that there is intelligence enough among the slaves of the South to maintain themselves under the Government of the United States, and the equal protection of its laws, and maintain good and peaceable relations among yourselves and with your neighbors?

Answer. I think there is sufficient intelligence among us to do so.

6. State what is the feeling of the black population of the South toward the Government of the United States; what is the understanding in respect to the present war, its causes and object, and their disposition to aid either side; state fully your views.

Answer. I think you will find there is thousands that are willing to make any sacrifice to assist the Government of the United States, while there is also many that are not willing to take up arms. I do not suppose there is a dozen men that is opposed to the Government. I understand as to the war that the South is the aggressor. President Lincoln was elected President by a majority of the United States, which guaranteed him the right of holding the office and exercising that right over the whole United States. The South, without knowing what he would do, rebelled. The war was commenced by the rebels before he came into the office. The object of the war was not, at first, to give the slaves their freedom, but the sole object of the war was, at first to bring the rebellious States back into the Union, and their loyalty to the laws of the United States. Afterwards, knowing the value that was set on the slaves by the rebels, the President thought that his proclamation would stimulate them to lay down their arms, reduce them to obedience, and help to bring back the rebel States; and their not doing so has now made the freedom of the slaves a part of the war. It is my opinion that there is not a man in this city that could be started to help the rebels one inch, for that would be suicide. There was two black men left with the rebels, because they had taken an active part for the rebels, and thought something might befall them if they staid behind, but there is not another man. If the prayers that have gone up for the Union army could be read out, you would not get through them these two weeks.

7. State whether the sentiments you now express are those only of the colored people in the city, or do they extend to the colored population through the country, and what are your means of knowing the sentiments of those living in the country?

Answer. I think the sentiments are the same among the colored people of the State. My opinion is formed by personal communication in the course of my ministry, and also from the thousands that followed the Union army, leaving their homes and undergoing suffering. I did not think there would be so many; the number surpassed my expectation.

8. If the rebel leaders were to arm the slaves, what would be its effect?

Answer. I think they would fight as long as they were before the bagonet, and just as soon as they could get away they would desert, in my opinion.

9. What, in your opinion, is the feeling of the colored people about enlisting and serving as soldiers of the United States, and what kind of military service do they prefer?

Answer. A large number have gone as soldiers to Port Royal to be drilled and put in the service, and I think there is thousands of the young men that will enlist; there is something about them that, perhaps, is wrong; they have suffered so long from the rebels, that they want to meet and have a chance with them in the field. Some of them want to shoulder the musket, others want to go into the quartermaster or the commissary's service.

10. Do you understand the mode of enlistment of colored persons in the rebel States, by State agents, under the act of Congress; if yea, state what your understanding is?

Answer. My understanding is that colored persons enlisted by State agents are enlisted as substitutes, and give credit to the States, and do not swell the army, because every black man enlisted by a State agent leaves a white man at home; and, also, that larger bounties are given or promised by the State agents than are given by the States. The great object should be to push through this rebellion the shortest way, and there seems to be something wanting in the enlistment by State agents, for it don't strengthen the army, but takes one away for every colored man enlisted.

11. State what in your opinion is the best way to enlist colored men for soldiers.

Answer. I think, sir, that all compulsory operations should be put a stop to. The ministers would talk to them, and the young men would enlist. It is my opinion that it would be far better for the State agents to stay at home, and the enlistments to be made for the United States under the direction of General SHERMAN.

In the absence of General SHERMAN, the following question was asked:

12. State what is the feeling of the colored people in regard to General SHERMAN, and how far do they regard his sentiments and actions as friendly to their rights and interests, or otherwise?

Answer. We looked upon General SHERMAN, prior to his arrival, as a man, in the providence of God, specially set apart to accomplish this work, and we unanimously felt inexpressible gratitude to him, looking upon him as a man that should be honored for the faithful performance of his duty. Some of us called upon him immediately upon his arrival, and it is probable he did not meet the Secretary with more courtesy than he met us. His conduct and deportment towards us characterized him as a friend and a gentleman. We have confidence in General SHERMAN, and think that what concerns us could not be under better hands. This is our opinion now from the short acquaintance and intercourse we have had.

[*Mr. Lynch* states that, with his limited acquaintance with General SHERMAN, he is unwilling to express an opinion. All others present declare their agreement with Mr. *Frazier* about General SHERMAN.]

Some conversation upon general subjects relating to General SHERMAN's march then ensued, of which no note was taken.

APPENDIX G.

DEATH OF JUSTICE E. M. STANTON.

From the Boston Herald.

WASHINGTON, *April 21, 1879.*

THE following communication was to-day handed to the Secretary of War by William J. Dupee, who is at this time a messenger in the War Department, and was the private messenger of the late Secretary Stanton. Summaries of the affidavits which accompany the letter are sent you with it. The revival recently of the absurd and malicious tale that Mr. Stanton committed suicide is the occasion of this publication, as well as of a letter from Surgeon-General Barnes, who was Mr. Stanton's physician, and who was at his bedside when he died. There was never the least ground for the suicide story, which was the malicious invention of men who hated him for his devotion to the Union cause, and could find no other way to gratify their baseness than to circulate a tale which could not hurt him, but was intended to annoy and distress his widow and children:

DUPEE'S LETTER.

WASHINGTON, *April 21, 1879.*

To the Hon. Secretary of War.

SIR: I respectfully ask that the inclosed affidavits of William S. Dupee and David Jones, relating to the manner of the death of the late Edwin M. Stanton, formerly Secretary of War, be admitted to the files of the War Department. For the first time since the death of Mr. Stanton, a permanent character and a responsible name have been lent to a story that found utterance in some obscure newspapers, shortly after his death, that he had committed suicide, and that the fact had been carefully concealed from the public. General Richard Taylor, of the late Confederate army, among his "Personal Experiences of the Late War," asserts, with much obscurity of language but equal directness of meaning, that the former Secretary of War died by his own hand. The widow and adult son of Mr. Stanton are both dead, and I therefore feel at liberty to act upon my own view of what is right to be done in refuting the malicious and slanderous tale repeated by General Taylor. Very respectfully,

WILLIAM S. DUPEE.

SYNOPSIS OF AFFIDAVIT OF WILLIAM S. DUPEE.

Messenger in office of Secretary of War, and has been since 1864; much with late Secretary Stanton during his last illness; mind all the time clear and strong; disposition cheerful, hopeful of recovery; death, however, a foregone conclusion with members of the household, and surprise that he lasted so long; after death of Mr. Stanton, and while body still warm, affiant shaved his throat and face and dressed his hair; no marks of violence on him, nor could any have escaped observation of affiant; affiant had much intercourse with the family servants, and never saw or heard anything to lend countenance to the story of Mr. Stanton's death by suicide, and when the story first made its appearance, soon after the death, it was the subject of mingled indignation and ridicule among those who had been about Mr. Stanton at the time of his death.

The affiant quotes the passage from Dick Taylor's late book, "Destruction and Reconstruction," which has led him to make his affidavit. It is as follows:

"1. The War Secretary I did not meet. . . . I never saw him. In the end, conscience, long dormant, came as Alecto, and he was not." . . .

SYNOPSIS OF AFFIDAVIT OF DAVID JONES.

Lives at No. 1807 T street, Northwest; was waiter in family of Edwin M. Stanton at the time of his death, and in constant attendance on him till he died; no signs of weak or wandering mind till a day or so before his death, when the patient was feverish, and his mind would now and then wander for a short time; after fever appeared, patient was never a moment alone at any time of day or night. (He names six or seven persons who used to relieve him and each other in occasional attendance.) Affiant saw nothing in the appearance of Mr. Stanton to indicate death till almost at the moment of death, and had no idea he was in imminent danger till Surgeon-General Barnes told him to go for Dr. Starkey, minister of the Episcopal Church, about half an hour before death; when Dr. Starkey arrived, Mr.

Stanton was conscious and able to speak in a low voice, and so remained till about the moment of death, affiant rubbing him at the time; affiant assisted in dressing and preparing the body, and is positive there were no marks of violence anywhere; the corpse was laid out in a front room up-stairs, and for three days was viewed by a great number of personal friends of the deceased; there is no foundation whatever for story of the suicide.

LETTER OF SURGEON-GENERAL BARNES.

WASHINGTON, D. C., *April 16, 1879.*

The Hon. EDWARD McPHERSON, *Philadelphia.*

DEAR SIR: In reply to your inquiry, the late Mr. Edwin M. Stanton was for many years subject to asthma in a very severe form, and when he retired from the War Department was completely broken down in health. In November, of 1869, the "dropsy of cardiac disease" manifested itself (after a very exhausting argument in chambers, in a legal case), and from that time he did not leave his house, rarely his bed. For many days before his death I was with him almost constantly, and at no time was he without most careful attendance by members of his family or nurses. On the night of December 23d the dropsical effusion into pericardium had increased to such an extent and the symptoms were so alarming that the Rev. Dr. Starkey, rector of the Church of the Epiphany, was summoned and read the service appointed for such occasions; he, with Mrs. Stanton, Mr. E. L. Stanton, the three younger children, Miss Bowie, their governess, myself, and several of the servants, were by his bedside until he died, at 4 A. M., December 24, 1869. After the pulse became imperceptible at the wrist, I placed a finger on the carotid artery, afterward my hand over his heart, and when its action ceased I announced it to those present.

It is incomprehensible to me how any suspicion or report of suicide could have originated, except through sheer and intentional malice, as there was not the slightest incident before or during his long sickness indicative of such a tendency nor a possibility of such an act. Fully aware of his critical condition, he was calm and composed, not wishing to die, while unterrified at the prospect of death. During the lifetime of his widow and of his son, Mr. E. L. Stanton, I did not feel called upon to make any written contradiction of the infamous and malignant falsehoods you allude to; but now, in view of your letter of April 14th, and in behalf of Mr. Stanton's minor children, I do most emphatically and unequivocally assert that there is not any foundation whatever for the report that Mr. Edwin M. Stanton died from other than natural causes, or that he attempted or committed suicide.

Very respectfully yours,
Joseph K. Barnes, M. D.

APPENDIX H.

MILITARY COMMISSIONS.

October 8, 1846.

The within draft of a letter it may be proper to address to each commander of an army now operating against Mexico. I am aware that it presents grave topics for consideration, which is invited.

It will be seen that I have endeavored to place all necessary limitations on *martial law:* 1. By restricting it to a foreign hostile country; 2. To offenses enumerated with some accuracy; 3. By assimilating *councils of war* to courts-martial; 4. By restricting punishments to the known laws of some one of the States, etc.

Respectfully submitted to the consideration of the Secretary of War.   WINFIELD SCOTT.

PROJET.

HEADQUARTERS OF THE ARMY,
WASHINGTON, *October* —, *1846.*

SIR: It can not but happen that many offenses, not cognizable by courts-martial, under the "act for establishing rules and articles of war for the government of the armies of the United States," approved April 10, 1806, will be committed by or upon the army under your command while in the enemy's country. I allude to crimes which, if committed in our own organized limits, would, as heretofore, be referred to the ordinary or civil courts of the land.—*Cross*, p. 107.

Our land-forces take with them, when on service beyond the limits of the Union, its organized Territories, and the "Indian country," as defined by the first section of the act approved June 30, 1834, no statutory code for the punishment of offenses, other than the said recited act of 1806, with its amendments.—*Cross*, p. 204.

Murder, willfully stabbing and maiming, and assault and battery, committed upon any "*superior officer*," and no one else; or the drawing and lifting up any weapon against, or the offering of any violence to, such officer (he being in the several cases "*in the execution of his duty*"), by any "officer or soldier," or other person subject to said articles, are all clearly within the ninth of those articles.—*Cross*, p. 208.

Wanton disturbance of religious worship is made punishable by the second article, without reference to place or country.—*Cross*, p. 107.

So are spies (not citizens of the United States), by the second section of the said act of 1806.—*Cross*, p. 123.

Other capital offenses against the general safety of the Union and army are expressly referred to courts-martial by the fifty-sixth and fifty-seventh articles.—*Cross*, p. 116.

The fifty-first and fifty-fifth provide for a few other capital offenses which may be committed abroad; and the fifty-second abroad or at home, upon persons or property, by individuals of the army; and the ninety-ninth article refers numerous non-specified crimes, "*not* capital," but merely "disorders and neglects to the prejudice of good order and military discipline," to courts-martial, whether such offenses be committed at home or abroad.—*Cross*, pp. 115, 116, 123.

It is evident that the ninety-ninth article, so qualified or limited, can not apply to the numerous omitted offenses in question, many of which, if committed, ought no doubt to be punished with death, or otherwise severely; for it is enacted in the eighty-seventh that "no person shall be sentenced to suffer death" by general courts-martial, "except in the cases herein expressly mentioned"—a limitation which has been universally applied to the *commissions* of officers also.—*Cross*, p. 120.

Articles 32, 33, and 54, seem to be limited to the general maintenance of good order at home and abroad, and to the protection of persons and property *within* the United States.—*Cross*, pp. 112, 115.

Assassination, willful murder, stabbing, maiming, wounding, assault and battery (except under the strict limitations of the ninth and fifty-first articles); rape, willful destruction of houses, or other private property; robbery and theft, or plunder and pillage (except in the limited cases under the fifty-second and fifty-fifth articles); and desecration of religious edifices, fixtures, and monuments, are all, whether committed by or upon the army, at home or abroad, unprovided for by our written military code; and they are offenses which, of course, could not, in a foreign hostile country, often, if ever, be safely turned over to the courts of such country, whether the offenders belong to the latter or to the army.

The good of the service, the honor of the United States, and the interests of humanity, demand that the numerous grave offenses omitted, except to a limited extent as above, should not go unpunished because committed in a foreign country, on or by our army.

The British mutiny act, and articles of war founded thereupon (which had their origin at the Revolution of 1688), omit the same offenses, and to the same extent, because, as Lord Loughborough (2 H. Blackstone, 98) remarks, "In this country, all the delinquencies of soldiers are not triable, as in most countries of Europe, by martial law" (which, he says in the same opinion, had, in the Continental sense, been "totally exploded" from that kingdom since 1688; "but, where there are ordinary offenses against the civil peace, they are tried by the common-law courts" (and such also has always been done in the United States).

But when a British army is abroad, in a hostile country, the omissions in the British penal code (the same as in ours, and to the same extent, for our articles of war are borrowed *in extenso* and with but slight verbal variations therefrom), that army supplies those omissions by the supplemental, unwritten, and undefined code, called *martial law.*

This law can have no constitutional, legal, or even necessary existence, *within* the United States. At home, even the suspension of the writ of *habeas corpus,* by Congress, could only lead to the indefinite incarceration of an individual or individuals who, if further punished at all, could only be so punished through the ordinary or common-law courts of the land.

But abroad, and in hostile countries, it is believed that the commanders of our armies, like those of Great Britain, may, *ex necessitate rei*, enforce martial law against any of the grave offenses indicated above, which may be unprovided for in our statutory code, whether such offenses be committed by persons appertaining to those armies, or by the inhabitants of the hostile country.

Accordingly, no matter by whom such offenses may be committed in the hostile country occupied by the army under your immediate command, or in which it may be engaged in military operations, whether by persons appertaining to that army upon the persons and property of each other, or by such persons upon the persons or property of the inhabitants of the hostile country, or by the latter upon the persons or property of the army and its followers, all such offenses, if against the laws of war, and not provided for in our rules and articles of war, will be duly brought before *councils of war* and by them tried and sentenced, according to the nature and degree of such offense, and according to the known laws of any one of the States of this Union.

Every council of war, for the trial of such offenses, will be appointed in the same manner and by the same authority that appoints courts-martial, whether general, regimental, or garrison, and will, as far as practicable, be governed by the same limitations, rules, principles, and procedure, including reviews, modifications, meliorations, and approval of sentence.—*Articles 65, 97.*

The proceedings of councils of war will, of course, be kept in writing, and sent to the adjutant-general's office, as in the case of the proceedings of courts-martial.

GENERAL ORDERS, No. 287.

HEADQUARTERS OF THE ARMY,
NATIONAL PALACE OF MEXICO, *September 17, 1847.*

The general-in-chief republishes, with important additions, his General Orders, No. 20, of February 19, 1847 (declaring martial law), to govern all who may be concerned:

1. It is still to be apprehended that many grave offenses not provided for in the act of Congress, "establishing rules and articles for the government of the armies of the United States," approved April 10, 1806, may be again committed by, or upon, individuals of those armies, in Mexico, pending the existing war between the two republics. Allusion is here made to offenses, any one of which, if committed within the United States or their organized Territories, would, of course, be tried and severely punished by the ordinary or civil courts of the land.

2. Assassination, murder, poisoning, rape, or the attempt to commit either; malicious stabbing or maiming; malicious assault and battery; robbery, theft, the wanton desecration of churches, cemeteries, or other religious edifices and fixtures; the interruption of religious ceremonies, and the destruction, except by order of a superior officer, of public or private property—are such offenses.

3. The good of the service, the honor of the United States, and the interests of humanity, imperiously demand that every crime, enumerated above, should be severely punished.

4. But the written code, as above, commonly called the *Rules and Articles of War*, does not provide for the punishment of *one* of those crimes, even when committed by individuals of the army upon the persons or property of other individuals of the same, except in the very restricted case in the ninth of those articles; nor for like outrages,

committed by the same class of individuals, upon the persons or property of a hostile country, except very partially in the fifty-first, fifty-second, and fifty-fifth articles; and the same code is absolutely silent as to all injuries which may be inflicted upon individuals of the army, or their property, against the laws of war, by individuals of a hostile country.

5. It is evident that the ninety-ninth article, independent of any restriction in the eighty-seventh, is wholly nugatory in reaching any one of those high crimes.

6. For all the offenses, therefore, enumerated in the second paragraph above, which may be committed abroad—in, by, or upon the army—a supplemental code is absolutely needed.

7. That *unwritten* code is *martial law*, as an addition to the *written* military code prescribed by Congress in the Rules and Articles of War, and which unwritten code all armies in hostile countries are forced to adopt—not only for their own safety, but for the protection of the unoffending inhabitants and their property, about the theatres of military operations, against injuries on the part of the army, contrary to the laws of war.

8. From the same supreme necessity, martial law is hereby declared as a supplemental code in, and about, all cities, towns, camps, posts, hospitals, and other places which may be occupied by any part of the forces of the United States, in Mexico, and in and about all columns, escorts, convoys, guards, and detachments, of the said forces, while engaged in prosecuting the existing war in and against the said republic, and while remaining within the same.

9. Accordingly, every crime, enumerated in paragraph No. 2 above, whether committed—1. By any inhabitant of Mexico, sojourner or traveler therein, upon the person

or property of any individual of the United States forces, retainer or follower of the same ; 2. By any individual of the said forces, retainer or follower of the same, upon the person or property of any inhabitant of Mexico, sojourner or traveler therein ; or, 3. By any individual of the said forces, retainer or follower of the same, upon the person or property of any other individual of the said forces, retainer or follower of the same—shall be duly tried and punished under the said supplemental code.

10. For this purpose it is ordered that all offenders, in the matters aforesaid, shall be promptly seized, confined, and reported for trial, before *military commissions*, to be duly appointed as follows :

11. Every military commission, under this order, will be appointed, governed, and limited, as nearly as practicable, as prescribed by the sixty-fifth, sixty-sixth, sixty-seventh, and ninety-seventh of the said Rules and Articles of War, and the proceedings of such commissions will be duly recorded in writing, reviewed, revised, disapproved, or approved, and the sentences executed—all, as near as may be, as in the cases of the proceedings and sentences of courts-martial : *provided*, that no military commission shall try any case clearly cognizable by any courts-martial ; and *provided*, also, that no sentence of a military commission shall be put in execution against any individual belonging to this army, which may not be, according to the nature and degree of the offense, as established by evidence, in conformity with known punishments, in like cases, in some one of the States of the United States of America.

. . . .

13. The administration of justice, both in civil and criminal matters, through the ordinary courts of the country, shall nowhere, and in no degree, be interrupted by any officer or soldier of the American forces, except—1. In cases

to which an officer, soldier, agent, servant, or follower of the American army may be a party; and, 2. In *political* cases—that is, prosecutions against other individuals on the allegations that they have given friendly information, aid, or assistance to the American forces.

． ． ． ． ． ． ．

By command of Major-General Scott:
H. L. SCOTT,
Acting Assistant Adjutant-General.

THE END.